The Plays of Beth Henley

The Plays of
Beth Henley

A Critical Study

GENE A. PLUNKA

McFarland & Company, Inc., Publishers
Jefferson, North Carolina, and London

An earlier version of Chapter 4 is ©2002 from *Beth Henley: A Casebook* by Julia A. Fesmire. Reproduced by permission of Routledge/Taylor & Francis Books, Inc.

Portions of Chapter 5 appeared in an earlier version as "Beth Henley's *The Debutante Ball* and the Modern Neurosis" in *Southern Quarterly* 42.4 (2004): 19–34. Used by permission of *Southern Quarterly*.

Portions of Chapter 7 are to be published as "Freudian Psychology and Beth Henley's Popular Culture Satire: *Signature*" in *The Journal of Popular Culture* 38.5 (forthcoming, 2005). Used by permission of Blackwell Publishing.

LIBRARY OF CONGRESS CATALOGUING-IN-PUBLICATION DATA

Plunka, Gene A., 1949–
    The plays of Beth Henley : a critical study / Gene A. Plunka.
        p.   cm.
    Includes bibliographical references and index.

    ISBN 0-7864-2081-2 (softcover : 50# alkaline paper)

    1. Henley, Beth — Criticism and interpretation.   2. Women
and literature — United States — History — 20th century.
3. Henley, Beth — Knowledge — Psychology.   4. Drama —
Psychological aspects.   5. Existentialism in literature.
6. Despair in literature.   I. Title.
PS3558.E4962Z84   2005
812'.54 — dc22   2005000095
British Library cataloguing data are available

On the cover: Beth Henley (*courtesy Gersh Agency, Los Angeles*)

Manufactured in the United States of America

McFarland & Company, Inc., Publishers
 Box 611, Jefferson, North Carolina 28640
  www.mcfarlandpub.com

Contents

Preface

This is the first critical book on the theater of Beth Henley. One might find it odd that no critical book has been written on Henley to date, given the fact that she has been writing plays for a quarter of a century, including more than a dozen dramas and screenplays for three films. The Pulitzer Prize-winning playwright has been one of the most successful contemporary American dramatists, with her plays being consistently staged worldwide. Perhaps no book has yet been written on Henley because critics and scholars who argued early in her career that Henley was a Southern gothic writer or a feminist playwright cannot sustain the argument over the full range of her plays. If a book requires a thesis or a prolonged argument, critics obviously find the stereotyped notion of Henley as Southern gothic icon or feminist banner carrier somewhat difficult to sustain throughout Henley's canon, particularly with regard to some of the later plays. My book attempts to dispel these critical stereotypes as I argue that her plays can best be understood to delineate a deeply rooted existential despair manifested in what Sigmund Freud described as the modern neurosis; read as universal statements about the *angoisse* of modern civilization, Henley's plays (all of them, not merely the early ones) will be more accessible to modern audiences.

I would first like to thank Beth Henley for granting me an interview that I conducted with her on June 29, 2002, near her home in Westwood, California. When I contacted Ms. Henley about my proposed book project, she eagerly agreed to help without any hesitation. The book could not have been completed without her valuable support.

I am indebted to the now-retired Gilbert Parker, Henley's former agent, of the William Morris Agency for acting as a liaison who initially helped me establish contact with Ms. Henley. The Gersh Agency has also been helpful, particularly in acquiring the photo of Henley for the cover of this book. I want to thank Henley's current agent, Lee Keele, and her assistant, Michelle Lange, for encouraging Henley to supply a photo of herself for my book.

A University of Memphis Faculty Research Grant awarded in summer 2002 enabled me to complete the writing of the book's last chapters. University of Memphis travel funds partially covered the expenses of my summer 2002 trip to Los Angeles to interview Ms. Henley. A University of Memphis Professional Development Award in spring 2005 allowed me to usher the manuscript through to production. I also want to acknowledge the assistance of Wayne S. Key of the interlibrary loan office at the University of Memphis for his help in ordering difficult-to-locate newspapers, magazines, and journals during the research stage of the book's preparation.

Chapters of this book appeared earlier in slightly different forms. I want to thank Julia A. Fesmire for publishing my essay on *Crimes of the Heart* in her anthology, *Beth Henley: A Casebook* (Routledge, 2002); Noel Polk, who kindly included my article on *The Debutante Ball* in the summer 2004 edition of *Southern Quarterly: A Journal of the Arts in the South*; and Gary Hoppenstand, who accepted my essay on *Signature* for publication in a 2005 issue of *The Journal of Popular Culture*.

Last, I am indebted to my colleagues in the Department of English at the University of Memphis, Dr. Naseeb Shaheen, Dr. Jackson R. Bryer, Dr. Robert Feldman, Dr. Stanley and Mrs. Rhona Plunka, Mark Lapidus, Ted Musiker, Lillian Siegel, and Harry R. Plunka, for their encouragement and support. I especially want to thank Dr. Stephen Tabachnick for being a good friend, a strong motivator, and a wonderful colleague who has made my life so much more pleasant since he became chair of the Department of English at the University of Memphis.

Introduction

Even before her Pulitzer Prize–winning play, *Crimes of the Heart*, made it to Broadway, scholars and critics were beginning to stereotype Beth Henley into a recognizable niche for the purpose of easily categorizing her plays. John Simon's review of the Off Broadway production of *Crimes of the Heart* began the trend when he deemed Henley's writing to be "demented" yet humorous and "believable," with touches of Anton Chekhov, Flannery O'Connor, and Tennessee Williams.[1] Although Henley admitted to having had Chekhov's *Three Sisters* in mind when she wrote *Crimes of the Heart*,[2] she had not read O'Connor and was only remotely familiar with Williams. Nevertheless, the stereotype was firmly planted in the minds of critics, who associated her bizarre, eccentric, or "demented" characters from the tradition of O'Connor, Williams, and (added later) Eudora Welty with the recognizable, and thus more acceptable, genre of Southern Gothic.

The Southern Gothic epithet has become a favorite of Henley's critics. William W. Demastes writes, "In Henley's case, being raised in Mississippi has certainly cultivated in her a penchant for 'whoppers.' But more important is her keen Southern sense of the grotesque and absurd experienced in daily existence, a sense that has often triggered loose comparisons between her and other Southern writers like Eudora Welty and Flannery O'Connor."[3] Matthew C. Roudané echoes Demastes's sentiments: "Her [Henley's] characters, spiritual descendants of those of Eudora Welty or Flannery O'Connor, fill the stage with the vernacular, mannerisms, and ethos of the South. Enacting fears and anxieties in realistic sets, her characters skirt the edges of the absurd, the grotesque, and the bizarre."[4] Both Demastes and Roudané have associated the absurd and the demented with

3

the "grotesque," adding to the ubiquitous notion that Henley's writings stem from the Southern Gothic tradition. There are many other such examples in the literature on Henley. Tish Dace notes, "As Henley's exotics pursue their unfulfilled dreams, they inhabit a Southern, gothic, whimsical world likely to make us laugh and wince in about equal measure. When she appears primed to veer into pathos, Henley generally undercuts sentimentality with eccentric characters or grotesque action."[5] Scott Haller, in a widely read and often-cited essay in the November 1981 edition of *Saturday Review* that initially introduced Henley to the general public, seemed to brand the Southern-bred playwright for life: "Henley's comedy has elicited comparisons with the works of such distinguished Southern writers as Eudora Welty and Flannery O'Connor, in part because she writes with wit and compassion about good country people gone wrong or whacko."[6] Perhaps Haller was merely reiterating what Frank Rich, the drama critic for the *New York Times*, had stated about *Crimes of the Heart* on Broadway earlier that month: Southern gothic humor worthy of Flannery O'Connor and Eudora Welty.[7] During the last twenty years of the twentieth century, critics and reviewers who write their précis seem to follow lock-step the leads of Simon, Haller, and Rich by paying homage to Henley's Southern Gothic playwriting. For example, Kay K. Cook states, "Her [Henley's] style has been described as 'southern gothic,' a regional literary idiom that combines dark humor with the grotesque to achieve an effect of laughter tempered with tragedy."[8] Gerald M. Berkowitz acknowledges as matter of fact, "Clearly, Henley is drawing on the same tradition of gothic and grotesque that has inspired southern writers from Faulkner to Williams, though with a particularly benign and loving humour that assures all will be well."[9] Even when Henley is compared to a contemporary playwright such as Marsha Norman, the emphasis is still placed on the stereotype; for example, Lisa J. McDonnell infers, "Related to the playwrights' [Henley and Norman] characteristically southern storytelling is their handling of southern gothic humor. Although Henley and Norman both draw on the tradition of Flannery O'Connor and Eudora Welty, their comedic styles differ: Henley's humor is wild and outrageous, Norman's dry and sardonic."[10] These examples can be repeated ad nauseam (and perhaps I am guilty of this already); however, although stereotypes can be useful at times, they can also be misleading, particularly with regard to the pigeonholing of playwrights into a mainstream tradition, such as Southern Gothic, that carries its own baggage and expectations.[11]

The other noteworthy stereotype embedded in the criticism on Henley's plays is that she represents a feminist ideology. Given the fact that most of Henley's protagonists are females whose collective bonding has been viewed as a means of struggling against an omnipresent patriarchy (the males in her plays assume subordinate roles, yet they occupy positions of authority), as well as the fact that the women in her dramas certainly have the best lines, she has been allied with feminist causes. Jonnie Guerra asserts, "Henley turns a spotlight into the shadow and gives central importance to the dilemmas of women, to their conflicts and suffering within the family, and to their questions about personal identity and the meaning of life."[12] Guerra argues that, despite Henley's use of the conventions of realism of the family-play genre, a form shunned by most feminists, she portrays women on a quest to redefine their sense of nothingness resulting from a patriarchal society that forces women to question their self-worth and dignity.[13] Alan Clarke Shepard mentions that Henley's black comedies study the effects of the feminist movement on a few mostly proletarian women in rural Mississippi. He ascribes their coping with the residual scars of emotional abandonment to a latent anger with a firmly solidified patriarchy: "We are invited to sympathize with isolated heroines whose fantasies demonstrate the difficulty of conceiving female subjectivity while entrenched in patriarchal epistemes, whose resilience is expressed in their canny, survivalist compromises with the codes of passive southern womanhood."[14] Criticism of *Crimes of the Heart*, considered by many scholars to be Henley's finest achievement in the theater, adds fuel to the notion of Henley as a feminist playwright. For example, Sally Burke presents this overview of the play: "Beneath its surface presentation of the crimes committed by the MaGrath [*sic*] sisters, Lenny, Meg, and Babe, the play, set in Mississippi, critiques the crimes of the patriarchy, including the father's abandoning the family; Babe being physically and verbally abused by her husband, Zackery; Zackery's racism; sexual double standards; and the suffocating control exercised over the sisters by the figure and symbol of patriarchy, their Old Granddaddy."[15] Helene Keyssar argues that *Crimes of the Heart* "has many of the ingredients of a strong feminist drama," but the sisterly bonding is undercut by women who have yielded to caricatures while making themselves objects of derision by a patriarchal society.[16] Karen L. Laughlin disagrees, viewing the play as a vision of female assertiveness and bonding as an alternative to self-destruction and a means of rejecting patriarchal forces.[17]

This book attempts to dispel the critical stereotypes that depict Henley as a Southern Gothic or feminist playwright. Instead, I will argue that Henley can best be perceived as a dramatist who delineates a deeply rooted existential despair manifested in various forms of what Freud described as the modern neurosis; her plays thus can be read not as regional drama ("Southern Gothic") or as sociological treatises ("feminist") but as universal statements about the *angoisse* of modern civilization. The thesis will be discussed in detail in chapter 2. Since this is the first single-authored critical book published on Henley's plays, I will begin with information about her life, her approach to playwriting, and the critical reception of her plays.

1

A Career Overview

Elizabeth (Beth) Becker Henley was born 8 May 1952 in Jackson, Mississippi, the second oldest of four daughters. Her father, Charles Boyce Henley, was an attorney with a passion for history and later a judge who served in both houses of the Mississippi legislature; his family was originally from Hazelhurst, which is approximately thirty miles south of Jackson. Beth's mother, Elizabeth Josephine (maiden name, Becker; nickname Lydy) was a housewife with a passion for acting; her parents were from Brookhaven, farther south of Hazelhurst. Beth spent considerable time in Hazelhurst and Brookhaven, as well as in Biloxi, where her family vacationed nearly every summer. During her childhood in Jackson, Beth was shy, overweight, asthmatic, and heavily sedated with antihistamines because of her susceptibility to allergies; she also spent a lot of time getting shots and lying in bed. Henley recalls, "At night, Mama'd come into my room and ask me why I was crying. I'd tell her I was pretending to be Heidi."[1] She was very much a quiet child adept at listening to her mother gossip with friends at home; Henley acknowledges that many of her stories are derived from this oral tradition prevalent in the South, where people were more inclined to sit around the kitchen table and talk rather than watch television.

Henley went to St. Andrew's Day School until third grade, then to Duling Elementary, followed by Bailey Junior High School in Jackson. Her early years were spent living in her own little world. She would come home from school, sit in the closet, and cut pictures out of books. She also collected rocks and bottles, but she admitted the process was rather arbitrary, keeping the unattractive rocks merely because she felt sorry for them. Although her father was a politician, Henley developed no interest in politics, viewing

it as a sham even when she was a child. She recalls the hypocrisy involved
with politics:

> We were taken around to politic for my father at a very early age, and I
> just loathed it. And I became cynical about politics because of it. But my
> mother loved it. When we'd go to a hick town, she'd say, "Beth, those shoes
> look a little too nice. Put some mud on 'em, girl." Or, "Okay, Beth, you've
> got a broken arm this summer. Play it up. Let's get the sympathy vote."
> You always knew it was show biz.[2]

Henley recalls that politics was disenchanting to her because "I began to
feel it didn't matter if this man won or that man won — they were still the
same fools."[3]

Henley was much more influenced by her mother, who performed at
the Jackson Little Theatre and then later at the New Stage Theatre. Her
mother was often on the play selection committee, so Beth habitually
picked up and read the Samuel French and Dramatists Play Service edi-
tions that her mother was perusing to make her choices for the next theater season. When her mother acted in a play, Beth often coached her on
the dialogue and thus became familiar with play scripts. Beth also attended
rehearsals quite frequently, which is where she learned that the theater was
the venue for excitement, glamour, and wonder, quite unlike the otherwise mundane life in Jackson. In the theater, Beth watched as her mother,
decked out in a beautiful dress, would get kissed by a handsome man,
which certainly was awe-inspiring for a young girl. Beth saw the magic of
the theater transpire as she witnessed the sets being built and torn down,
as well as the actresses dressing in fancy costumes while she was backstage
or at home hanging on the doorknob while her mother got dressed for performance. The theater became a magical place for her — a refuge or sanc-
tuary (her mother occasionally performed in a small converted church)
from reality and an inspired world where people were passionate about
life — laughing, clapping, and crying. Beth wanted to act in plays like her
mother and did actually have a bit role in *Summer and Smoke* when she
was in fifth grade. Instead she was enrolled in piano classes; embarrassed
by being on plastic keys while the others played on regular ones, Beth gave
it up. She was then enrolled in ballet class; however, her unsightly legs and
lack of coordination forced her to withdraw again. While in sixth grade,
she wrote a musical comedy titled *Swing High, Swing Low*, about a girl
running off to live with beatniks, which was targeted for rehearsals in her
garage; however, her inability to talk with boys forced her to renege on
that project as well. She was also reading scripts her mother brought home,
such as *Who's Afraid of Virginia Woolf?* Afterwards, her mother took her

for an achievement test, the results of which determined that Beth was tone deaf, color blind, and had no creative talent. To compensate for such devastation, Beth dyed her hair orange and became a junior high cheerleader. During her junior high school years, Beth dreamed of becoming a writer, but because she was poor with grammar and spelling, she thought acting would be more suitable for her. At one point, she was enrolled in a creative writing class, which resulted in disaster because when forced to read one of her incomplete short stories to the class, she bolted from the room in frustration. Perhaps the highlight of her junior high years occurred when Beth was twelve and her family vacationed in New York City (to see the World's Fair) instead of Biloxi; Beth had the opportunity to see *Funny Girl, Hello, Dolly!*, and *After the Fall* on Broadway.

During her high school years, Henley was a mediocre student, shy and withdrawn. She graduated from Jackson Murrah High School in 1970, but those years, when the average student was attending pep rallies and when being a cheerleader meant continued popularity, were miserable for her. Henley was essentially a loner, participating in no clubs or school activities. She recalls that she was not even in an Advanced English class. Her goal was to avoid causing trouble, so she spent much of her time alone, reading, writing, and listening to music; she did not go to homecoming and was dateless on prom night. When her parents divorced during this period, she tried to be less of a burden. Henley refused to commit herself to anything because she feared being tied down, much like her mother was; thus, in high school she refused to take home economics and refrained from learning how to cook, sew, or type. The highlights of her high school years included reading *Waiting for Godot*, which Henley later admitted nearly "blew my mind,"[4] acting in *Stop the World* at the New Stage (she did not participate in any high school theatrical productions), and winning a Gold Key for a picture she drew: "It almost means more to me than the Pulitzer prize. That's when I needed it badly, some sort of meager scrap of affirmation."[5] During her senior year, Henley enrolled in an acting workshop at Jackson's New Stage Theatre, thinking that, like dancing lessons, the acting class would rejuvenate her; bored and depressed, Henley was cheered up by the class, which inspired her to pursue an acting career in college.

Henley matriculated at Southern Methodist University in 1970 (she chose the school largely because their application form was easy to fill out), majoring in theater with a specialization in acting. Henley seemed to find her niche in college, where she took theater history courses and classes in production. Her boredom and indifference turned to ecstasy as she grappled for the first time with plays from all periods, including Shakespeare, Chekhov, Shaw, and Beckett. When *Three Sisters* was about to be produced at the university, Henley began to read Chekhov more closely, and after seeing an all-black production of *The Cherry Orchard* starring James Earl Jones and Gloria Foster, she recognized the seeds of black comedy that changed her life: "It was just absolutely a revelation about how alive life can be and how complicated and beautiful and horrible; to deny either of those is such a loss."[6] In her sophomore year, she took a playwriting class and wrote her first drama, *Am I Blue*, a one-act play originally titled *No, I Don't Have a Cat*, as part of the course requirements. Henley admits, however, that she learned more about playwriting from acting and reading plays than from the class, yet she also acknowledges that the course taught her the discipline needed to develop characters and find direction for them. Meanwhile, Henley pursued acting both at Theatre Three, a Dallas repertory group, during 1972 and 1973 (she had a bit role in *The Oresteia*) and as a member of the acting ensemble at the university. During her senior year, Henley rewrote *Am I Blue* for production on campus at the Margo Jones Theatre; the bashful playwright refused to put her name to the play, so she used a pseudonym — Amy Peach.[7] Her recently divorced parents came to see the production, and her father, who was rather indifferent to the play, suggested that the title should be a statement of fact rather than a question; this turned out to be Henley's only play that her father would ever see performed. Henley graduated in 1974 with a bachelor of fine arts degree.

After finishing her undergraduate degree, Henley taught creative dramatics and acted at the Dallas Minority Repertory Theatre in 1974 and early 1975. To earn money, she worked temporarily as a waitress, as a file clerk for a dog food company (Meg's profession in *Crimes of the Heart*), and as a Christmas photographer of children in the local Sears, Roebuck and Company store. Before she left Dallas, she wrote the book for *Parade*, a 1940s musical for which her friends Mark Hardwick and Stephen Tobolowsky composed the music and created the lyrics, respectively; Southern Methodist University gave them six hundred dollars to have the production performed for the students. Henley enjoyed this experience tremendously, although her father, having read the script, thought the information on World War II was historically inaccurate and perhaps too fanciful (his brother was killed during the War) and thus did not think his daughter was suited to being a writer. In 1975, Henley enrolled in the master's degree program in theater with Tobolowsky at the University of Illinois at Urbana-Champaign, where, on a scholarship, she taught acting and Lessac voice technique. Tired of school at this point, Henley dropped out after one year, realizing how ridiculous it was to get a master's degree in acting. During the summer of 1976, she acted in the *Great American People*

Show, a historical pageant about Abraham Lincoln presented by the New Salem State Park Theatre in Illinois.

Many of Henley's friends from her undergraduate years at Southern Methodist were going to New York or Los Angeles to pursue their dreams of acting. Henley and Tobolowsky moved to Los Angeles in 1976 to be with several of their friends while trying to break into the movie industry. She attended auditions, standing in line with various sleazy characters, only to be told that they did not like the way she looked or how she talked; she realized that acting in plays by Shakespeare or Chekhov could be realized in college but was difficult to do in Los Angeles, where performers would pray for any role, even a commercial for McDonald's. Furthermore, Henley found it demeaning to make photos of herself and then send them out to strangers. Henley recalls that at first, "Los Angeles was just another long bout with depression. I guess I took it too seriously, but I couldn't take the rejection."[8] Rather than subject herself to everyone's mercy, Henley decided to do something creative. While keeping her hand in the production side of theater as a member of the board of directors at the Met Theatre in Los Angeles, Henley wrote *The Moonwatcher* (later retitled *Nobody's Fool*), a screenplay based upon her experience in the Lincoln pageant of the New Salem State Park Theatre a year earlier. The script went unnoticed because producers refused to touch it unless it came through an agent, and Henley had trouble getting an agent because they were not taking on new clients at the time.

While working at the Broadway Department Store (Henley never did get any jobs as an actress but was offered nude modeling roles instead), she turned her attention to writing a play that might get performed in one of the local small theaters in Los Angeles. When Henley's father passed away in 1978, she was finishing the first draft of *Crimes of the Heart*, originally titled *Crimes of Passion*, which took three months to write. She based the play on the tale of her grandfather having been lost in the woods for two nights during Hurricane Camille, resulting in a manhunt replete with helicopters sent out to search for him. Her grandfather was eventually found unharmed, but that event, a crisis that reunited the family, became the starting point for the play, which Henley completed while working in the parts department for TRW, the computer manufacturer. To make the play producible for repertory theater groups on a tight budget (as was true of her friend Frederick Bailey's play, *Gringo Planet*, which was being mounted for five hundred dollars at La Mama Hollywood), Henley limited the number of cast members required, confined the locale to one set, reduced the props to unbreakable items, and even sought to have the lights fade out before the cutting of the cake so as to avoid purchasing a new cake for each performance.

She modeled the drama upon Chekhov's *Three Sisters*, hoping that both plays could be done in repertory with Irina as Babe, Masha as Meg, Olga as Lenny, Natasha as Chick, and Vershinen as Doc.[9] After a reading of the play at her home, Sharon Ullrich, Henley's friend, got her agent to turn the play over to Gilbert Parker from the William Morris Agency (Henley's agent until recently). Henley, feeling somewhat discouraged after submitting the play to regional theaters, such as San Francisco's ACT Company, to no avail, then showed the play to Bailey, who had earlier directed her when she performed as a fairy in a summer stock production of *A Midsummer Night's Dream*. Bailey, whose play, *The Bridgehead*, had won the best play contest at the Actors Theater of Louisville the year before, submitted *Crimes of the Heart* to Jon Jory, the artistic director of the Louisville contest, for production there. Bailey was so confident of the play that he did not submit a self-addressed stamped envelope with the text.[10] *Crimes of the Heart* was selected as co-winner of the Actors Theatre of Louisville's Great American Play Contest over four thousand competitors, which meant a prize of three thousand dollars and a 1 February 1979 debut of the play as part of the company's annual Festival of New American Plays. Henley attended the preview during a snowstorm and wondered why people would get dressed up, hire babysitters, and pay good money to see her play. This production, which featured Kathy Bates (Lenny), Lee Ann Fahey (Babe), and Susan Kingsley (Meg), received slight attention from the national media: Jack Kroll (*Newsweek*) was the most positive; Julius Novick's one-paragraph summary in the *Village Voice* reduced the drama to a wacky sentimental comedy in the tradition of Eudora Welty; and T. E. Kalem (*Time*), writing only two sentences about the play, praised the production but declared the drama to be little more than an afternoon soap opera.[11]

Crimes of the Heart was next performed on 26 April 1979 by the California Actors' Theater at Los Gatos, California, under direction by J. Ranelli.[12] Subsequent productions were at the Loretto-Hilton Theater in St. Louis (October 1979) and at Baltimore's Center Stage (18 April 1980); Henley removed scenes from the St. Louis production, then restored most of them when the play moved to Baltimore. However, when Henley's agent tried to peddle the play to New York producers, it was universally rejected. Lynne Meadows of the Manhattan Theatre Club refused to stage the play but relented when she learned that Melvin Bernhardt was interested in directing it. Henley did another rewrite of the play, cutting out a character named Uncle Watson, before the play was ready for New York. *Crimes of the Heart* ran for thirty-five performances (until 11 January 1981) Off Broadway at the Manhattan Theatre Club's Upstage Theater after debuting on 9 December 1980. Bernhardt's direction inspired fine performances from Mia Dillon

(Babe), Mary Beth Hurt (Meg), Lizbeth MacKay (Lenny), Peter MacNicol (Barnette), Julie Nesbitt (Chick), and Stephen Burleigh (Doc). John Lee Beatty designed the set, Patricia McGourty made the costumes, and Dennis Parichy supervised the lighting.

The Off Broadway production of *Crimes of the Heart* received very high praise from the New York press, with no dissenting opinions. John Simon led the charge with his review in *New York*, claiming that the play's energy, sagacity, and generosity toward people and life restored his faith in the theater; he praised Henley as a playwright of charm, warmth, style, unpretentiousness, and individual vision.[13] Humm (*Variety*) lauded Henley's natural ear for dialogue, the original and unforced writing, and the revelation of common humanity that underlies desperate behavior.[14] Edith Oliver's review in the *New Yorker* singled out Henley's talented and original writing,[15] while Marilyn Stasio (*After Dark*) noted how Henley carefully crafted Southern Gothic craziness into something rational and beautiful.[16] Terry Curtis Fox (*Village Voice*) had reservations about the play as "an almost mechanical comedy which would be perfectly in place in Norman LearLand," as did Frank Rich (*New York Times*), who viewed the play as a bit murky at times, yet both reviewers joined their colleague Glenne Currie (*Los Angeles Times*) in praising a cast that marveled under Bernhardt's able direction.[17]

Although Henley's agent was impressed with the reviews of the Off Broadway run at the Manhattan Theatre Club, he did not think *Crimes of the Heart* received strong enough press for a Broadway mounting of the play. In April 1981, *Crimes of the Heart* won the Pulitzer Prize for Best Drama of the 1980-1981 season, a very unusual distinction for a play that had not yet graced Broadway and for a playwright so young (age 29) and writing her first full-length drama.[18] Henley became the first woman in twenty-three years to win the award for playwriting (her predecessor, Ketti Frings, won for *Look Homeward, Angel* in 1958) and only the sixth woman to ever do so. In June, the New York Drama Critics Circle voted *Crimes* the Best New American Play of 1980-1981, and in August, the play captured the prestigious George Oppenheimer/*Newsday* Playwriting Award as well. Melvin Bernhardt also won an Obie Award for Best Direction. Henley reportedly received over a million dollars to write the screenplay for the film version of the play. Plans were quickly made for a Broadway opening with the same Off Broadway cast and production team, but there was a slight delay to allow Mary Beth Hurt to play Shakespeare's Juliet at the Long Wharf in New Haven.

Crimes of the Heart debuted on Broadway at the John Golden Theater on 4 November 1981 with Bernhardt directing largely the same cast that worked with him during the play's production at the Manhattan Theatre Club.[19] Later, during the play's run of 535 performances (closing on 13 February 1983), Holly Hunter replaced Mary Beth Hurt. The vast majority of the critical response to the Broadway production was positive, including reviews by Clive Barnes (*New York Post*), Robert Brustein (*New Republic*), Brendan Gill (*New Yorker*), Hobe (*Variety*), T.E. Kalem (*Time*), Stanley Kauffmann (*Saturday Review*), Howard Kissel (*Women's Wear Daily*), Jack Kroll (*Newsweek*), Don Nelson (*Daily News*), Frank Rich (*New York Times*), John Simon (*New York*), Marilyn Stasio (*Penthouse*), and Edwin Wilson (*Wall Street Journal*).[20] Rich discussed how Henley used comedy to show human absurdity,[21] Kauffmann wrote that *Crimes* said much about the state of the world and about human chaos,[22] Kroll claimed the play's strength was its subtlety in fusing humor and pathos,[23] and Simon suggested the drama was about constricted living and confined thinking, resulting in a love story that is never sappy or piously cloying.[24] Several of these critics extolled Henley's wit, heart, off-beat humor, and ability to create unpretentious characters with depth; Bernhardt's suave and textured direction; and the admirable performances of the cast members.

However, since the Broadway production of *Crimes of the Heart* received more critical attention than the Manhattan Theatre Club performances, the critical assessment was not unanimous in praise of the play. Walter Kerr's review in the *New York Times* was neutral; Kerr had no complaints about the production, yet, although he acknowledged that Henley's play is the work of a gifted writer, he could not tolerate the offbeat humor that he thought went beyond the Southern grotesquerie typical of perhaps a Flannery O'Connor.[25] John Heilpern (*Times*) saw Henley's characters as Southern "types" out of a cartoon; Gerald Weales, in his one-sentence review in the *Georgia Review*, claimed that the play was overwritten and overacted; and John Beaufort (*Christian Science Monitor*) was amazed that what he deemed Southern fried Gothic comedy, part soap opera and part patchwork plotting, could have won the Pulitzer Prize and the New York Drama Critics Circle Award as Best Play.[26] Leo Sauvage, writing in the *New Leader*, perhaps represented the minority view of those who disliked the play because they felt the humor was sick, not black, particularly when the Magrath sisters (referred to as the "Magrade sisters" in his review) laugh at Old Granddaddy's falling into a coma.[27] Finally, Michael Feingold's review in the *Village Voice* was negative largely because he complained of Henley's pity and mockery of her characters: "The play gives the impression of gossiping about its characters rather than presenting them, and the playwright's voice, though both individual and skillful, is the voice of a small-town southern spinster yattering away on the phone, oozing pretended sympathy and real malice for her unfortunate subjects, and never at any point coming close to the truth of their lives."[28]

After receiving a Tony nomination for Best Play, *Crimes of the Heart* had a successful regional run in the United States and Great Britain. Melvin Bernhardt once again directed the play for a Los Angeles production at the Ahmanson Theater, debuting on 4 May 1983. The play also ran in London at the Bush Theatre during May 1983, where it was first runner-up for the Susan Smith Blackburn Prize for Playwriting.[29] During December 1983, the play first premiered in Chicago, at the Blackstone Theatre, and in May 1984, Jane Brody directed a beautifully understated production of the play at the Immediate Theatre in Chicago.[30] Productions were soon mounted at the Stanford Theater in Palo Alto (featuring John Lee Beatty's scenic design),[31] at the Olney Theater outside of Washington, D.C.,[32] at the Oregon Shakespearean Festival in Ashland, and at the Addison Stage Company in Berkeley.[33] In May 1989, a distinctly Southern rendition of the play was staged by the Southern Repertory Theater in New Orleans.[34] In August 1989, *Crimes* played briefly at the Man in the Moon Theatre in London but did not generate much attention from the press[35] and was on the East Coast again in January 1990 at the Nickerson Theater in Boston and simultaneously at the Little Theatre in Alexandria, Virginia.[36] Throughout the 1990s, *Crimes of the Heart* was also performed at smaller community and regional repertory theaters, such as the Littleton Town Hall Arts Center near Denver (September 1991), Harmony Hall in Fort Washington, Maryland (February 1993), and the Manchester Royal Exchange Theatre in Manchester, England (June 1995). *Crimes of the Heart* returned to New York in 2001, when it ran from 16 April to 14 May in a Second Stage production directed by Garry Hynes. The play has been popular worldwide, with productions staged in France, Australia, China (performances in which Henley attended the year after the protests in Tiannamen Square), Turkey, Peru, Japan, and Israel.

Meanwhile, during the period from 1979, when *Crimes of the Heart* was staged in Louisville, through its run on Broadway, Henley was involved with other projects. In 1979, she was busy writing *Morgan's Daughters* for a television pilot to be produced by Paramount Pictures. She continued acting also, most notably taking the role of a bag lady in a summer 1981 production of Frederick Bailey's radical farce about the Depression of the 1980s, *No Scratch*, at the Odyssey Theater in Los Angeles. Henley was also becoming more comfortable with life in West Hollywood, where she lived with Tobolowsky, an actor/musician/writer who played keyboard with a rock group called the L.A. Slugs. When she was interviewed on 10 March

1981 by John Griffin Jones, she remarked, "I have a Mississippi driver's license, Texas license plates and Illinois car insurance. I refuse to say L.A.'s my home."[37] However, during the early 1980s, Henley gradually settled in to California culture, and despite her dislike of smog, the crowds, and the weather in Los Angeles, she became fond of her back yard, surfcasting, Dodger baseball, going to David Bowie concerts, jazz sessions at the Parisian Room, and living in a neighborhood where the children come to the door selling things. Gradually, Henley became like a den mother for transplanted Southern Methodist graduates who were trying to make their livings as actors and actresses in Hollywood.

On 10 January 1982, *Am I Blue* and two other one-act plays (Lanford Wilson's *Thymus Vulgaris* and John Bishop's *Confluence*) were presented at the Circle Repertory Company in New York City. With *Crimes of the Heart* on Broadway at this time, Henley thus had two plays running simultaneously in New York. Stuart White, who initially staged *Am I Blue* the year before at the Hartford Stage Company in Hartford, Connecticut, directed the play again for the New York performances, which featured June Stein as Ashbe and Jeff McCracken as John Polk, with set design by Bob Phillips and costumes by Joan E. Weiss. The "Confluence" program was fairly heavily reviewed by the New York press, but because Henley shared the evening with two other playwrights, *Am I Blue* did not receive any in-depth commentary. Most of the reviews, however, were favorable, with particular attention paid to comedienne Stein's dazzling performance as a pint-sized Ashbe, and Henley's writing described as "poignant," "promising," "sentimental" yet "bracing," and "not believable but constantly amusing."[38] *Am I Blue* has been infrequently staged since 1982, with varying degrees of success.[39]

The Wake of Jamey Foster germinated in Henley's mind soon after her father's death, and the unduly long time to bury him, which was painful for Henley's mother, gave her the idea for the play. Henley did not finish it until before she won the Pulitzer Prize, probably in late winter 1981. Henley sent the script to director Ulu Grosbard, who liked the play so much that he immediately optioned it for Broadway with the stipulation that it be tried out first in Hartford, Connecticut. Grosbard was meticulous about casting the play, spending three months auditioning twelve hundred actors and actresses and having a particularly difficult time finding someone suitable to play Pixrose, Marshael's confidante. Grosbard even went to a funeral home to make sure that the flowers would be arranged properly on stage. *The Wake of Jamey Foster* debuted 1 January 1982 at the Hartford Stage Theatre, where it ran for five weeks. The cast included Susan Kingsley (Marshael Foster), Stephen Tobolowsky (Leon Darnell), Belita

Moreno (Katty Foster), Adam LeFevre (Wayne Foster), Patricia Richardson (Collard Darnell), Amanda Plummer (Pixrose Wilson), and Brad Sullivan (Brocker Slade); Moreno was a former Southern Methodist graduate for whom Henley had written the role of Katty. The only review of this production to appear in a national publication was Markland Taylor's précis in *Variety*. Taylor complained that Henley needed to tighten the roles for Pixrose and Katty, giving us stronger reasons for both characters' presence, and warned that they play was not yet ready for Broadway.[40]

Nevertheless, four producers helped Grosbard raise $650,000 to mount the Broadway production, including funding for advertising the play. They had to wait for Susan Kingsley, for whom Henley had written the role of Marshael after seeing her play Meg in the Louisville production of *Crimes of the Heart* (Kingsley was worth waiting for, having created a sensation in Marsha Norman's *Getting Out* Off Broadway three years earlier), who decided to spend some time with her family in Kentucky. Anthony Heald took over the role of Wayne for Adam Lefevre, and Holly Hunter, now introduced to Henley for the first time during her Broadway audition, played Pixrose (Amanda Plummer had taken a role in *Agnes of God*); the remainder of the cast was the same as in Hartford.

The Wake of Jamey Foster had its Broadway premiere on 14 October 1982 at the Eugene O'Neill Theater, thus giving Henley two plays appearing on Broadway at the same time—certainly one of the youngest playwrights to ever achieve such a feat. The only positive review of the play was written by Clive Barnes of the *New York Post*, who argued that Henley's new drama struck deeper and with far more passion than *Crimes of the Heart* yet with as much humor and appeal as her first play. Unfortunately, Barnes's colleagues did not share his sentiments; the play was vilified by the New York press, including negative reviews from Robert Brustein (*New Republic*), Curt Davis (*After Dark*), Brendan Gill (*New Yorker*), Humm (*Variety*), Howard Kissel (*Women's Wear Daily*), Julius Novick (*Village Voice*), Frank Rich (*New York Times*), Leo Sauvage (*New Leader*), John Simon (*New York*), Douglas Watt (*Daily News*), and Edwin Wilson (*Wall Street Journal*).[41] Despite the fact that Henley finished the play before she won the Pulitzer, Gill, Rich, and Simon wrote that she was trying to rewrite her first success, and Rich noted that the "desperate" writing precluded her from firmly establishing her people, plot, or themes; Watt also claimed that Henley was straining to write and suggested that she probe deeper into her characters.[42] Kissel complained that the characters were cartoonlike and without coherence, providing the play with a disjointed quality, while Novick found Henley's oddities humorous but without substance.[43] Sauvage questioned the limits of black humor, wondering where to draw the line between what is humorous and what is tasteless.[44] Gill wrote that the dialogue was implausible and blamed Grosbard for bungling the direction.[45] Brustein claimed that the play was fine for a homespun television series, but for the stage, Henley needed to be bolder and do more than merely hang crepe on regional family pictures or black out the teeth of Norman Rockwell portraits.[46] Humm summed up the views of most critics when he stated that the cast was adept (reviewers had particular praise for Hunter, Moreno, and Kingsley), but Henley failed to realize that eccentric characters and regional flavor do not compensate for characters that need further development and stage action that is limited to static rhetoric about betrayed relationships.[47] The play closed after twelve performances. After the fiasco, Frank Rich wrote another column, analyzing *The Wake* in retrospect; he stated that the play, misproduced and perhaps misdirected because of Grosbard's unfamiliarity with rural regional comedy, should have waited for the availability of an intimate Broadway theater rather than the Eugene O'Neill, a house large enough for musicals where Santo Loquasto's set looked puny.[48] Henley, however, enjoyed the production and Grosbard's direction; she even went to the performances every evening and later admitted, "It was the best experience I've *ever* had, working on *any* play."[49] When *Crimes of the Heart* premiered on Broadway, Henley had no idea of what to expect from the critics, and its success forced her to be self-effacing. Although the reviews for her second play on Broadway were disastrous, Henley's wonderful feelings for a play that was dear to her made her feel stronger and more brazen. *The Wake of Jamey Foster* later had a successful production at the Studio Theater in Washington, D.C., during June 1984 but was negatively received when it was performed at the Alliance Theatre in Chicago during April 1985.[50]

In 1983, shortly after *The Wake of Jamey Foster* closed on Broadway, Henley continued her acting career, appearing as a Bible pusher in the film *Swing Shift*, released in 1984 by Warner Brothers. As an author-actor, Henley joined an impressive group that included Sam Shepard, Christopher Durang, and Bill C. Davis. As an actress, Henley learned how to make dialogue stageworthy and began to incorporate in her plays things she herself would like to do on stage. Henley admits, "Being an actress really helped me writing plays particularly.... You just get into a character, and what that character wants, what are their greatest dreams, their greatest fears, what would they feel at this moment or in this scene...."[51] In short, acting was a primary means for Henley to keep in touch with her imagination.

Henley began writing *The Miss Firecracker Contest* after she returned from the Louisville production of *Crimes of the Heart* in 1979, but with the regional productions of *Crimes* keeping her busy with out-of-town appearances, she could not get much work done on the play; however, she managed to finish it in late 1979 because she always wanted to at least work on a second play while another was in production. Henley admits, "I'm heartsick when I don't have a play that I'm working on, 'cause I don't know what to think about when I'm in the shower or in the grocery line. Or even how to survive the night without being able to dream about my characters."[52] *The Miss Firecracker Contest* premiered at the small (estimates range from seventy-three seats to ninety-nine seats) Victory Theater in Burbank, California, in March 1980, where it ran through May 11.[53] Maria Gobetti directed a cast that included Mary McCusker (Carnell), Belita Moreno (Popeye, the role that Henley created for her), Cheryl Anderson (Elain), and Stephen Tobolowsky (Delmount). Henley was pleased with the production, although it was not well attended.[54] *The Miss Firecracker Contest* then was staged by the New Stage Theatre in Jackson, Mississippi (which Henley swears was better than the New York version because the Southern actors had a better feel for the play than the New York cast), followed by a brief run in Dallas at Theatre Three, where it was directed by Larry O'Dwyer, before it received a college production by the University of Illinois at the Krannert Center in Urbana during October 1981.[55] The play was next performed by the Studio Arena Theatre in Buffalo (opening 30 October 1981), under direction by Davey Marlin-Jones, with Tobolowsky again playing Delmount in a reworked edition of the play with an otherwise different cast than the original version that played in Burbank.[56] This was followed by a creditable British staging of the play at the Bush Theatre in London during Spring 1982, with notable performances by Gayle Hunnicutt (Elain) and Sally Watts (Popeye) under Simon Stokes's authentic direction.[57] The last stop on the tryout tour before New York was at the Steppenwolf Theater in Chicago, where it opened on 30 June 1983 under direction by Gary Sinise.[58]

The Miss Firecracker Contest had its Off Broadway debut on 1 May 1984 at the Manhattan Theatre Club's small (one-hundred-seat) theater. The play, directed by Stephen Tobolowsky with costume design by Jennifer von Mayrhauser and set design by John Lee Beatty, featured Holly Hunter (Carnell), Belita Moreno (Popeye), Patricia Richardson (Elain), Mark Linn-Baker (Delmount), Budge Threlkeld (Mac Sam), and Margo Martindale (Tessy Mahoney). Most of the New York press gave the production fine reviews. Frank Rich of the *New York Times* provided the most in-depth insight on the play, claiming that for all of this drama's hyperbolic comedy, Henley never loses sight of the sad, real people fighting the specter of death until the moment they die.[59] Edith Oliver (*New Yorker*) joined Rich in praising the performers and the distinguished production work on the sets, costumes, and lighting, while agreeing with Richard Schickel (*Time*), who singled out Holly Hunter's fine performance as the highlight of the production.[60] Benedict Nightingale, who reviewed the British production in 1982 and now was asked to do so again, this time for the *New York Times*, disagreed with Frank Rich's assessment of the casting when he wrote that Henley, a born anecdotist, writes with poignancy and pathos, yet the cast failed to deliver either in a farce that he characterized as "thoroughly beguiling."[61] Other positive reviews followed from Clive Barnes (*New York Post*), John Beaufort (*Christian Science Monitor*), and David Richards (*Washington Post*).[62] Sylviane Gold of the *Wall Street Journal* and Ron Cohen of *Women's Wear Daily* offered neutral reviews of the play, with Gold lamenting that *Miss Firecracker* lacked the structural elegance of *Crimes of the Heart* while Cohen claimed that Henley's exaggerated regional types wear thin, yet the production maintained a clarity of vision that the author lacked.[63] The two negative reviews were written by Douglas Watt (*Daily News*) and John Simon (*New York*).[64] The former insisted that, except for Carnelle, the characters in the play do not ring true, and although the play might be ready for Broadway, Henley's script needs more work to blend the pathos and humor more effectively; Simon complained that Henley's wit and touching insight was lost in the bizarreness, which was coy at first, then cloying, and finally, intolerable. The theater-going public, finding the play much more palatable than *The Wake of Jamey Foster* (funerals are often difficult to make palatable for audiences), disagreed with the few dissenting critical voices and made the play a success. After only one month, the production moved to the Manhattan Theatre Club's larger stage before it transferred to the West Side Arts Theater. The play closed Off Broadway on 25 August 1984 after 131 performances and then played for another 113 performances and 13 previews during Fall 1984 at West Side.

After being published in *The Ten Best Plays of 1983-1984*, *The Miss Firecracker Contest* went on to do well in regional theaters throughout the United States. The play was next directed by James Waring at the Olney Theater outside Washington, D.C., in August 1985, then staged by Phase One Productions at San Francisco's Nova Theater during May 1986, revived at the Greenwich Theatre in England in July 1986 with the original London cast that played it four years earlier at the Bush Theatre, was performed by the Boston Post Road Stage Company in Fairfield, Connecticut, in March 1988, was given an uneven production at the McCarter Theater at Princeton University (July 1988), and also was mounted at Theatre 40 in Beverly Hills during September 1993.[65] *The Miss Firecracker Contest* has played internationally as well, including performances in Germany, Mexico, Sweden, and the Netherlands.

In the early and mid–1980s, Henley was busy with miscellaneous writing projects. Her playlet, *Hymn in the Attic*, was presented by the Back Alley Theatre in Van Nuys, California, in 1982, as one of twenty-four plays arranged in chronological sequence (each treating a different hour of the day), which was part of the *Twenty-Four Hours* program; these dramas were published in 1985 as *West Coast Plays*. That year, after Henley was still feeling depressed by the poor reviews of *The Wake of Jamey Foster* on Broadway, she co-authored a script for PBS's *Survival Guides* with comic Budge Threlkeld, who collaborated with Henley to help her out of her stupor. The half-hour television play, directed by Jonathan Demme and starring Rosanna Arquette and David Byrne (songwriter of The Talking Heads), kicked off the 1985 PBS comedy anthology series. The script was based on producer Jon Denny's idea, which principally involves a girl's first meeting with her future in-laws.

Henley began doing more writing for television and film. In 1985, she sold the rights to *Strawberry* (begun in spring 1984), a screenplay about the misadventures of a comedienne from a small town in Texas who, after her husband leaves her, ventures to Los Angeles with her two children. Written as a vehicle for Sissy Spacek, *Strawberry* has yet to be filmed. In 1986, she co-authored with David Byrne and Stephen Tobolowsky *True Stories*, a screenplay for a 1986 film produced by Warner Brothers. Henley actually does not take much credit for the writing, for she merely helped Tobolowsky organize his ideas, and Byrne, who directed and narrated the film, used whatever parts of the script he needed, shaping it to his songs and discarding the rest. Another major project in 1986 was the November release of *Nobody's Fool*, a 107-minute film directed by Evelyn Purcell based upon Henley's original 1977 script, *The Moonwatcher*.[66] The film concerns Cassie (Rosanna Arquette), a frustrated waitress in Buckeye Basin, Arizona, who lives a dull life with her mother (Louise Fletcher) and bizarre younger brother (Stephen Tobolowsky). Cassie has had a child as a result of an unhappy affair with Billy (Jim Youngs), stabbing him when he suggested that she have an abortion. Cassie meets Riley (Eric Roberts), who is in town for the summer working as a set designer for an outdoor Shakespeare festival. The hot-tempered Riley develops an affair with Cassie, who has trouble breaking with a grim past that includes her unusual relationship with Billy. The screenplay was written when Henley was angry about not being able to support herself as an actress in Los Angeles. Henley admitted, "*Nobody's Fool* was real, real personal to me. It's about someone who's in despair and is looking for meanings and has made mistakes and is looking for salvation."[67]

When Henley rewrote the script, she was removed from the initial angry mode and thus became peeved at Cassie's constant whining, so she changed the focus to allow Cassie to give the baby up for adoption and try to overcome her depression by leaving Arizona and going to California with stage technician Riley: the theater is indeed liberating after all! Cassie's suicide attempt gone awry, similar to Babe's ludicrous suicidal machinations, becomes black comedy as Cassie's rope breaks and she falls into the dumpster.

Another half-hour television script, "How to Survive a Family Tree," was again co-authored with Threlkeld as part of PBS's *Trying Times*, a series of six original comedies each with its own director. Jon S. Denny created the idea of these skits, written by playwrights such as Henley, Christopher Durang, and Wendy Wasserstein, each tackling a 1980s trauma, such as getting a job, moving, dealing with a husband's former girlfriend, etc. Produced by KCET's Phylis Geller, "A Family Tree" (the title was shortened from the original) aired on 18 October 1987 under direction by Jonathan Demme. Rosanna Arquette played a woman who spends an evening as an unwelcome guest at an anniversary party of her medical school boyfriend (John Stockwell), where one disaster leads to another, as is typical in Henley's scripts.

In December 1986, the film version of *Crimes of the Heart* was released. Henley had sold the film rights to an independent producer in 1980, who, in turn, sold them to the eventual producer, Dino De Laurentiis, at United Artists. Director Bruce Beresford shared Henley's vision for the film, and they developed a good rapport on the set while filming her screenplay (in Southpoint, North Carolina, instead of Mississippi). The film starred Diane Keaton (Lenny), Jessica Lange (Meg), Sissy Spacek (Babe), Sam Shepard (Doc), and Tess Harper (Chick). Beresford's most difficult task was to create a sense of self-effacement for three Hollywood (read non–Southern) actresses who had each won Academy Awards, and Henley believed he accomplished that goal: "They play the characters; they don't play as *stars*. It's not Diane Keaton being Diane Keaton and Sissy Spacek being Sissy Spacek and Jessica Lange being Jessica Lange. You even end up believing that they're sisters."[68] Critics lauded Keaton, Spacek, and Lange for putting their hearts into the acting, providing strong, unabashed performances, and although Lange seemed to tower over Spacek at times, the latter certainly held her own during the film. Most critics praised the screenplay as well, although a few suggested that Henley needed to flesh out the script a bit more, noting that monologue-driven dialogue is anathema to the cinema. Whatever criticism there was of the film was blamed on Beresford, who was cited for using misty lighting and rueful music while laboring comic moments and denying us the intimacy of the play through his heavy-handed camera work.[69] Nevertheless, the film grossed $22 million and garnered three Academy Award nominations: Henley for Best Adapted Screenplay, Spacek for Best Actress, and Harper for Best Supporting Actress. Spacek also won the Golden Globe Award and the New York Drama Critics Award for Best Actress. Also, in 1986, Claudia Reilly's novel, *Crimes of the Heart*, was published by New American Library, based on Henley's screenplay.

During the mid–1980s until the early 1990s, when Henley was writing scripts for television and film (she adapted Reynold Price's *A Long and Happy Life* in 1989 and John Kennedy Toole's *A Confederacy of Dunces* in summer 1990), she enjoyed the idea that screenwriting allowed her to zip from one image to another, create lots of characters, and change scenery at will. However, she also acknowledged that screenwriting meant that you lost control over the text to a director who had the authority to change what you have written, and, of course, the writer has no control over the casting of a film as a playwright might when she selects her own performers. With regard to writing for television, Henley realized, "You go in with a committee of people and each one gets one of their own ideas in. It's like nailing them all together and trying to patchwork the thing. And it comes out brown dishwater: non-specific, bland. I mean, they *work* at getting things bland for TV."[70] With enough income from the national tour of *Crimes of the Heart*, as well as from selling the film rights of the play, Henley was able to turn her attention momentarily away from screenwriting and back to the theater.

After *The Wake of Jamey Foster* was excoriated by the New York press, Henley retreated to Los Angeles to begin work on her next play, *The Debutante Ball*, almost with a vengeance. However, because of other commitments, Henley could not finish *The Debutante Ball* until late Spring 1984 after the play had gone through dozens of drafts—certainly Henley's most difficult drama to write. The play was based upon a true story that Henley heard while growing up in Jackson about a society woman who "took the rap" for her daughter's alleged murder of her father and thus went to jail in her stead. When Henley showed the play to her agent, he had reservations that it was too risqué and perhaps offensive to the deaf community (Frances Walker being the deaf character who appears foolish at times); as it turned out, Gilbert Parker was right about his reservations—twenty-eight theaters rejected the play before it was picked up by the South Coast Repertory in Costa Mesa, California. In 1984, *The Debutante Ball* had its first workshop reading at South Coast. Before the play premiered, it was given a sit-down reading at Henley's house followed by a staged reading before rehearsals; Henley was still revising the play at this point. *The Debutante Ball* premiered at South Coast Repertory on 9 April 1985 and ran through May 12.[71] Despite a good cast that featured Phyllis Frelich as Frances Walker (for whom Henley had written the part after seeing her in *Children of a Lesser God*), Kurtwood Smith (Hank Turner), Penny Johnson (Violet Moore), and Ann Hearn (Teddy Parker), as well as an adept production team that included Robert Blackman's costumes, Tom Ruzika's lighting, Mark Donnell's sets, and Stephen Tobolowsky's direction, the play itself did not gel. Although the drama received good reviews from *Variety* and the *Los Angeles Times* (the only nationally distributed media sources to cover this production),[72] Henley thought the script rambled too much; after the first preview, she left the auditorium at intermission to vomit in a jade bush behind the theater.

Three years later, in 1988, Henley worked with director Norman René to revise *The Debutante Ball* for a New York production. Henley eliminated several extraneous characters and placed the focus on the relationship between Jen and her daughter Teddy. The revised version of the play debuted at the Manhattan Theatre Club's Second Stage on 26 April 1988. René directed a cast that featured Carol Kane (Bliss White), Ann Wedgeworth (Jen Turner), and Kellie Overbey (Teddy). Critics were not allowed to attend in order for Henley and the production team to work out the kinks, and by doing so, eventually transfer the play to the main stage. However, the producer felt that the play was too extreme for mainstream audiences, so *The Debutante Ball* never made it to Off Broadway, which meant that critics did not review this production.

Although *The Debutante Ball* has never been produced in New York City, it has had several productions worldwide. The play was produced by the New York Stage and Film Company at the Powerhouse Theater, Vasser College, in Poughkeepsie, New York, on 28 July 1988. The London production debuted at the Hampstead Theatre on 30 May 1989 under direction from Simon Stokes, who was an old hand at directing Henley's plays for British audiences. The British press gave it mixed reviews ranging from an assessment of the play as high-camp nonsense played by an excellent company to reviews describing it as sentimental, ghoulish, grand guignol, arch, inane, and ponderously "unfunny."[73] *The Debutante Ball* has been successful overseas, particularly in Germany (Hamburg), where it was a smash hit.

Soon after Henley had finished writing *The Debutante Ball*, she began work on *The Lucky Spot* in 1985. The two-act play was first staged under Norman René's direction in Summer 1986 at the Williamstown Theatre Festival in Williamstown, Massachusetts, with Holly Hunter as Cassidy

Smith, and then opened 28 April 1987 Off Broadway at the Manhattan Theatre Club, where it ran until 17 May. Stephen Tobolowsky directed a cast that included Mary Stuart Masterson (Cassidy), Alan Ruck (Turnip Moss), Ray Baker (Reed Hooker), Lanny Flaherty (Whitt Carmichael), Belita Moreno (Lacey Rollins, a role that Henley again wrote specifically for Moreno), Amy Madigan (Sue Jack Hooker), and John Wylie (Sam); John Lee Beatty designed the sets, Dennis Parichy supervised the lighting, and Jennifer von Mayrhauser made the costumes. *The Lucky Spot* was not heavily reviewed by the New York media, and, except for the virtually unanimous praise given to the performances by Madigan and Masterson, the half-dozen reviewers who did write were divided in their assessments. Henley's most vociferous supporter was John Simon, whose review in *New York* was nothing but superlatives, claiming that Henley wove feyness, wit, and pathos drowned in humor extremely well so that we care about these characters presented to us in a breathtaking production, making *The Lucky Spot* Henley's best play since *Crimes of the Heart*.[74] Henry Popkin (*Plays and Players*), John Beaufort (*Christian Science Monitor*), and Edith Oliver (*New Yorker*) also favorably reviewed the play, paying particular attention to the remarkable acting by the ensemble.[75] Negative opinions of the production were shared by Humm (*Variety*), Julius Novick (*Variety*), and Frank Rich (*New York Times*). Humm complained that Henley's overwrought depiction of goofy Southerners was becoming tedious because of too much sentimentalizing and not enough fresh comic dialogue; his counterpart from *Variety*, Novick, writing one week after Humm's review was printed, also found too much sentimentality and recycled, unconvincing typed characters, although he did acknowledge that Henley wrote with an individual voice and penned some good dialogue.[76] Rich characterized the play as pseudo Tennessee Williams, artificially sweetened for mass consumption, disingenuously upbeat, and misdirected by Tobolowsky, who permitted overacting and failed to establish a tone to unify "a literary marriage between Strindberg and Al Capp."[77] *The Lucky Spot* has been staged with varying degrees of fortune since the production in New York, including a successful run at the Center Theater in Chicago from November 21 to December 22, 1990, and a somewhat disappointing set of performances by Boston's Delvena Theatre Company in December 1998.[78] After it was staged in a small London theater, Lewis Gilbert, a British director who went to see the play, asked Henley to write the screenplay for a film version destined for Paramount; Henley completed the script in 1991, but it has yet to be filmed.

In 1988, Henley's screenplay, *Miss Firecracker*, based on *The Miss Firecracker Contest*, was being filmed in Yazoo City, Mississippi, the new location now replacing Brookhaven. Henley was working closely with first-time director Thomas Schlamme, who suggested that oogle-eyed Alfre Woodard, an African-American, play Popeye, for she certainly looked the part. Henley had written a blues scene into the screenplay, but it had to be dropped because the film's $3.5 million budget did not allow the expense of its shooting. Other new wrinkles in the film included Schlamme's suggestion to have Carnelle work on a catfish farm (determined by the location filming) and his desire to have Carnelle confront Elain at the end of the film, which does not occur in the play and thus required a rewrite that had Elain bringing the red dress to Carnelle yet not giving it to her to wear during the contest.[79] Of course, Henley's play was written as a type of Greek tragedy where most of the action occurs offstage, but the visual orientation of a film required that the audience see more of the contest, even though the change of title puts the emphasis squarely on Carnelle rather than on the contest. The other important revision permitted Carnelle to watch the fireworks alone, without Popeye or Delmount, therefore allowing the two lovers to be together while Carnelle is spiritually separated from the others. *Miss Firecracker* was released by Corsair Pictures in May 1989 with a cast that included Holly Hunter (Carnelle), Woodard (Popeye), Mary Steenbergen (Elain), Tim Robbins (Delmount), and Scott Glenn (Mac Sam). The critics praised Schlamme for getting the maximum out of the performers, especially Robbins, Hunter, Steenbergen, and Woodard, some of whom were even accused of overacting The overall assessment of the script was that Henley's appetite for the Southern Gothic was insatiable and somewhat sentimental, but underneath there was compassion for her indomitable, lonely dreamers.[80]

Henley spent five years doing research on nineteenth-century frontier life for her next play, *Abundance*, which was commissioned by the South Coast Repertory Theater. The play was a major departure for Henley because its epic form that spans twenty-five years was a new adjustment for a playwright typically confined by a classical structure that followed unity of time. *Abundance* had its world premiere at South Coast Repertory in Costa Mesa, California, on 21 April 1989 and ran through 25 May. Ron Lagomarsino directed O-Lan Jones as Bess and Belita Moreno as Macon in an appropriately subdued and spare production. Although the premiere received little critical attention, the consensus was that the play, although improbable at times, was a thoughtful and accomplished piece of writing.[81]

Abundance had its New York debut at the Manhattan Theatre Club on 4 October 1990, again under direction by Lagomarsino but now with a cast that included Amanda Plummer (Bess), Tess Harper (Macon), Michael Rooker (Jack Flan), Lanny Flaherty (William Curtis), and Keith Reddin

(Elmore Crome). The production crew consisted of Adrianne Lobel (sets), Robert Wojewodski (costumes), and Paule Jenkins (lighting). The critics made sure that the play would have a limited run Off Broadway. The only positive reviews were from Mimi Kramer (*New Yorker*), Frank Rich (*New York Times*), and James S. Torrens (*America*). Torrens lauded the play's imaginative vision, intriguing Victorian language, and inventive staging, while Kramer gave Henley credit for a strong script brought to life by solid acting and a haunting set that featured slow-moving turntables.[82] Rich was the play's most eloquent yet cautious defender, citing, on the one hand, an overabundant production with languorous set changes and too many repetitions and prosaic transitions, yet, on the other hand, admitting that the actors hold the audience's attention in what he deemed Henley's most provocative play in years; Rich saw the play as a revisionist Western, spiced with Gothic humor, that presented the specter of disfigured dreams, thus unearthing the dark underside of American mythology about the West.[83]

Unfortunately, most reviewers did not take the time to assess the Off Broadway production of *Abundance* as thoughtfully as Rich did. The play received negative press from Clive Barnes (*New York Post*), Robert Brustein (*New Republic*), Melanie Kirkpatrick (*Wall Street Journal*), Howard Kissel (*Daily News*), David Richards (*New York Times*), John Simon (*New York*), and Linda Winer (*New York Newsday*).[84] Several critics claimed that the play sent conflicting signals about its purpose, allowing the focus to shift from an exploration of failed American mythology to the strange ways destiny works and then to the effects of female bonding. Richards complained about Harper's extroverted sunny California presence not fitting into Henley's sense of the macabre; Simon noted that Plummer's repertoire was limited because her performance conveyed no connection with the role or with her fellow actors, while Kissel characterized it as "the contemporary notion that acting is a form of neurosis."[85] Barnes depicted Henley's script as unconvincing yet intriguing but was confused by the tone (like Winer, who found it uneven), which he suggested ranged from a comedy, a farce, or an epic Western — albeit sans the usual Henley wit and imagination.[86] Simon's comments were certainly the most perplexing in his attempt to convince us that the play was a catharsis for Henley, a reckoning with an ex-husband and a female friend, with Bess (read Beth) transformed from 1868 to 1968.[87]

Abundance was also staged at the Actors Theater in San Francisco during September and October 1992, by the Signature Theatre in Washington, D.C., from 20 March to 23 April 1994 in an entertaining production directed by Dorothy Neumann that featured Lou Stancari's barren sets and Rosemary Regan's fine performance as Bess, at London's Riverside

Theatre (November 1995) in performances highlighted by Maryam d'Abo as Macon, and from 27 May to 11 June 2000 in Pamela Moller Kareman's production at the Schoolhouse Theater in Crofton Falls, New York.[88] Henley adapted the play for the 1998 film, *Come West with Me*, which was directed by Marleen Gorris.

During the early 1990s, Henley began writing experimental drama both that was no longer set in the South and that deviated from her Southern Gothic, classically structured plays, thus requiring an alternative venue rather than the commercially oriented Broadway or Off Broadway; besides, after the negative reception of *Abundance* Off Broadway, Henley was probably not too eager to repeat the experience. She began writing *Signature* in 1990 after she paid a graphologist on Melrose Avenue to read her handwriting, and he proclaimed that it was indicative of a "petty, selfish, measly, talented egotist" and then added, "I don't mean any of this as a value judgment."[89] *Signature* was first performed in a workshop by the New York Stage and Film Company in Poughkeepsie, New York, during Summer 1990. Thomas Schlamme, who directed *Miss Firecracker*, put the actors through their paces, including Kurtwood Smith (Boswell), Mark Linn-Baker (Maxwell), Carol Kane (William Smit), Christine Lahti (L-Tip), Damon Anderson (C-Boy), and O-Lan Jones (Reader). This low-budget production got a bit ragged when the company ran out of money for costumes and when actors were forced to wear their street clothes; Henley, the Pulitzer Prize winner, meanwhile, stayed in a dorm room in Poughkeepsie. The first full-scale production of the play occurred in Charlotte, North Carolina, from 29 March to 9 April 1995. The Charlotte Repertory Theatre staged the play at the Performing Arts Center under direction from Steve Umberger. *Signature* was next performed by the Passage Theater Company at Mill Hill Playhouse in Trenton, New Jersey, during May 1996, with Jim McGrath directing.[90] Stephen Stout, the artistic director of the theater, had been at Southern Methodist with Henley and thus was able to get a copy of the play and do a staged reading in February 1995 before actually producing the play and also acting in it as Boswell.

Henley wrote *Control Freaks*, her most daring play, shortly after she finished the last draft of *Signature*. Henley, who was on the board of directors for the Met Theatre in Los Angeles, wrote *Control Freaks* with four characters and one rather sparse set so it could be staged at the Met with Holly Hunter, who had previously starred in five of Henley's dramas, as Sister Willard. Henley did not have the heart to try to explain her motivations for her most experimental play to a director, especially since much of the writing was intuitive, so she thought it best to direct it herself. However, to gain confidence before attempting a production in Los Angeles, she workshopped the play for ten days at Center Theater in Chicago during January 1992 before its September 1992 debut (Henley knew the artistic director at Center Theater, Dan LaMorte, from her student days at the University of Illinois). In his review of the play for the *Chicago Tribune*, Richard Christiansen praised the production but stated that Henley's direction was over the top and mainly required her getting control of these freaks portrayed on stage; Hedy Weiss, however, thought the play was unredeemable, degenerating into an "atrocious amalgam of self-indulgence and gratuitous sexual rage."[91] After writing letters to friends trying to raise money for the production in Los Angeles and after securing financial help from Holly Hunter as the co-producer with David Beaird, *Control Freaks* eventually premiered at the Met Theatre in Santa Monica under Henley's direction in a run from 16 July to 8 August 1993. The fine cast included Hunter as Sister (fresh from winning a Best Actress award at the Cannes International Film Festival for her role in Jane Campion's film, *The Piano*), Carol Kane as Betty Willard, Bill Pullman as Carl Willard, and the lesser known Wayne Pere as Paul Casper. Henley viewed her directorial debut as "Very challenging. And really sort of monumental for me because I had to take responsibility to communicate and to really go with a vision without leaning on a director and being able to leave when things got boring or heated. It was a big leap — but hard."[92] Her patience with *Control Freaks* paid off; in his review of the play (the only national attention the Met Theatre's production received), Tom Jacobs of *Variety* wrote that Henley's superb direction inspired the cast to do wonders with a text that he described as "darkly hilarious" and "startling wonderful."[93] Don Shirley's review in the *Los Angeles Times* was also laudatory with the caveat that the play falters in the denouement because Sister's plight is revealed too late in the play for us to get very emotionally involved.[94]

In fairly quick succession, Henley wrote *Revelers* (1993) then *L-Play* (1994). *Revelers* received its first production by the New York Stage and Film Company in Poughkeepsie, New York, in 1994, under director Leonard Foglia's guidance. In 1996, *Revelers* was next staged at the Center Theater in Chicago, with Dan LaMorte directing. These productions went unnoticed by the national media,[95] and Henley herself has expressed reservations about the play.[96] Consisting of twelve vignettes of ninety minutes' duration without intermission, *L-Play* was directed by Eric Hill at the Unicorn Theatre, the second stage of the Berkshire Theatre Festival, in Stockbridge, Massachusetts, during Summer 1996.[97] Despite fine acting by the six-member cast and Hill's animated direction, *L-Play*, hardly noticed by the press, was reviewed negatively because of complaints that Henley's message was half-hidden, the characters' motives were difficult to discern (making them seem as if they lacked humanity), and the form was a confusing mélange alternating between naturalistic and hallucinatory.[98] *L-Play* was also staged as a benefit performance at the Met Theatre in 1996, featuring cast members Alfre Woodard, Holly Hunter, Amy Madigan, James Gammon, Ed Harris, and Bill Pullman.

During 1995, when Henley was pregnant with her first child, she was commissioned to write a play for the Roundabout Theatre, whose staff was seeking to stage the work of established playwrights who were not being produced much any longer in New York. Henley's mother urged Beth to write a comedy because she was pregnant and did not want the baby to be put under stress, so the result was *Impossible Marriage* set in a wooded fantasy world outside of Savannah, Georgia — a sort of *Midsummer Night's Dream* with Edwardian repartee derived from the theater of Oscar Wilde. She did most of the work on the play in 1995 but held off getting it finished and polished for performance because she was busy rearing her son (born in August 1995), writing a movie script about Canadian bank robbers, and recovering from a strength-sapping illness. *Impossible Marriage* opened at the Roundabout Theatre on 15 October 1998 — eight years since Henley had had a play staged in New York (*Abundance*). Stephen Wadsworth directed the ninety-minute play featuring Daniel London (Sidney Lunt), Holly Hunter (Floral Whitman),[99] Lois Smith (Kandall Kingsley), Jon Tenney (Jonsey Whitman), Gretchen Cleevely (Pandora Kingsley), Alan Mandell (Reverend Larence), and Christopher McCann (Edvard Lunt).

Clive Barnes of the *New York Post* was grateful that the Roundabout Theatre brought Henley out of hiding; Barnes and Fintan O'Toole (*Daily News*) were the only critics to argue that the subtext of the play was slow and thoughtful, deftly brought to the surface by Wadsworth.[100] Charles Isherwood (*Variety*) had reservations about the believability of the characters and the quirky comedy that he claimed fell flat at times, but he praised the direction, the "impeccable" cast, and Henley's dialogue, which he called "insufferably precious" and "disarmingly charming."[101] Barnes and Isherwood, however, were definitely in the minority because most of their colleagues did not find merit in the play. Donald Lyons (*Wall Street Journal*) dismissed the writing as "desperate," "threadbare," and "incoherent," claimed that Donald Lynch's lush vegetative set was "pointlessly excessive," and stated that only Smith and Hunter were believable in their roles.[102] John Simon (*New York*) disagreed with Lyons's assessment of the production, stating that it was handsomely designed and operatically staged but calling it "coagulated whimsy" that failed to sustain the interest of the audience; David Patrick Stearns, in turn, disagreed with Simon's opinion with regard to the play's staging, stating that the performance was "engaging," but the flippant nonsequiturs passing for dialogue, the mercurial characters, and the nonsensical wit were too much to bear.[103] Edward Karam (*Times*) claimed that at times the play echoed Chekhov and Marivaux, but otherwise it sounded like a clumsy collaboration of J.M. Barrie and Tennessee Williams; he suggested that Henley rewrite and then mount the play in a more astute production.[104] Finally, Ben Brantley of the *New York Times* praised Henley as a virtuosic wordsmith but put the blame on the acting, arguing that the performers seemed uncomfortable, even distanced, from the dialogue, in a play where the most convincing character (Jonsey) is the most superficial.[105] *Impossible Marriage* has also been staged most recently in Minneapolis's Theatre in the Round — a lackluster July 2000 production that opened the theater's forty-ninth season.[106]

On 16 April 2000, Henley's *Family Week* opened Off Broadway at the 299-seat Century Center for the Performing Arts. Under direction by Ulu Grosbard, the ninety-minute play featured performances by Rose Gregorio (Lena), Angelina Phillips (Claire), Carol Kane (Rickey), and Julia Weldon (Kay). The play concerns the effects of a teenager's murder on three generations of women who have come to a treatment center in Arizona for one week to exorcize their demons through therapeutic games. *Family Week* closed on 16 April after running only eight performances.[107] As of this writing, the play remains unpublished, and Henley confided to me in an informal conversation that she plans to revise the play; thus, since *Family Week* is a work in progress without a definitive text, I cannot examine it critically in this book.

Henley currently lives in Los Angeles with her young son, who, as one might imagine, has slowed her writing considerably. To get ideas for plays, Henley carries a notebook to record images, interesting costumes, furniture for the set, etc. She usually begins with ideas she is tormented with, is wrestling with, or perhaps images that she is perplexed with or have been difficult for her to grasp rather than images that she understands; thus, in essence, her plays are largely somewhat autobiographical. A dominant image for her to start with may be, for example, a funeral, a beauty pageant, or someone getting arrested. Without having a clear-cut sense of characters at first, she does a lot of pre-writing in notebooks to record various smells, images, and bits of dialogue. She prepares excessive notes, character charts, and plot outlines — all ritualistic activity — before attempting to write any dialogue; she thinks in terms of character and story rather than thematically. Henley writes almost daily, mostly at her office during the afternoons. She relies on her acting experience to get to know her characters by envisioning how she would play them on stage, noting how they will think (usually about the dominant image she has in mind from the beginning), and what they will say, much like an improvisation in which one character recites the first line, and the other responds accordingly. Henley develops her characters by making long lists of what they might say, do, or wear. In an interview with Cynthia Wimmer-Moul, Henley stated, "Every character has a secret, every character has a reaction to the other characters, every character has a greatest fear, and every character has a greatest dream; and I want to know what their sense of humor is and what their sexuality is and how they dress and how they talk."[108] Once she understands her characters and the plot, the dialogue comes easy to her since that is her forte. Henley writes intuitively and for herself, which is partly why her vision is so true. With regard to writing intuitively rather than thematically, Henley admits, "I'm like a child when I write, taking chances, never thinking in terms of logic or reviews. I just go with what I'm feeling."[109] Each day, Henley rereads the previous day's dialogue and refers to her notes and sketches about the plot and characters. After fleshing out the characters and their relationships, Henley maps out the first scene; the remainder of the play is usually sketchy since Henley likes to leave things open for surprises, especially the denouement, which always seems to cause trouble for her. She begins writing in longhand in spiral notebooks and then edits it before copying the draft neatly in another notebook. Once she gets the first act typed on her IBM Selectric (she does not use a word processor or computer), she photocopies it, then makes corrections before turning it over to a typist. Next, she shows the draft to one of her close friends, who Henley trusts will overpraise it; she acknowledges, "The last thing you want after working on something for five months is to have someone tell you it's no good."[110] Henley then shows the manuscript to friends who are more critical; after the first draft, she usually does not do major rewrites, though she will make minor adjustments.

Henley prefers a low-key approach to readings of her manuscripts, which usually occur at her house or in the residences of her friends. During these readings, she notes problem points that need work. Once the play is in rehearsals, Henley attends them regularly, for she loves being in the theater, watching actors discover things about themselves or about the play. She refrains from talking to the performers (who usually get upset when the playwright criticizes them), choosing instead to work more closely with the director by passing him or her notes. She has definite ideas about the costumes but is more reticent about interfering with sets and lighting, which she knows much less about. To Henley, the writing and rehearsal process is part of her necessary existence, a means of occupying her mind during the daily mundane tasks of life, as well as a vital practice that makes her feel alive.

2

Henley and the Modern *Angoisse*

In *Civilization and Its Discontents* (1930), Freud argued that modern society is largely responsible for the creation of misery, in direct contrast to the psyche's id, which seeks pleasure. In Freudian psychoanalytical theory, the ego (the self or "I" that is in contact with the external world through perception) and the superego (the component of our personalities that forms our ethical and moral judgments) are established through social structures. However, the id, which relates primarily to sex and aggression — the primitive bodily instincts that are established in humans at birth — is oblivious to the external world or the norms and values of society's institutions. The push and pull of the conscious socialization felt directly on the ego and superego diminish or mask our unconscious libidinal desires represented by the id, and thus we become conflicted or anxious. Freud characterized the *angoisse* or angst as neurotic: "It was discovered that a person becomes neurotic because he cannot tolerate the amount of frustration which society imposes on him in the service of its cultural ideals, and it was inferred from this that the abolition or reduction of those demands would result in a return to possibilities of happiness."[1] In the early stages of development, during the formative years when the child is being nurtured by the mother, the satisfaction of happiness is the major goal; however, once the individual is socialized and integrated into community norms and values, cultural restrictions are formed. Thus, the libidinal urge toward human happiness eventually conflicts with the purpose of civilization, which is to create a unity out of individual human beings. Freud wrote, "If more is demanded of a man, a revolt will be pro-

33

duced in him or a neurosis, or he will be made unhappy."[2] Freud understood the neurosis to be endemic to modern society, a universal condition among civilized nations: "If the development of civilization has such a far-reaching similarity to the development of the individual and if it employs the same methods, may we not be justified in reaching the diagnosis that, under the influence of cultural urges, some civilizations, or some epochs of civilization — possibly the whole of mankind — have become 'neurotic?'"[3] The reaction to this dichotomy between individual happiness and the socializing norms of civilization has been a deeply rooted existential despair manifested in *angoisse*, alienation, isolation, and various neurotic behaviors, such as narcissism, depression, Manic Depressive Disorders, Borderline Personality Disorders, Antisocial Personality Disorders, and schizophrenia — all of which will be discussed in detail in various chapters throughout this book.

Freud discussed how societies have developed religion, science, and art to assuage the neurotic condition — all to no avail because these means of achieving pleasure misrepresent life delusionally. Religion, science, and art merely offer us a mild narcosis, which is a temporary relief from the modern neurosis. Individuals may also turn to sexual relationships to pursue the pleasure principle; however, modern society places restrictions on sex, thereby diminishing the ego. Love is also a major source of pleasure that individuals pursue to negate the neurotic condition that permeates modern society. Unfortunately, innate human aggressiveness opposes Eros in its attempt to unite human beings into a world of peace, harmony, and happiness. Civilization merely promotes the illusion that humans are loving and caring rather than aggressive. Destructive aggression is turned against the ego in the form of a superego, which produces guilt and thus discontent. As civilization advances, the price we pay is a loss of happiness through this sense of guilt. Cynical about the consequences of World War I when he was writing *Civilization and Its Discontents* and believing that reason and intelligence were merely masks for human aggressiveness, Freud understood that humans are not gentle creatures who want to be loved but rather aggressive individuals capable of defending themselves if attacked, and their friends and neighbors are often someone who tempts them to satisfy their aggressiveness; this primordial hostility of humans against humans Freud termed the death instinct. This natural aggressiveness, the hostility of each against all and of all against each, opposes the goals of civilization, thus creating an absurd condition. The struggle becomes one of Eros versus Death, between the instinct of life and the instinct of destruction, essentially a neurotic condition that can never be resolved. Civilization is counterproductive in this struggle, for it tries to create a mastery over the individual's dangerous desire for aggression by increasing one's individual guilt over it; this exacerbates the discontent peculiar to the life of modern culture and civilization. In his book on Freud, Paul Ricoeur summarizes the modern *angoisse* that Freud discussed in *Civilization and Its Discontents*: "And now culture comes upon the scene as the great enterprise of making life prevail against death: its supreme weapon is to employ internalized violence against externalized violence; its supreme ruse is to make death work against death."[4] Thus, we pay for advances in civilization that further increase our sense of guilt and concomitantly cost us our sense of happiness—hence, the discontent that Freud postulated is the modern *angoisse*. As Gerald Levin notes, "Freud's major theme is that the original unity of ego and the external world gradually shrinks as man surrenders the pleasure principle for the reality principle; man is thus a diminished being, ridden with conflicts that civilization heightens rather than alleviates, not the creature of unlimited potentiality whose natural instincts are sources of happiness."[5] Humanity is thus plagued with the constant imbalance and conflict of having to contend with perpetually irreconcilable forces, thus exacerbating the neurotic condition. The modern neurosis leads to impaired social contacts, contempt for others, and perhaps an inability to work and love. Psychiatrist Samuel I. Greenberg also notes that the neurotic often ignores the means by which modern civilization forces us to sublimate and reject our aggressive tendencies and therefore projects anger onto others, leading to their neglect.[6] Neurosis no longer is the disease of the traumatized but is instead a general condition of humanity's progress in the twentieth century.

In *The Myth of Sisyphus* (1940), Albert Camus tried to explain philosophically the modern neurosis that Freud discussed ten years earlier in psychoanalytic terms, which Camus deemed the absurd condition. Camus claimed that the world itself is not absurd, but, as Freud realized, humanity's longing for clarity cannot be achieved, thus creating the neurotic condition where antimony and *angoisse* reign. Camus argued, "I can therefore say that the Absurd is not in man (if such a metaphor could have a meaning) nor in the world, but in their presence together."[7] If the Absurd is the fundamental condition of humanity, Camus posed the question of whether life was worth pursuing. Camus, in effect, wanted to explore the notion of whether suicide — which Freud would argue would be equivalent to succumbing to the death instinct — would be viable. He stated, "The subject of this essay is precisely this relationship between the absurd and suicide, the exact degree to which suicide is a solution to the absurd."[8]

Camus used the Greek myth of Sisyphus to demonstrate that the absurd condition or the modern neurosis could be, if not negated, then

temporarily challenged. The gods had condemned Sisyphus for his transgressions by forcing him to push a rock up a hill; when the rock reached
the pinnacle, it would roll back down, forcing Sisyphus to begin the labor
yet another time. The metaphor is that, like the modern neurosis, which
Freud argued was futile and hopeless to counteract, Sisyphus's labor is
cyclical and interminable. Camus applies Sisyphus's fate to modern civilization: "The workman of today works every day in his life at the same
tasks, and this fate is no less absurd. But it is tragic only at the rare moments
when it becomes conscious."[9] In defiance of the absurd condition, Sisyphus revolts by refusing suicide as a viable alternative. Camus depicts Sisyphus in the worst possible scenario—condemned to an absurd existence.
Sisyphus could decide not to cooperate with the gods, and since he is
already dead (brought back from the underworld), what fate could be
worse as his punishment? Instead, Sisyphus decides to revolt through
momentary consciousness as he walks back down the hill to prepare to
begin the arduous task again ad infinitum. In his recognition of the modern neurosis, Sisyphus revolts, and by doing so, believes that he creates
his own fate in defiance of his condemned status. Camus concludes, "The
struggle itself toward the heights is enough to fill a man's heart. One must
imagine Sisyphus happy."[10] In short, as Freud assured us, the absurd condition can never be abrogated by human behavior, but it can be temporarily mitigated by consciousness that helps us to revolt against it,
simultaneously nullifying any desires we have to commit suicide.

The anomie and *angoisse* of the modern neuroticism is manifested in
the theater of the absurd in which humanity is shown to be cut off from
its religious, transcendental, and metaphysical roots—lost in an inexplic-
able universe. In *The Theatre of the Absurd*, Martin Esslin stated that the
goal of playwrights of the absurdist theater was to find dignity in modern
society in which generally accepted integrating principles were now no
longer present.[11] Theater of the absurd was performed essentially to make
humanity aware of its precarious position in the universe. Henley's theater, as we shall soon see, has the same purpose and the same result as theater of the absurd: her plays make us aware of the modern neurosis (what
Camus deemed the absurd condition), and the revolt that Camus discussed
is essentially what Esslin postulated and what Henley demonstrates to be
a quest for dignity amidst the *angoisse*. However, I do not presume to
equate the theater of the absurd with Henley's dramas, for their fundamental assumptions, forms, and language are different. As Esslin aptly
notes, the theater of the absurd derived its distinctiveness from other forms
of drama, not through Freud's notion of the modern neurosis, but from
the impression that these playwrights had of a disjointed, purposeless world

in which logic and reason failed to explain the chaos that occurred during World War II. This resulted in communication being depicted in the theater of the absurd in a state of breakdown in which language is devalued; Henley's plays do not pinpoint World War II as the source of the breakdown and thus do not mock logic, reason, or language. Moreover, the loss of religious beliefs after the War, resulting in characters depicted in absurdist theater as lacking motives, a past, and concomitantly empathy from the audience, is absent from Henley's dramas. Obviously, the form of theater of absurd, which is structured by poetic images that work like a jigsaw puzzle for the audience to piece together, is also anathema to Henley, who works largely within the confines of conventional theater. However, despite the differences in language, content, and structure, the *goals* of the theater of the absurd and Henley's theater are the same. Esslin stated, "In the Theatre of the Absurd, the spectator is confronted with the madness of the human condition, is enabled to see his situation in all its grimness and despair."[12] As I will argue throughout this book, Henley strips the illusions behind our masks, forcing us to confront the modern neurosis in all its horror and despair. Moreover, the solution she proposes to fight against the modern *angoisse* is derived from the revolt that Camus discussed in *The Myth of Sisyphus*, a philosophy that became the underlying assumption for absurdist playwrights as the means to combat the absurd. Rather than submit to the modern *angoisse,* protagonists in the theater of the absurd come face to face with the modern neurosis, much in the same manner that Sisyphus revolted against insurmountable forces. Esslin explains, "But by facing up to misery and despair and the absence of divinely revealed alternatives, anxiety and despair can be overcome."[13] As we shall see, Henley's protagonists, like Sisyphus and his disciples from the absurdist theater, engage in a quest for dignity and meaning in a world defined by the neuroticism that produces the existential despair, anomie, and *angoisse* endemic to our lives in modern society.

One may find it difficult to perceive Henley as sharing the same philosophy as absurdist playwrights who allow audiences to participate in the modern neuroticism because the latter portray the condition as universal while Henley's plays are stereotyped as regional dramas. There is no question that Henley's Southern heritage influenced the language, tone, and character development of the early plays. These dramas have a definite sense of place, unlike the theater of the absurd, which often occurs in nondescript locales (e.g., *Waiting for Godot, Endgame, The Bald Soprano, The Chairs, Rosencrantz and Guildenstern Are Dead, The Room, The Birthday Party,* etc.). Henley's early plays occur in the South: *Am I Blue* (New Orleans), *Crimes of the Heart* (Hazlehurst, Mississippi), *The Wake of Jamey*

Foster and *Hymn in the Attic* (Canton, Mississippi), *The Miss Firecracker Contest* (Brookhaven, Mississippi), *The Debutante Ball* (Hattiesburg, Mississippi), and *The Lucky Spot* (Pigeon, Louisiana). These are places Henley grew up with: her father's family was from Hazlehurst (population 3,000); her mother's kin from Brookhaven; her aunt, uncle, and cousins lived in Hattiesburg; she went to camp in Canton; and New Orleans was a getaway place for Southerners, merely two hundred miles from Henley's home in Jackson. Even in the late plays, she returns to her Southern roots, for part of *L-Play* occurs in south Louisiana, while *Impossible Marriage* is set in Savannah, Georgia. There is no doubt that the oral tradition of telling tales ("whoppers") is indigenous to the region and plays a large part in Henley's dramas. Henley confided to Scott Haller how this oral tradition supplied her with the material for her early plays, especially when she left Los Angeles to return home:

> I get off the plane, and the stories are just incredible. All sorts of bizarre things are going on. It's in the air. Oh, Lord, the stories I hear about just who has died in town. There are dope fiends living next door. Hermits live over here. The police are out after people breaking in windows. Somebody's drowned, and somebody's shot themselves. And that's just the houses on my block.[14]

Henley speaks endearingly of her Southern heritage: "I love the people: They're so vivid in the way they speak and the stories they tell...."[15] She does not mock small-town Southern life nor does she believe it to be parochial. Instead, several of her plays do indeed have a sense of place that is distinguishable from the venues of absurdist theater. Henley's view of the South is not sarcastic or mocking: "It was hard growing up for me, but I still love the place I came from. I love the people and the way they tell stories. I love the romance and the smell of the air."[16]

There are, however, other reasons for Henley setting several of her plays in the South besides the fact that the oral tradition provides her with enough anecdotal ammunition for the diversionary tales that her protagonists tell. First, the South (and later the West) provides her with the poetic language that makes the plays flow, creating a unique resonance that rings true for audiences. Second, the "eccentricities" or stereotyped abnormal behavior associated with vices that are kept latent in the South make Henley's feelings about the modern neurosis more acceptable to a wide range of audiences. As Henley explained to Robert Berkvist, "If a play is set in the South, it can be kind of eccentric and people will accept it."[17] Third, and most importantly, the South has provided Henley with the model for the rebel, like Camus's Sisyphus, who fights the modern neurosis, usually to no avail, but who still insists on finding dignity in an absurd universe. Henley ascribes this condition to the South's unique reaction to its own history:

> There is something else, too, something I'm sure has to do with the South's defeat in the Civil War, which is that you should never take yourself too seriously. You may be beaten and defeated, but your spirit cannot be conquered. The South has gall to still be able to say we have our pride, but as a human characteristic it is admirable.[18]

This description sounds like Sisyphus's condition after he is condemned to death and forced to toil interminably by pushing the rock up the hill; yet Sisyphus becomes one with his rock by accepting his condition and making the most of it in defiance of the gods. Henley ascribes the South's destiny as beaten and defeated after the Civil War, yet Southerners seem to accept their fate, even relish it, thereby allowing the downtrodden to remain proud and dignified. Henley reiterates that this trait is endemic to the South: "I think Southerners, in a sense, being from the only part of the United States that's been defeated in war, have a certain resiliency and desire to survive defeat and remain dignified in the face of it."[19] Finally, the fact that Southern culture frowns on individuals who take themselves too seriously provides Henley with the perfect means to have her protagonists find the comic side to the agonizing reality of the modern *angoisse*.

Thus, Henley seems to employ the Southern setting as a viable locale to demonstrate the modern neurosis and an appropriate means of coping with it. We must not assume that a play set in the South merely has regional implications; instead, Henley's plays, often occurring in distinct settings, must be approached in the same manner that we might accept the more universal setting of absurdist dramas. The Southern milieu often invites critics to make misleading sociological or political inferences about her plays. For example, Jonnie Guerra asserts, "But the images of women the audience confronts in Henley's plays are predominantly negative ones of suffering, self-destructive females whose lives and identities have been shaped by male family members and the sexist values of the small southern towns in which they reside."[20] I agree with William W. Demastes who argues that the Southern setting creates a regional flavor to the plays, which usually does not coincide with the intellectual detachment of the absurdist theater; however, Demastes urges critics to view the domestic kitchen-sink Southern settings as a means of providing the absurd condition with a new relevance and immediacy to daily existence that is not found in theater of the absurd.[21] Associating Henley with the Freudian notion of the modern neurosis is particularly difficult because in the theater the absurd condition has been a European passion, rather than an American one, and certainly not of Southern distinction. Moreover, the absurd condition has generally been depicted in abstract settings rather than the specific middle-class Southern stomping grounds that Henley presents. Ayne C. Durham astutely notes, "Her [Henley's] plays realistically capture the Southern vernacular and take place in authentic Southern settings, yet they also exaggerate the recognizable and push the bizarre to extremes to reveal the underlying absurdity of the human condition. Whereas Henley's characters are rooted in her Southern heritage, the meaning of their experiences is not limited to time and place."[22] Finally, although Henley has used the Southern setting to good effect to create poetry in the dialogue and to portray the modern *angoisse* and an appropriate response to it, we must remember that nearly half of her plays do not occur in the South. As Gary Richards intimates, the plays written after 1990 codify Henley as a post–Southern writer:

> In the plays of this decade [1990s] [*Abundance, Signature, Control Freaks, Revelers, L-Play,* and *Impossible Marriage*], Henley consistently — if not always successfully — explores new concerns and preoccupations refreshingly unshackled from southern environs: gender roles in the nineteenth-century American West; the future of an ego-driven, media-controlled society; the complex relations of family, power, and eroticism; the dynamics of theater production itself; the inherent instabilities of the postmodern moment.[23]

To coincide with the stereotype of Henley as a Southern writer, critics have also labeled her plays "Gothic," which is usually synonymous with cutely dismissing them as eccentric, macabre, bizarre, dysfunctional, and/or "wacky." This mind set would allow us to believe that Freud's notion of neurosis is not endemic to modern civilization but rather that the pathological underside of life replete with jealousies, obsessions, madness, and behavioral disabilities are reserved for a few individuals who perhaps should be committed to mental institutions. Critics such as Benedict Nightingale wonder if Henley realizes that part of the appeal of her dramatic oeuvre is that Southern eccentricity, quaintly described as "Gothic," is being paraded in front of audiences (East Coast, West Coast, and international) that find these hidden perversions outrageous, even pathetic.[24] Henley, however, sees the walking wounded, the ostracized, the spiritually and physically maimed as typical of the repercussions resulting from the modern *angoisse* that Freud claimed was endemic to the human condition in the twentieth century. When asked to assess her plays as Gothic or her characters as eccentric, Henley denies the charge: "It seems real to me. I wouldn't find it interesting to be sitting around, making everything up. So many of my stories are from people I've known and tales I've heard."[25] This sentiment echoes what Henley told Ted Bent of *People* when trying to explain the public reaction to *Crimes of the Heart* on Broadway: "Almost everything in my plays is something I've heard of, seen, or known about. I don't think of my characters as wacky, I just think they're *vivid*."[26] Henley vows that her characters are representative of the modern anomie, alienation, suffering, and pain that reflects the human condition. To digest this daily in capsule form, one merely has to turn on the evening news. In short, when Mary Dellasega tried to get Henley to commit to the notion that her characters were strange, rather than vivid, Henley remarked, "Only in the sense that all human beings appear unusual to me. No stranger than anyone I know, certainly no stranger than people you see on the news."[27] Henley recognizes the dichotomy within individuals who seek happiness but are betrayed, in the Freudian sense, by modern civilization. In an interview in 1987, Henley remarked, "I try to understand that ugliness is in everybody. I'm constantly in awe of the fact that we still seek love and kindness even though we are filled with dark, bloody, primitive urges and desires."[28] The charm of Henley's characters suffering from this modern neurosis is exactly that they do not see themselves as different from anyone else because Henley refuses to see them as eccentric, strange, or wacky.

Besides being stigmatized as the queen of Southern Gothic drama, Henley has also been branded a feminist playwright. Feminists view the discord in Henley's plays as centered around the institution of marriage, arguing that her married couples do not display any intimacy or mutual understanding, and the women who are subservient in these relationships almost always exhibit insecurity with regard to their physical appearances and emotional well being. Moreover, Henley's females seem to repeat a pattern of adhering to patriarchal values to the extent that by mirroring the misery of their mothers, they make a statement about how the lack of progress for women is cyclical. Furthermore, there is no doubt that Henley's protagonists display an overabundance of violence and anger as a palliative, fantasizing about murder and attempting suicide; Alan Clarke Shepard argues that this aborted rage reflects the residual scars of emotional abandonment as a result of an inability to define their female subjectivity in an essentially patriarchal society.[29] When Mary Dellasega asked Henley why marriages fail to work in her plays and why her female protagonists are often in abusive relationships with males, she stated, "I think there are all aspects of human connections that I try to show in my plays. But I do very much believe that men and women have a hard row to hoe, connecting with each other, as do women and women and men and men.

But I think because of the sexual thing, there's something a lot more volatile."[30] Henley also mentioned that several male-female relationships in her plays do work well, including Barnette and Babe in *Crimes of the Heart* and Pixrose and Leon in *The Wake of Jamey Foster*; moreover she acknowledged that the aborted rage is not merely aimed at the patriarchy, for the females in her plays just as often direct their anger at other females. Dellasega pressed Henley, attempting to have her discuss how feminism is reflected in her plays. Henley responded definitively:

> I don't know. I cringe at that word, *feminist....* But I don't favor women over men characters when I write them. I try to understand each. I certainly like Delmount more than Chick, if you want to know the truth. I just try to look at people more than at just the sexes and hope that it'll be more a human point of view rather than having some sort of agenda to show that women are better, because I don't actually think they are.[31]

These comments echo Henley's statement that I cited in chapter 1 in which she rebels against any involvement with political or sociological issues because of the cynicism she displays as a result of her father's hypocrisy as a Mississippi politician. Henley states, "I like to write about people. The problems of just being here are more pressing and exciting to me than politics. Politics generally deal with the facades of our more desperate problems. I don't really feel like changing the world. I want to look at the world."[32] In other words, Henley's need to examine "the problems of just being here" seems to be a philosophical issue rather than a sociological or political one. Laurin Porter astutely realizes, "If her [Henley's] plays privilege women's narratives and occasionally reveal the destructive nature of patriarchal institutions and attitudes, in the last analysis Henley's female characters survive by adapting to the patriarchy and only dimly understand, if *at all*, their extent to which their lives have been shaped by a male-determined world."[33] By Henley's own admission, she is uninterested in writing plays that make sociological or political statements, and her "feminists" are essentially females who are more at home reading *People* or *Redbook* than they are with reading Gloria Steinem. Thus, the rage supposedly directed at the patriarchy, which I am arguing is actually a result of emotional disability from what Freud discussed as frustration accrued because of social constraints on the id, can no more be aborted than it can be sustained; asking Henley's neurotics to revolt against the patriarchy in their misery is like demanding that a partially blind person see clearly. If the only evidence to support Henley's claim as a feminist playwright is that most of her protagonists are female, then there is not much evidence at all.

Instead of considering Henley as a Southern Gothic or feminist playwright, I would like to change the focus of the debate by arguing throughout the remainder of this book that her dramas portray the modern neurosis that Freud views as a psychoanalytic dialectic between the bane of civilization and the id's antithetical desire for happiness—a fundamental plight of modern humanity, which Camus referred to as the absurd condition. Henley, of course, does not share the philosophical gaze of Camus or the scientific objectivity of Freud that allowed him to explore the etiology of the modern *angoisse*. Henley does not have a theoretical perspective on the absurd condition nor is it necessary for her to address the neuroticism directly during interviews; as an artist, she works intuitively and creates wonderful art, which should suffice. When Henley was asked in a 1987 interview why there are so few political plays written in the United States, she responded that she was not interested in political or social issues but instead was more concerned with the larger question of who we are in an absurd universe: "What is amazing to me is the existential madness we — everyone — are born into."[34] In her plays, Henley depicts this existential madness in various forms of emotional disabilities that range from depression to narcissism to various anxiety and personality disorders. Her afflicted personae are driven to extremes because of their neuroses and often are deemed insane — they are prime candidates for mental institutions (which they absolutely dread) or, in some instances, have recently been committed to the asylum. Henley acknowledges, "My favorite characters are the ones that screw up the most."[35]

Henley is a master of taking the modern neurosis and accentuating it to extremes. She admits, "I like to write about stressful situations, where people are not acting normally. These situations make people act bigger than life. They intensify the family situation, which is always volatile anyway."[36] Her plays often occur in the most traumatic situations that exacerbate the *angoisse*, such as a holiday, ceremony, or celebration of some sort — ritualistic events that often are highly charged. For example, *Crimes of the Heart* occurs when three sisters reunite to comfort Babe, who has shot her husband, and the trauma forces them to revisit their pasts and open old wounds. *The Wake of Jamey Foster* transpires during a funeral at Easter, *The Miss Firecracker Contest* unfolds during the annual carnival — Brookhaven's highly anticipated celebration — held on the Fourth of July, *The Lucky Spot* and scene 1 of *L-Play* take place on Christmas Eve (a terrible time for lonely people), *The Debutante Ball* is set amidst the atmosphere of Hattiesburg's most significant coming-out part, *Revelers* occurs during a memorial ceremony and reunion of Dash Gray's former acting students, and *Impossible Marriage* happens on the day and evening before a wedding. These special celebrations, reunions, and ceremonies create crises that bring individuals together to question their existences in an absurd universe. During these tense situations, Henley's protagonists engage in catharsis in which they trade stories that open old wounds while taking comfort in the neurosis that they gradually discover is shared by all humanity. The emotional crises inevitably elicit certain characters' physical deformities, which are gradually revealed by their on-stage presence or by the tales that surface through the catharses. Just as Henley exacerbates the emotional effects of the modern neurosis through crises, she also accentuates the physical effects of one's deformities by focusing on the ugliness in life. Henley admits, "I've always been very attracted to split images. The grotesque combined with the innocent, a child walking with a cane; a kitten with a swollen head; a hunchback drinking a cup of fruit punch. Somehow these images are a metaphor for my view of life; they're colorful…. It's a fascination with the stages of decay people can live in on this earth … the imperfections."[37] Henley's dramas offer us a staggering array of physical deformities and diseases that seem to complement the neurotic condition of her characters.

Although Henley's plays are often misperceived as simply comic by critics, her vision is fundamentally centered in a deep exploration of the modern neurosis. In an enlightening essay on American female playwrights, Barbara Kachur argues that Henley's main themes are ontological and are concerned with spiritual bankruptcy and individual isolation rather than sociological issues such as patriarchal conditioning, female rivalry, or domestic confinement.[38] Kachur notes that Henley makes us laugh but only in a world of "existential madness" in which we are inundated by pain, disappointment, and death.[39] The modern *angoisse* that Henley depicts onstage coincides with Freud's notion that the id is repressed by the socializing forces of civilization. The result is that Henley's characters are deeply wounded victims of broken dreams and unfulfilled lives.[40] Nancy D. Hargrove writes that in Henley's plays, "In many ways the vision is bleak indeed, portraying a chaotic and sterile world characterized by cruelty, suffering, and futility."[41] Images of death and dying create a pallor over these plays as Henley's heroines wonder if death remains the only viable escape from the suffering imposed on them by their neuroses. The Magrath sisters (*Crimes of the Heart*), Carnelle (*The Miss Firecracker Contest*), and Sue Jack and Cassidy (*The Lucky Spot*) have all lost their mothers; Pixrose (*The Wake of Jamey Foster*) and C-Boy (*Signature*) are orphans; Teddy has killed her father (*The Debutante Ball*); the dead father becomes the raison d'être of the family reunion in *The Wake of Jamey Foster* and perhaps for Jonsey's impotence in *Impossible Marriage*;

and we constantly hear of memories of dead animals (a horse and a cat, for example in *Crimes of the Heart*, a frog in *Hymn in the Attic*, a cat in *Control Freaks*), dead aunts (*The Miss Firecracker Contest*), dead brothers (*The Debutante Ball* and *Signature*), dead mentors (*Revelers*), and dead husbands (*Abundance*). Death certainly creates the necessary element for catharsis and leads to an Absence that only exacerbates the absurd condition. Henley's protagonists often feel intolerably alone, divorced, and depressed over their plights; they have a terrible need for the Other, for nurturing, or for love and affection to assuage, at least temporarily, the neuroticism. The needs that Henley's females have for love and the longing to be recognized by the Other often take the form of promiscuous behavior; when that temporary refuge fails, they resort to violence, and, as Camus argued, suicide must be considered an option to be weighed against the absurd condition. In an interview with Kevin Sessums, Henley discussed how she herself is suicidal and how her characters view suicide as a temporary solution to their neuroticism:

> I'm always thinking about killing myself.... Sometimes I just sit with a knife and wonder if this is the time I'm going to stab myself — you know, when I'm in the kitchen or something. I just can't imagine that people don't think about killing themselves or dying. I think it really saves you a lot of times. The fact that you have the choice to live or die is a triumph, in a way. When my characters try to kill themselves, it's always like, "Okay, I know how to solve this problem — I'll kill myself! That's what I'll do! I'm in control!" And it's an exhilarating feeling.[42]

However, Henley's protagonists engage in aborted suicide attempts that usually end up as comic interludes; in short, like Sisyphus, Henley's walking wounded find that suicide is not viable to counteract the universal angst of humanity's absurd condition.

Despite the fact that Henley's protagonists suffer interminably from an enduring *angoisse* that cannot be alleviated, they, like Sisyphus, battle against overwhelming odds to ease the pain at least temporarily. Their eternal struggle — a battle against a dialectic that cannot be overcome, yet one that increasingly inflicts pain and suffering — is endearing for audiences to watch. Like Sisyphus, Henley's characters fight for their dignity, grabbing for the isolated moment when they can share happiness by themselves or with others in a world of despair, knowing that the reality of pain and anguish is ubiquitous and enduring.[43] Questioning the modern neurosis, again much like Sisyphus who battled the absurd condition, Henley's protagonists can momentarily break the bond of absurdity as they enjoy brief interludes in which they gladly accept life's daily pleasures, such as laughter and love. As Colby H. Kullman aptly observes, "Confronting the ultimate futility and absurdity of life, the inescapable presence of anxiety and dread, death and the shadow it casts on life, Henley's existentialist protagonists never give up their quest to find out who they are, what they are here for, and where they are going."[44]

Although there is no solution to her characters' neuroses, what makes these plays endearing is that Henley consistently displays compassion for her walking wounded personae. Jon Jory, who produced *Crimes of the Heart* in Louisville, stated, "Most American playwrights want to expose human beings. Beth Henley embraces them."[45] In the Introduction to *Monologues for Women*, Henley succinctly expressed the optimism and compassion that she shares with her protagonists who suffer from their neurotic conditions:

> In performing these monologues, I would like to share the idea of hope. I feel all of these women are compelled and foiled, tortured and exalted by the never ending affliction of hope. Thus they are never tepidly depressed — they are despairingly anguished. [Lenny, Meg, Marshael, Bess, Carnelle.] They are not silly, sweet, or stupid — they are alive with burning poetic vision. [Babe, Pixrose, Popeye, Macon, Violet.] Even the characters who lack a certain spiritual enlightenment [Katty, Elain, L-Tip] are to me compelling in their dogged need to glorify the endless minutiae of everyday life and avoid their deep terror of being isolated and unworthy of love. In short, let me say that I care for all of the women in this book.[46]

Again, Henley does not see her protagonists as eccentric, bizarre, or grotesque, but instead she feels that they are as "normal" as anyone one might see on the evening news. Henley states, "It's about looking at these people and liking them for who they are. I don't talk down to them."[47] Henley's compassion for individuals who are desperately seeking solace and understanding amidst the pain and suffering in life ultimately produces tragicomedy. Her characters' resolve to laugh at life's foibles during aborted suicide attempts, shared memories with friends and relatives, special moments of contemplation or joy, and the comfort of playing musical instruments or dancing to music becomes the key to their survival and the means by which we empathize with them, sharing their glimmer of hope.

Henley's tragicomic vision is derived from Chekhov, her mentor.[48] Chekhov, one of the fathers of the modern theater and a precursor to the tragicomic genre that influenced absurdist dramatists, had an unusual ability to observe compulsive and pathological individuals through the comic and mundane activities of daily life. Chekhov, like Henley, allowed us to enter the souls of characters who were fighting to preserve a sense of dignity in their lives. As a physician, Chekhov would have understood Freud's concept of the modern neurosis, for his characters are seemingly conflicted with psychological problems, most often leading to unrequited love. Chekhov, the naturalist, began with a serious vision in which, as a scientist observing human nature, he sought to portray on stage life's miserable condition; however, humanity's foibles always led him to a comic vision as well. Similarly, Henley begins with the modern *angoisse*, but she admits that it always winds up as tragicomedy: "When I write the plays, they're real serious to me. And they're painful. I always think they're so, so sad, and so tragic — until people laugh at 'em."[49] Like Chekhov, Henley makes us laugh at the absurdity or existential madness of life; both playwrights undercut the seriousness of the modern neurosis through the pleasures that seem momentarily to assuage the absurdity and make it less horrifying. Henley seems to have Chekhov's larger perspective on life. She notes, "The darker side of life has always appealed to me. I like to have a big perspective on things: The reason things can be so funny is that they can be so sad; the reason they can be so beautiful is that they can be so ugly."[50] Moreover, the compassion that Chekhov displayed for all of his characters as if he were writing about members of his own family is a trait Henley seeks to emulate. Thus, understanding Henley's co-mingling of the grotesquely comic with the mundane, as well as her Chekhovian perspective in reducing serious issues to trivialities and concomitantly providing undue importance to the minutiae of daily life, helps us to see how her tragicomedy serves to mitigate, and perhaps to make us more aware of, the modern *angoisse*. In short, Henley begins with the modern neurosis as the basis for her plays, but when her protagonists seek to maintain their dignity against the inevitable, comedy results. In the tragicomic travails of her endearing, yet suffering, neurotics, Henley's vision is ultimately optimistic, much in the manner than Sisyphus rebelled against his fate in trying to make sense of an absurd universe. Henley realizes, "All these things that I feel inside are desperate and dark and unhappy. Or not *unhappy*, but searching. Then they come out funny. The way my family dealt with hardships was to see the humor or the ironic point of view in the midst of tragedy. And that's just how *my* mind works."[51] Henley, like Chekhov, has much to teach us about the pain of the modern *angoisse* and how to prevent it from unbearably encroaching on our daily existence.

3

Am I Blue and
The Wake of Jamey Foster

"Hey, stop spraying that! You know I'm not going to— well, you'd get neurotic, or pregnant, or some damn thing."[1] With these words, spoken by John Polk Richards to Ashbe Williams in the one-act *Am I Blue*, Henley began a playwriting career depicting the modern neurosis on stage. Of course, John Polk is not a psychiatrist and thus fails to specify the type of neurosis from which Ashbe suffers, yet his "diagnosis" seems to be fairly astute nonetheless.

Am I Blue begins during a rainy night in 1968 in the French Quarter of New Orleans, where sixteen-year-old Ashbe tries to pick up seventeen-year-old preppy college freshman John Polk in a bar. Successful in her attempt, Ashbe then brings her prey back to her dilapidated apartment; the two locales are linked in mood by the song "Am I Blue?," played on the piano in the back room of the bar and then sung by Billie Holiday or Terry Pierce on Ashbe's radio in the apartment.

Ashbe seems to suffer from manic behavior, particularly hypomanic syndrome. The *Diagnostic and Statistical Manual of Mental Disorders*, published by the American Psychiatric Association, defines a manic episode as an elevated or euphoric mood disturbance characterized by inflated self-esteem or grandiosity and manifested by, among other things, "excessive involvement in pleasurable activities with a high potential for painful consequences."[2] Manic-depressive mood disorders are not due to physiological effects of drug or medication use or from an otherwise diagnosed medical condition, such as a brain tumor or multiple sclerosis. Instead, the person's mood is excessive, which may be noted by unceasing and indiscriminate interpersonal or sexual contact with strangers.[3] For example, the person might "start extensive conversations with strangers in public places,"[4] perhaps offering advice in which they have no expertise. At times, there may be a flight of ideas with abrupt changes from one topic to another. Individuals suffering from manic disorders may also change their dress, makeup, or personal appearance to a more sexually flamboyant style.

Ashbe displays the overt characteristics of a manic-depressive disorder; Henley, moreover, has described the play as "about a girl who was sort of whacky...."[5] Outwardly, Ashbe dresses provocatively in an attempt to be noticed so as to pick up strangers. Her attire is described as what might be flamboyant but is perhaps garish to the more sophisticated: "*a flowered plastic rain cap, red galoshes, a butterfly barrette, and jeweled cat eyeglasses*" (68). One might even argue that these color schemes are incongruous and atypical yet something an individual who wants to be noticed would have to search for with some degree of difficulty, particularly the stylish glasses and the unusually colored boots. Ashbe is temporarily euphoric as she experiences the plight of many of Henley's protagonists: the absent father and the abandoned mother. Ashbe's parents are divorced; her mother lives in Atlanta, and her father is away on one of his frequent business trips. She is also divorced from her friends, for they are all at a school dance, which Ashbe rejects as being too parochial for her. The truth, however, is that Ashbe is usually dateless during these important social events; instead she fantasizes, like most hypomaniacs, into a world of her own creation. Ashbe dreams of going to an elegant ball instead of her high school dance: "I would prefer to wait till I am invited to an exclusive ball. It doesn't really matter which ball, just one where they have huge, golden chandeliers and silver fountains, and serve delicacies of all sorts and bubble blue champagne. I'll arrive in a pink silk cape. (*Laughing.*) I want to dance in pink!" (78). Ashbe resents the fact that her schoolmates are cliquish, often looking derogatorily upon orphans who lack the funds to dress stylishly. Instead, Ashbe dresses flamboyantly in total disregard for school styles; she even practices voodoo to put spells on the girls in the clique. Neglected by her parents and friends, Ashbe has retreated into a world of self-created eccentricities. She has become a loner, collecting sea shells, hoping to hear the "soul of the sea" in a vain attempt to find a soul for herself in a world where others have failed to provide any such nurturance. Like her mother, Ashbe has been "divorced" from relationships, which is again typical in Henley's plays where the offspring repeat the personal histories of their mothers. Ashbe laments, "Sure, everyone just views me as an undesirable lump" (84). To assuage the effects of the loneliness and despair,

Ashbe has retreated into a garish world of her own choosing that makes her stand out as an individual yet would also would be frowned upon by her "friends"— Tiger Claw perfume, hot Kool-Aid, colored drinking water, multicolored potholders, and paper hats.

Although Ashbe hides behind such eccentricities to help her escape the world, she actually hates herself and displays a penchant for much aborted rage. Her run-down room is described as "*a malicious pig sty*" (74), which latently reveals how she feels about her own self-esteem; she even admits that her mother "never was too good at keeping things clean" (74). Thus, Ashbe's calculated flamboyance is probably indicative of the manic-depressive's sudden change in personal appearance, an excessive involvement with pleasurable activities despite the sad loneliness that lies beneath the spunky exterior. Furthermore, her behavior is hypomaniac, for she relentlessly pursues sex with unusual determination for a virgin. Moreover, the hypomaniac condition she displays through this sudden burst of exuberant behavior is essentially revealed by the high potential for painful activities that may result from her euphoric condition. Ashbe has just stolen two ashtrays from Screw Inn — a subliminal statement from someone who is dateless for the school dance and wants to retaliate by stealing from a place of libidinal activity; instead, Ashbe does take John Polk to Screw Inn, which is synonymous with her own apartment (at least for this manic encounter). Ashbe defends her thieving, comparing herself to Robin Hood and thus justifying her righteousness in stealing from those who have wronged her.

Ashbe's temporary euphoria is associated with the violent, painful mentality of aborted rage that is endemic to manic-depressive behavior. She admits being a pickpocket, even though every time she engages in that activity, she gets caught and therefore must pay the consequences. En route to her apartment, Ashbe picks up a stray hat, wondering "Maybe it was a butcher's who slaughtered his wife or a silver pirate with a black bird on his throat" (74). Alan Clarke Shepard comments on Ashbe's potential for pain: "In Ashbe's terms, a pirate's violence both creates and signifies his autarkic self; and Ashbe, virtually alone in the world, vicariously produces one, too, through her well-developed fantasy life, which privileges the swashbuckler mode, where violence is glamorous, sovereign, and artificial."[6] In John Polk's mind, Ashbe's comment about the glamour of piratry, coupled with the fact that Ashbe's thievery was romanticized as a Robin Hood fantasy, forces him to associate her with the liability of violent behavior. John Polk thus wonders about accompanying Ashbe home, stating to her, "You've probably got some gang of muggers waiting to kill me" (73). Alone with John Polk in the apartment, Ashbe's rage extends to fantasizing about the result of going to Tokyo for an abortion of the child they might have together. She also recalls the aborted rage of smashing marshmallows in a grocery store. Ashbe associates the benign gesture of smashing marshmallows with the more serious notion of aborting her child: "I want to have my dear baby or at least get to Japan. I'm so sick of school I could smash every marshmallow in sight" (84); after hearing this, John Polk fears that Ashbe is nothing more than "sadistic" (84).

Alan Clarke Shepard associates Ashbe's impulses to smash marshmallows and abort babies to repudiated rage; in other words, she is expelling the pressures upon women to reproduce, to please and serve the patriarchy.[7] This notion would be supported by the fact that Ashbe, in seeking out a man that she can escort home, becomes the sexual aggressor, thus turning the tables on the socially imposed double standard. However, Ashbe does not disavow male aggression; instead, she fully embraces it, albeit subliminally. Moreover, if Ashbe were reacting negatively toward the patriarchy, she would not become so passive once she is in the arms of John Polk, whose fraternity-ascribed behavior is defined by reinforced patriarchal values. Instead, Ashbe is "blue" because of the anomie and *angoisse* that results from civilization and its discontents, and she can not cure these neurotic manic-depressive flings but at best may only assuage the suffering temporarily.

Ashbe seeks solace in mutual comfort with John Polk, another alienated and isolated individual. Ashbe's momentary increased self-esteem in seeking out men reflects how the manic-depressive condition masks an otherwise insecure person trying to escape recurrent patterns of low self-esteem. Abandoned by her friends and family and typically in the depressive state, Ashbe's manic condition becomes fully developed when she picks up strangers in bars, enlivens them with her rambling imagination, titillates them with tales that contain violent images, and then escorts them to her apartment for sex-talk while her father is out of town.

Ostensibly, Ashbe and John Polk have little in common. John Polk is a "straight" Sigma Alpha Epsilon fraternity boy and, as such, unlike Ashbe, he boasts of having lots of friends, including plenty of dates with women. Unlike Ashbe, who feels uncomfortable at social events, John Polk's fraternity brothers are always having parties for him to attend. While Ashbe seems to be divorced from her mother and father, John Polk is acculturated by his parents, who insist that he attend business school to be "management-minded" so as to eventually run his father's soybean business; success is thus equated with the social norms of having a secure job that will pay well. John Polk admits to Ashbe that he goes out on dates as a social requirement, although most of the time the dates end disastrously because of his inability to engage in conversation with females or because they are incompatible with him. In order to break the ice with females, John Polk's fraternity buddies have set him up with a whore in New Orleans as a type of coming of age present for his eighteenth birthday. When he meets Ashbe in the bar, he is trying to stay drunk to avoid nervousness as he approaches the midnight rite of passage with the prostitute.

At first glance, one might imagine that Ashbe and John Polk come from different socioeconomic backgrounds or "different sides of the track" and thus have little in common. Upon hearing of John Polk's plans to finish business school, Ashbe remarks, "I'd hate to have to be management-minded" (77). Ashbe rails against John Polk's desire to conform: "You think I want to be in some group ... a sheep like you? A little sheep like you that does everything when he's supposed to do it!" (80). She is particularly appalled that his conventional thinking runs counter to her bohemian lifestyle and tells him, "Not only are you a sheep, you are a NORMAL sheep" (80).

However, Ashbe senses there is loneliness and despair that lies beneath John Polk's mask of artificial veneer that he creates in order to belong. Colby H. Kullman astutely notes, "As high strung and flaky as John Polk is nervous and tentative, Ashbe initiates him into her fantasy world as she tries to bridge the loneliness engulfing them both."[8] Upon first meeting him at the bar, John Polk, "*a bit overweight and awkward*" (68), perhaps stood out in Ashbe's mind as being unlike the typical preppy fraternity boy. Ashbe intuitively seems to sense John Polk's angst, and she is fairly blunt about expressing it to him: "I just figured that's why you had the appointment with the whore — 'cause you didn't have any one else — to make love to" (70). As the evening wears on and John Polk becomes more comfortable with Ashbe, partly because of the effects of the alcohol, he loosens up and reveals the truth to her. He admits to being a sheep living a life of complacent bourgeois conformity in which he followed his family's advice about college and career, as well as his brother's advocacy of the benefits of fraternity life. Although John Polk is not the bohemian rebel that Ashbe purports to be, he does have in common with her the need to be his own individual free from the whims of others. He acknowledges, "I never used to worry about being a failure. Now I think about it all the time. It's just I need to do something that's—fulfilling" (81). Feeling ill at ease in college, especially when he realizes the effects of the false claims of fraternity life that have gotten him into this uncomfortable rendezvous with a whore, John Polk actually has much in common with Ashbe, who suffers from her own angst. Ashbe induces a catharsis in John Polk in which he reveals his hidden frustrations with the need to conform to fraternity life: "Hell, I would have told them a handkerchief, a pair of argyle socks, but, no, they have to get me a whore just because it's a cool ass thing to do. They make me sick. I couldn't even stay at the party they gave. All the sweaty T-shirts, and moron sex stories—I just couldn't take it" (82). John Polk finally breaks down and admits he is a virgin, like Ashbe, which cements the common bonds that they share. Ashbe then tells John Polk that his drinking to forget his meeting with the prostitute is a mask that will not alleviate the underlying loneliness of his life: "You're only trying to escape through artificial means" (83).

Although John Polk declines to have sex with Ashbe, the two of them do indeed bond, albeit through their shared loneliness. There may be some truth to the notion that Ashbe, alienated from her peers in school, date-less during school dances, divorced from parental guidance, and unable to penetrate the cliquishness of her colleagues, allows herself subliminally to belong to the "normal" through John Polk. More likely, however, is the fact that the two of them lose themselves temporarily in a tentative under-standing of their absurd condition. John Polk separates himself from the herd mentality, while Ashbe briefly realizes her unique individuality and divorces herself from the stereotyped negative image of an undesirable lump. They dance together past midnight (the hour of John Polk's supposed coming of age) while listening to the blues music of Terry Pierce/Billie Holiday singing "Am I Blue?" For one brief interlude, Ashbe and John Polk trade "feeling blue" for the blues. Thus, Henley's father was correct when he urged his daughter to change the title of the play from a question to a statement. The statement, "am I blue," is a fact of life, a result of the modern neurosis. Moreover, the bond shared by Ashbe and John Polk negates the feminist view that Henley's solution to problems that her female protagonists have with patriarchal society can be assuaged briefly through female bonding (seen in the denouement of *Crimes of the Heart*, which is often, yet unfortunately, the only Henley play that many critics ever explore in any depth). Ashbe never rails against patriarchal society, for her problem is more deeply rooted in the absurd condition that produces her alienation and isolation. Again, this neurosis can never be cured; it can only be temporarily assuaged. As Ashbe and John Polk merge together through the dance, they momentarily are aware of the absurd condition (or "feeling blue") and share an enlightening experience that temporarily stops time, similar to Sisyphus, happy in his under-standing of the existential dilemma that we all face but very few of us recognize. In this moment of security, Ashbe and John Polk, like Sisy-phus, insist on maintaining a sense of dignity in an otherwise absurd uni-verse.

The Wake of Jamey Foster occurs in Madison County, Mississippi, where neurotic thirty-three-year-old Marshael Foster, undoubtedly the protagonist of the play, has summoned the immediate family for the wake of her husband Jamey, who died after being kicked in the head by a cow.[9] The site is Marshael's home, which Henley depicts as rapidly deteriorating to coincide with Marshael's increasingly debilitating psychological condition: "*The house is an old rambling country home that is in distinct disrepair with faded drapes, peeling paint, old furniture, worn-out rugs, and so on.*"[10] The play takes place at Easter when the family pays its respects to the deceased lying in a coffin in Marshael's house the day before the funeral.

At one point in the play, Pixrose, a guest of Leon Darnell, Marshael's brother, states, "We've all had cruel, sad, unbearable things happen to us in this life" (126). This sentiment sums up the essence of Marshael's neurosis. In Freudian terms, Marshael's id is suppressed by the cultural ideals expected of her, reducing any chance for happiness while exacerbating her angst or *angoisse*. The crisis situation of the immediate death of her husband followed by the social demands of the wake have aggravated Marshael's neurosis. The result is that she manifests Borderline Personality Disorder, a form of anxiety characterized by unstable and intense relationships and problems with one's self-image. The *Diagnostic and Statistical Manual of Mental Disorders* lists some of the major symptoms of Borderline Personality Disorder as frantic efforts to avoid real or imagined abandonment, recurrent self-mutilating behavior, chronic feelings of emptiness, inappropriate intense anger due to sudden changes of mood, and self-damaging behavior such as binge eating or substance abuse.[11] Individuals suffering from Borderline Personality Disorder are negatively affected by impending separation or rejection, which usually leads to profound changes in self-image. Their abandonment fears result in an intolerance of being alone and a need to enjoy the company of others.

The Wake of Jamey Foster is essentially a two-day catharsis or tale telling for Marshael Foster; ironically enough, during this time of crisis when she needs help the most, Marshael can receive none from her relatives, who unleash their own tales of woe into the maelstrom.[12] Marshael is particularly upset that her husband died so young — at age thirty-five with a lot of living ahead of him. When they were first married, Jamey showered Marshael with gifts and kept her dreaming through the inspired stories he would tell. Jamey wanted to be a renowned historian whose revolutionary ideas about humanity were carefully crafted through research that he was trying to get published. Marshael, with her conflicted personality, sent his incomplete manuscript to a New York publisher while simultaneously telling her husband that it was superficial and sophomoric. After the rejection letter came, Jamey's life seemed to fall apart. He took a job selling real estate and never finished his master's degree. Jamey and Marshael seemed to endure nevertheless, raising three children. Gradually, he began to put on weight, lose his hair, drink heavily, and develop a rash over his knuckles, much of his afflictions due to a relationship he was having with Esmerelda Rowland,[13] a twenty-two-year-old twice-divorced baker (whose wonderful pies inspired him to gain the weight). His marriage with Marshael soon deteriorated as the couple began arguing all the time over what appeared to be trivialities. Two weeks before Jamey died, Marshael filed for divorce. Moreover, Jamey's notorious escapes made him the talk of the community. During the wake, Brocker, Marshael's friend, admitted, "He appeared to me to be a miserable, bewildered man" (114). Collard, who as Marshael's sister, shared her sibling's secrets, remarked, "I never liked him. He had a genius IQ and all the promise in the world, but he was a lazy coward with no guts and never finished a thing he'd start. He lied to himself and to everyone else" (114).

Jamey's corpse remains on stage throughout most of the play as a grim reminder of his legacy that seems continually to haunt Marshael and make her misery interminable. Miriam M. Chirico astutely writes, "The corpse wears a ridiculous bright orange-and-yellow plaid jacket, casting it as an object of derision."[14] Marshael is also terribly conflicted about the ordeal, having loved her husband and choosing to remember the idyllic time when Jamey first declared his love to her under the seemingly purple trees, but now she feels "abandoned" (103) — one of the characteristics of Borderline Personality Disorder. As Marshael puts Jamey's clothes away, she begins talking as if Jamey's corpse could hear her: "Damn you, leaving me alone with your mess. Leaving me again with all your goddamn, gruesome mess t'clean up. Damn, you, wait! You wait! You're not leaving me here like this. You're gonna face me! I won't survive! You cheat! I've got t'have something ... redemption ... something" (134). Interestingly, Marshael's neuroticism forces her to confront the issue of survival after emotional abandonment. When she first realized that her husband would rather be with Esmerelda, Marshael refused to recognize the truth, rationalizing, "Well, I just kept thinking if the blood ever dried he'd be back home. Foolish notion" (103). Instead, Marshael gradually realized that Jamey deceived her in the last months of their marriage, making her feel worthless: "It fiercely hurt me and my pride — like I wasn't even a woman" (127). As is true of those afflicted by Borderline Personality Disorder, Marshael feels an emptiness due to abandonment. As she sorts Jamey's ties, Marshael seems to be losing her mind as she wonders if her abandonment has left her without an identity and without redemption: "Treating me like nothing! I'm not ... nothing. Hey, I'm talking. I'm talking to you. You'd better look at me. I mean it, you bastard! (*She pulls the lid off the coffin.*) Jamey. God, your face. Jamey, I'm scared. I'm so scared. I'm scared not to be loved" (134). Marshael is further conflicted because she realizes that her dreams and aspirations were not the same as those of her husband. She tells her sister-in-law Katty, "I wanted children so badly. I was like some giant sea turtle looking for a place in the warm sand to lay my eggs. I felt all fertile inside. I wanted a home and babies and a family. But Jamey never wanted all that" (131). Thus, as Nancy D. Hargrove notes, as is typical of Henley's plays, marriage, a relationship supposedly based upon romantic love, causes pain and anguish instead.[15]

Upon viewing Jamey's corpse, Marshael's neurosis is compounded by the sudden realization that her dreams and aspirations have never been met, thus reproducing a vicious cycle of disappointment. In Freudian terms, happiness has been subsumed by the demands of civilization, which force the id to be rechanneled into more suitable cultural norms, such as marriages that must be made even though the idyllic dream of happiness usually results in grief. As Jonnie Guerra mentions, Marshael's life replicates the miserable existence of her mother: both had three children (two girls and a boy), both were married to alcoholics, and both marriages deteriorated.[16] Marshael tells Pixrose, "My parents fought all the time when I was little. Yelling and crying in the night. I wanted a different kind of life; but it didn't work out" (120). Moreover, this same sense of duty to tradition now further delineates Marshael's *angoisse*: due to the Southern convention of displaying the deceased in an open-lid coffin at the wake, Marshael's initial grief and depression gives way to an examination of a deeply rooted *angoisse* that she traces through several generations. She is now trying to maintain a sense of dignity in a world that has reduced her to sewing drill team uniforms and selling household improvement ornaments such as place mats and salt and pepper shakers shaped like crocodiles.

The Wake of Jamey Foster is primarily concerned with the neurosis resulting from loss and abandonment, questioning the possibility of dignity and renewal in modern society. Ulu Grosbard, who directed the play in New York, says, "It has to do with the theme of being able to bear your losses, to go on and make something of your life. Marshael is struggling to survive her ambivalent feelings, so she can go on."[17] Marshael, like Sisyphus, is trying to determine whether there can be dignity in an absurd universe. Her *angoisse* in what should be a time of mourning instead is exacerbated by relatives who come not to grieve, but to increase her angst by reminding her that she is partly to blame for her own misery. Wayne,

Jamey's brother, accuses Marshael of contributing to Jamey's frustrated life full of unrequited dreams: "Hey, listen, Missy, you're the one who saddled him with those three children and that job he despised. You're the reason he never got his damn Master's degree" (111). Wayne also accuses her of sabotaging Jamey's manuscripts by informing his publishers that the writing was superficial. Marshael even begins to believe that her seeming compliance with Jamey's idyllic dreams masks her deeply rooted fear about their deteriorating marriage. She confides to Pixrose, "I was afraid to ask him for anything. I never wanted him to know how scared I was. I just kept on telling him how, until all his theories were finished and started selling, that real estate was fine with me" (120). Marshael begins to internalize the idea that Jamey blamed her and the children for his dissipated dreams. After she sent his manuscript to a publisher and Jamey's hopes of becoming a widely recognized scholar were dashed, he ran off with Esmerelda. The wake thus literally becomes a rude awakening for Marshael, who, through a cultural norm that ostensibly is supposed to be a time of support for a grieving widow, in reality becomes a catharsis for one trying to survive the intimidating scrutiny of relatives flaming the neurosis.

The effects of Marshael's Borderline Personality Disorder include canker sores on her mouth, erratic eating habits, and insomnia. The purple trees that she recalls at the start of her love affair with Jamey have now figuratively degenerated to painful purple canker sores. Marshael's neuroticism has forced her to develop ambivalent attitudes toward food. During the early stages of her marriage, Jamey brought Marshael barbecued chicken every Saturday as one of the gifts with which he showered her. However, when Jamey gained weight as a result of Esmerelda's pastries, Marshael began to resent food as a spiritual offering. She became even more conflicted when Jamey began to use food as a means of expressing his fondness for Esmerelda's cooking while simultaneously subliminally convincing his wife that she had a problem with food and eating. Marshael recalls how Jamey taunted her about food: "'Hey, Marshael, why don't you try one of those delicious caramel pecan balls Essey brought? You could stand some weight on those saggy bones'" (127). During the wake, which is the only time we are confronted with Marshael's strange eating habits, she refuses to touch her food during dinner but instead eats erratically and without regard to nutrition, consuming only the ears of a chocolate Easter bunny (91) or jellybeans (104); she even rejects the ham Leon offers her and retreats to her candies. This craving for sweets unconsciously reflects a need for nurturing, a desire to return to the oral phase of childhood in which food from a loving mother meant happiness; this need for nurturance has been lost for Marshael in her anxiety and despair.

Marshael's ambivalent attitude toward food has caused her to throw it, which is a means of directing her internal violence against others. She tosses jellybeans all over the house and throws Esmerelda's blueberry pie from upstairs to the floor below — each incident reflecting the constant mood swings endemic to persons afflicted with Borderline Personality Disorder. Moreover, individuals suffering from Borderline Personality Disorder are substance abusers, and Marshael's constant gin drinking certainly falls within this category. The alcohol becomes another substitute for nurturance, artificially providing Marshael with a means of security to bolster her feelings of abandonment and worthlessness.

To assuage her suffering, Marshael briefly turns to the violin, which Henley has stated is often depicted as a metaphor for the creative impulse in several of her plays.[18] However, playing the violin for Marshael is equivalent to Babe's flirtation with the saxophone in *Crimes of the Heart*— temporary salves that do not diminish the deeper need to assuage the anguish in the darkest days of their lives. Individuals suffering from Borderline Personality Disorder desperately need to be with others who can provide solace and comfort rather than try to fight their neurosis alone. This is especially true for Marshael, whose almost daily feelings of abandonment are now exacerbated by the death of her husband. However, the irony that Henley presents is that family members who attend the wake ostensibly to pay their respects to the deceased and comfort the widow not only fail to do so, but instead bring their own bitterness and bickering with them, offering anxiety instead of solace to Marshael's house of mourning.

Marshael's younger brother, Leon Darnell, has been left to make arrangements for the wake. Slow-witted Leon, who works as a turkey jerker full-time in a chicken factory (having left his former job delivering newspapers) and part-time cashing in soda bottles, lacks the necessary social graces to make the proper funeral arrangements; he could not have done worse if he had hired the Marx Brothers to set the decorum for the solemn ritual. Leon assumes the role of one of Henley's favorite stock characters— the somewhat retarded brother who harasses his neurotic sister (similar, for example, to Cassie's sibling in *Nobody's Fool*). Leon has decked the corpse out in what he calls "a nice cheerful suit" (122), which consists of a bright orange and yellow plaid jacket, thus displaying the body prominently in the cheapest pine box available. Leon is incapable of helping Marshael cope with her neurosis. Instead, he chooses to focus both on Pixrose, his guest at the funeral, and on his dire need to turn in Coke bottles. Leon follows Pixrose around during the wake, brings her flowers, and defends her honor among his relatives. His comments about her are self-centered: "See, we're exactly alike. Pixrose and me. We're exactly the same.

Both of us enjoy public transportation and both of us have bumps right here on our heads" (92); he also says to Wayne, "We both hate Dr. Peppers and Orange Crushes are our favorite beverage" (93). When he is not praising Pixrose or his efforts to establish what he believes is decorum for the wake, Leon is arguing with Wayne, who wants "things done with class and dignity and respect" (94) for his brother. Leon thus creates more tension during the wake, first by bringing a stranger into family affairs and second by being a catalyst for Wayne's seething anger. Wayne calls Leon "a brainless imbecile" (108) and loathes being in the company of such a lower class lout: "Goes around picking up trash just for the fun of it. It near t'killed him when they brought out those no deposit bottles—cut his income clean in half. Isn't that so, Leon?" (108). Wayne constantly ridicules Leon: "It's no surprise to me that you've never held down a job — have to live in a shack —" (108). Leon, in turn, makes the wake more intolerable for all by defending himself like a child, throwing food, for example, at his tormentor.

If Marshael's younger brother cannot provide her with support during the wake, even less can be expected from her younger sister, Collard Darnell. In fact, Collard Greens, as she is affectionately called by family members, herself is ill prepared for the wake and is more likely to need support than to offer it. Luckily for Collard, the wake occurs at Easter, when she is off from her job of taking school portraits of the children (which was a brief foray for Henley as well). She enters the solemn setting unkempt with wild hair, dirty face, and inappropriate attire consisting of a muddy red evening gown and men's cowboy boots several sizes too large for her. During the morning of the funeral, she apparently has to borrow a dress, shoes, and hat that obviously do not fit and thus make her look ludicrous. Upon initially seeing Collard the day before the funeral, Wayne remarks, "Nothing you do surprises me much less your lack of concern for your bereaved sister" (94). Ironically, then, because of cramped quarters, Collard is forced to sleep with Marshael in her room but is the least likely to offer the bereaved any support. As a photographer, she is most qualified to take photos of the funeral, but she declines: "I just don't like t'look at dead people" (98). Collard admits that she despised Jamey as a liar and a lazy coward, which, of course, is not what Marshael needs to hear; moreover, she regrets having to socialize with the family, which she must do only at deaths and at Christmas, because otherwise, in her own words, "I don't like to affiliate myself with the rest of this menagerie" (114). Even when forced to grieve under the shadows of the coffin, Collard's nonchalance is overbearing as she pays her final respects: "Oh, hell, I may as well have one last look at the son of a bitch" (114).

Collard can offer Marshael no means to assuage the angst and despair because she has spent her own life being bitter. Collard's father wanted her to follow in his footsteps and become a lawyer, but after having received a score twenty points lower than Leon on an IQ test that she took when she was twelve years old, she lost faith in herself. Collard remembers her father's disappointment in her lack of achievement: "I was nothing in his eyes from then on! Just dumb and stupid and nothing!" (127). Collard's life consisted of a history of abandonment; she even recognizes herself as "a black sheep" with "a black, black soul" (103). First, she abandoned her own family, leaving the responsibility to Marshael to care for their aging parents. Marshael accuses her sister of abandonment: "You're the one who ran off and left me to keep care of Mama the six months she was sick, and then later, when Daddy was dying, you were here just long enough to upset everyone, then you ran off again!" (121). Collard flunked out of college and then went on a promiscuous tear, in her own words, caressing "death and danger with open legs" (122). She uses men, then discards them, and by aborting her own fetus, she in effect abandons any attempt at having children as well. Upon hearing about Jamey's death, she abandoned her responsibilities, fleeing to Memphis for a wild party in which the clothes she was planning to wear for the funeral were stolen. Collard's bitterness and the resulting wild and carefree spirit that she exudes make her incapable of providing Marshael with any support for her own neurosis. Collard prides herself as being the lone wolf of the family, the carefree spirit or rebel who disdains order and refuses to meet cultural expectations: "Oh yeah — I've slept with married men, I've slept with priests, I've stolen from stores, I've killed animals in the road, lied and cheated just to win at a game of cards" (129). She winds up drinking more gin than Marshael, which certainly suggests that she is the least likely to help her sister master her oral fixation. Thus, Collard, feeling no need to grieve for Jamey and concomitantly an icon for the spirit of bitterness and depravity, cannot possibly console Marshael, who herself suffers from the disposition of abandonment that her sister so relishes.[19]

Wayne Foster, Jamey's younger brother, cannot provide spiritual comfort for his sister-in-law; instead, his presence at the wake serves to create more tension for Marshael. In what is perceived as a family crisis and time of mourning, Wayne does nothing more than exacerbate the tense situation. Wayne mocks Leon as a "jerky turkey" whose pitiful income confines him to living in a shack, tries to seduce Collard after reminding her that her IQ has always been low, refers to Marshael's father as a drunken lawyer, complains to Marshael about the funeral arrangements that make Jamey look like a clown in a box, and accuses his sister-in-law of ruining her husband's career aspirations. Moreover, Wayne's attempted embrace of Collard has forced his wife Katty to retreat to the bathroom, and coaxing her out becomes an anxiety-ridden moment that Marshael can do without in this otherwise crisis situation; indeed, when the women engage in storytelling that indicates empathy for Katty's feelings of loss of self-worth, Marshael's story of Jamey's infidelity with Esmerelda — more unwanted cathartic angst for her — finally is the salvific dose that Katty needs. Marshael at least is aware of Wayne's status as a prominent banker whose monogrammed three-piece suits, genuine cow leather briefcase, and business cards mark him as a star rising from the white trash background from which he ascended. The truth is that Wayne wants to be recognized as the successful sibling, even though his mother praised Jamey for being more intelligent and creative than his brother. In short, Wayne has come to resent Jamey, whom he refers to as "that stinking bastard" (130), for belittling his job at the bank after his own dreams of getting manuscripts published never materialized, and Marshael, accusing Wayne of being disingenuous, is aware of his hypocritical attitude of concern for the way the body has been displayed: "I mean all this sudden deep show of concern and respect when you never even liked Jamey! You never even cared for him at all. It made you happy watching him struggle and fail!" (111). In turn, Wayne accuses Marshael of saddling Jamey with children, refusing to recognize his dreams to succeed, discouraging him from getting his master's degree, and ultimately reducing him to an alcoholic; his advice to his neurotic sister-in-law is to get "professional help" (112). Wayne, of course, cannot provide Marshael with any means to assuage her neurosis, and, as an instigator of trouble at the wake, he compounds his sister-in-law's anxiety. Furthermore, his own physical and psychological deportment are in disarray, leading to nosebleeds and excessive drinking, respectively, so he is in no position to provide Marshael with any type of constructive psychological support.

Katty Foster, Wayne's twenty-nine-year-old wife, is the social agent of acculturation who takes it upon herself to become the superego for Marshael and the family attending the wake. Henley has stated that she modeled Katty after Chick Boyle in *Crimes of the Heart*, whom Henley believed warranted further development than she was accorded in the earlier play.[20] Like Chick, Katty is overly concerned about portraying the proper public image for the family. Unlike Collard whose clothes for the funeral were stolen in Memphis, Katty has carefully selected the proper attire for the social occasion: "I mean, I'm wearing this outfit all day today, and then tomorrow I'm wearing my navy blue suit with my navy pumps and my navy dress hat with the white piping" (97). Collard sarcastically remarks that Katty is a Windsor from northeast Jackson, which makes her "real quality folk" (106) able to set the standards of decorum for the wake. Katty perceives Marshael's period of mourning as nothing more than a social event, or, as Marshael puts it, a "ghastly tea party" (105) in which she becomes the grand hostess, telling people how to dress properly for the event, where to sit in the limousine, or how the flowers should be arranged. Marshael mocks her as a misguided maître d'hotel: "'Here's a coaster and a fresh napkin for your drink. Do you need some more ice cubes? Oh, by the by, the deceased is residing in the parlor'" (105). However, underneath Katty's hypocritical exterior of hiding behind a mask of social graces lies an individual seething at the world. When the women trade stories of cruelest things they have done, Katty recounts a tale of revenge on the impoverished Dooley family, who, having despised her for being from the upper class, shoved her in a mudhole while she was en route to church in her finest Easter outfit. Katty responded by yanking the chirping heads off every one of their colored Easter chicks. As Nancy D. Hargrove states, Katty, seemingly the most humane of those attending the wake, exhibits the cruelest behavior.[21]

Katty cannot help Marshael cope in this time of crisis because beneath the somber, sweet exterior of social graces, she is actually domineering, critical of others, and insecure. Henley has stated that Katty is a controlling person who needs to be liked; but even going beyond the Willy Loman syndrome, Katty needs, moreover, to be perfect.[22] Since her life is mired in social graces and decorum, she must adhere to those standards herself to be a role model for others. Her main dilemma is that she is incapable of having a child, having gone through three miscarriages already. She bases her self-worth on the ability to have children, lamenting to her husband, "If we only could have a child. You'd see I had so much to give" (115).

When Wayne makes advances to Collard, Katty locks herself in the bathroom for an hour and a half, refusing to come out. In other words, Katty seems to be in need of psychiatric help as much as Marshael. Even after she is coaxed out of hiding, she remains insecure, reiterating to Marshael, "I hate the me I have to be with him. If only I could have the baby it would give me someone to love and make someone who'd love me. There'd be a reason for having the fine house and the lovely yard" (131). Although Katty's plight can be argued to be the impetus for female solidarity — the women having to tell tales to pry her loose from the bathroom — there is nothing to suggest that Marshael is in any way changed by Katty's presence,[23] which, if anything, more clearly delineates the neurosis rather than inhibiting it from flourishing.

Ironically, Marshael gets help with her Borderline Personality Disorder through contact with Pixrose and Brocker Slade, the only two attending the wake who are outsiders rather than family members. Pixrose Wilson, a seventeen-year-old, is visiting her friend Leon during the time of the wake. Pixrose is an orphan and a virgin, which immediately makes her stand out from the rest of the women in the play who all have families and who have children (Marshael), define themselves through their ability to produce a fetus (Katty), or have aborted babies (Collard).[24] Pixrose is also the youngest onstage, and as such, she has her life ahead of her and thus aspires to the future, albeit in the role of dog bather once she graduates from high school. Her mother was a pyromaniac who burnt down the family's house, killing herself and scarring Pixrose for life with burns over the lower part of her body. Moreover, she lost her father in a fiery automobile accident that left her arms maimed and her brother Franky with permanent brain damage, which confines him to wearing a football helmet all day in a mental asylum.

Pixrose seems to be someone who has a black cloud constantly hanging over her, for her luck is miserable. During dinner the night before the funeral, she accidentally sets the kitchen on fire, and when offering to compensate Marshael for the damage, she breaks her dinner plate. Fire seems to thrice-plague Pixrose: when her friend at the orphanage found out that she was afraid of fire, she burned down two wings of the building, which left Pixrose seared and in bandages because she sacrificed herself to save several small children. Pixrose thus has been abandoned by family and friends, which speaks directly to Marshael's symptoms personified by her Borderline Personality Disorder. Pixrose, however, is stoical in her endurance, realizing that despite a psychologically damaging legacy of a mother and father who tried to murder their own children, she has the will to survive: "But — but they shouldn't a' tried burning me and Franky away with them. First at home and then in that car. Still though, we survived! We survived —" (133). Pixrose is like Sisyphus, who, condemned to spend the rest of his life in turmoil, makes the best of a terrible situation by accepting life's harsh reality while trying to maintain his sense of dignity. Pixrose, a stranger and thus different from the rest of Marshael's family, presents a contrast to Marshael's familiar environment: she demonstrates the need to live with the neurosis. Moreover, she finds solace in Leon, whom she sees only rarely. The irony for Marshael is that even the most miserable can find brief happiness by bonding with the pathetically dim witted.

Marshael, suffering from the latent fear of being abandoned and thus not being loved, learns from Pixrose that she must be stoical and thus must be herself despite the possible rejection. On the day of the funeral, Marshael refuses to attend, choosing instead to enjoy a moment of grace with Brocker Slade, who was once her close friend. Brocker, at age fifty-three and thus twenty years her senior, understands abandonment. To the others attending the wake, Brocker is nothing more than a gruff, vulgar pig farmer with tattoos covering his body; he is described in the stage directions as *"big, tired, and worn-out"* (113). He originally came to Mississippi with a woman who knew all about raising hogs, but after financing the venture, she eventually abandoned him; forced to fend for himself in a business he knew little about, Brocker was not surprised when the pigs exploded from overeating. In turn, Brocker abandoned Marshael when her husband was paralyzed in the hospital and she "was all in distress" (133). Brocker recalls, "I leave the one woman I love alone in a great, unrelenting deluge. I give her nothing. Nothing" (133). Immediately after telling this to Leon, Marshael, talking to herself in front of the coffin, sighs to Jamey, "You're not ... nothing. (*She moves away from the coffin, realizing it contains nothing of value.*) Still I gotta have something. Still something..." (134). Marshael begins to understand what Brocker views as the modern neurosis; as he retires for the night to sleep in a ditch with his dog, Brocker exclaims, "Jesus! YUK!!! It's a madhouse" (135). Thus, Marshael refuses to go with the family to the funeral and instead spends time with Brocker, who serenades her with wooden spoons as he sings "This Old Man Comes Rolling Home."

Billy J. Harbin misinterprets the denouement: "She [Marshael] and her funeral guests end the play as they began it, floundering in isolation and low self-esteem, no more able to establish bonds with others than their parents before them."[25] Indeed, although Alan Clarke Shepard frames Marshael's solace in sociological terms as "a conservative, paradigmatic strategy for recuperating an emotionally dysfunctional man," he also acknowledges that she takes comfort from the "implicit promise of Slade's enduring paternal presence."[26] Nancy D. Hargrove argues that the play, set during Easter, reinforces the idea of Marshael's emotional resurrection, spiritual healing, and renewal: "What specifically she has learned is unclear, but her endurance is unquestionable as is the implication that she and Brocker together may be able to salvage some meaning, even though it may not be as heady as exaltation or triumph, from otherwise dreary and futile lives."[27] Marshael seems to have learned what Pixrose demonstrates: one needs to endure and enjoy brief moments of solace amidst the overbearing *angoisse* that we suffer from daily.[28]

Again, Henley explores the question of whether we can avoid feeling worthless and abandoned to find dignity in an absurd universe that constantly denies us happiness and makes us all neurotic. Henley begins with a crisis situation and then increases the tension and violence as emotions seethe in a macabre setting dominated by a corpse on stage as the ever-present reminder of what will eventually be the culmination of the chaos. As the "mourners" reflect on their past lives, they tell tales about abortions, fires that killed their parents or caused brain damage to their siblings, miscarriages, cows that kicked people in the head, exploding hogs, automobile accidents, Easter chicks and turkeys that are dismembered, and animals that are left for dead on the road. The tales are accompanied by physical violence, including the throwing of Easter bunnies, jellybeans, gin bottles, vegetables, pies, and scissors, as well as visible physical illnesses, such as canker sores, nosebleeds, backaches, bodily scars from fires, and borderline mental illness—all seen in the shadow of Jamey's stroke. Marshael, however, manages to survive the crisis and the chaos, and her neurosis, at its peak due to her interaction with family members unable themselves to cope and thus incapable of offering support, is temporarily assuaged through a brief moment of happiness with a stranger. Like Ashbe and John Polk who dance into the night amidst the terror, Marshael, refusing to go to the funeral, therefore rejects the past in favor of a brief interlude in which she finds dignity in an absurd universe.

4

Crimes of the Heart

On the whole, critics and theater reviewers have not depicted the plight of the Magrath sisters in *Crimes of the Heart* as the result of the anomie and *angoisse* that Freud notes is the neurotic impulse of modern society. Instead, critics such as Karen L. Laughlin see the play as a feminist vision of female assertiveness and bonding as an alternative to crimes that are self-destructive.[1] Jonnie Guerra agrees with Laughlin's view of the play as a feminist statement but one that reacts specifically against the patriarchy instead of emotional crises that are personal.[2] Helene Keyssar argues that the patriarchal forces are so omnipresent that the Magrath sisters cannot bond effectively since their subservience to norms and values defined by the patriarchy reduces them to caricatures and objects of derision.[3] Janet L. Gupton's thesis is that *Crimes of the Heart* depicts unruly women who "make spectacles of themselves, and in doing so, challenge the tropes of femininity validated by traditional Southern culture and offer models of transgressive, alternative behavior."[4] Susanne Auflitsch maintains that Henley's notion of a nonhierarchical union of women in the denouement is a statement against the traditional Southern family structure and the patriarchal subjugation of women.[5] Janet V. Haedicke further delineates the play as the domesticity of kitchen-sink drama, which ultimately becomes a sociological treatise on battered women, with Babe's attempted homicide as the focal point for Henley's statement about violence to women in the family.[6] Critics who see the drama as contemporary sociology are also supported by Alan Clarke Shepard's view that the play "studies the origins and effects of domestic abuse," depicts culturally sanctioned violence against women, exposes the link between sexism and racism, and suggests the grave consequences of women who begin to realize themselves "as wholly volitional beings."[7] Yet these feminist interpretations often seem inadequate because the play's supposed message of power in female bonding in the denouement coincides with the fact that the patriarchal values are still in place; moreover, one could argue that the patriarchy is hardly even realized by the Magrath sisters. Alan Woods astutely notes that although the play may ostensibly celebrate the power of the individual over a repressive society, the problems are at best only temporarily resolved: Babe still must await court action (through a male-dominated system of justice), Meg is far from finding happiness despite her realization that Old Granddaddy's wish for her singing career was misguided, and Lenny's joy is clearly in the hands of a male suitor, Charlie Hill.[8] Thus, Laurin Porter seems to be correct when she argues that *Crimes of the Heart* may initially focus on women's narratives in the context of patriarchal assumptions of womanhood, yet Henley never seriously examines the sociological institutions that shape modern society. Porter concludes, "Ultimately, however, the play fails to challenge patriarchal structures or even acknowledge that they have been the root of the problem."[9] Porter's views coincide with Henley's response to Mary Dellasega (cited in chapter 2), in which she refused to assess her plays as feminist statements.[10]

Instead of viewing the play from a feminist perspective, I want to argue that *Crimes of the Heart* represents Freud's notion of the modern neurosis, and the denouement effectively provides a response to the *angoisse* and alienation that permeates throughout society and which typically prevents human beings from achieving happiness. Barbara Kachur's analysis of the play is particularly informative, asserting that the focus is mainly ontological and that rather than being concerned with patriarchal conditioning, female rivalry, domestic confinement, or women' s issues, *Crimes of the Heart* is about spiritual bankruptcy and individual isolation.[11] Kachur notes that the Magrath sisters are striving to find meaning for their unfulfilled lives in a world of existential madness underscored by pain, disappointment, and death.[12] This approach seems to concur with the way Henley views the neurotic modern world, stating in an interview cited in chapter 2 that the political/sociological perspective is moot compared to the psychological ramifications of the modern *angoisse*.[13]

What is unusual about Henley's essentially Freudian notion of the search for happiness deterred by the demands of modern civilization producing the ubiquitous neurosis is that the tradition is rarely represented in modern American drama, except perhaps excluding the dramas of O'Neill and the early plays of Edward Albee. This existential despair and modern angst have been mainly represented in European drama, beginning with Chekhov, extending through the philosophical ideas of Camus and Sartre, and eventually culminating in the anomie and alienation felt in the theater of Beckett, Ionesco, Genet, Pinter, and Stoppard. Critics may be confused about Henley's intentions because the setting of *Crimes of the Heart*—a middle-class kitchen—is unlike the bare stage or abstract sets usually associated with absurdist dramas or their precursors (witness the bare nursery in *The Cherry Orchard*, for example). However, William W. Demastes puts Henley in perspective with regard to the setting she employs: "As such, her work escapes the intellectual detachment of the French absurdists and existentialists, and because it takes the horrors of life out of the lecture halls and puts them in a kitchen, it argues that the absurd has an immediacy and relevance to daily existence that other works can't claim to argue."[14]

Particularly apropos in relating Henley's theater to the existential tradition that has led to an examination of the modern *angoisse* is the comparison between *Crimes of the Heart* and Chekhov's plays, especially since Henley has stated that Chekhov influenced her more than any other dramatist.[15] Henley also has stated, "When I wrote *Crimes*, I was thinking mainly of Chekhov and *The Three Sisters*. I always thought both plays should be done in repertory."[16] Jean Gagen and Joanne B. Karpinski have each written detailed analyses exploring the relationships between *Crimes of the Heart* and *Three Sisters*.[17] Karpinski hints at the neurotic condition that both playwrights seem to understand almost intuitively: "Both plays raise the Lamarckian question of whether acquired characteristics (a culture, a psychosis) determine the behavior of the next generation."[18] Just as important, however, is Gagen's comment that both playwrights incorporate bizarre humor into essentially dramas of frustration, alienation, and sorrow.[19] Thus, Henley's black humor can be compared to the tragicomedy of Chekhov in which both playwrights use comedy to assuage the guilt, loneliness, and despair of the essentially neurotic modern condition resulting from cultural expectations that negate the natural drive for human happiness. As Matthew C. Roudané has noted, "Indeed, laughter becomes the key to her [Henley's] characters' very survival, a laughter filled with compassion, one that keeps at bay the loneliness, frailty, and loss that otherwise would destroy these offbeat creations."[20] Like Chekhov, who demonstrated compassion for all of his characters despite their frailties, Henley views her protagonists as part of one big family whose offbeat comic pathos helps them to maintain a sense of dignity in a neurotic, absurd universe. Understanding Henley's co-mingling of the grotesquely comic with the mundane, as well as her Chekhovian perspective in reducing serious issues to trivialities and concomitantly providing undue importance to the minutiae of daily life, helps us to see how her tragicomedy serves to mitigate, and perhaps to make us more aware of, the modern *angoisse*. Critics who fail to see Henley as part of the European tradition associated with the existential despair often confuse her plays with sick, rather than black, humor. For example, Leo Sauvage, in his review of the Broadway production of *Crimes of the Heart*, found nothing enthralling in what he deemed the badly adjusted, if not mentally retarded, Magrath sisters,[21] while Anthony Masters, commenting on the 1983 London staging, noted that only someone with a sick sense of humor could relate to the play.[22] Several critics were appalled when the Magrath sisters laughed at the news that their grandfather was in a coma, and even a few noted wryly that Lenny reacted more shockingly to the death of her horse than to the patriarch lying comatose. Again, what is overlooked is the way Chekhov, Henley's mentor, uses tragicomedy — often bizarre yet incisive — to understand humans who are searching for dignity in a neurotic world that denies the individual happiness at every turn. As was discussed in chapter 2, Henley sees the bizarre, the grotesque, the pathos of human existence as everyday reality. Henley uses tragicomedy as a means of understanding humanity's search for dignity in a bizarre, absurd, neurotic universe.

Henley stacks the cards against her protagonists from the very beginning of *Crimes of the Heart*, suggesting that the neurosis that Freud described in *Civilization and Its Discontents* imbues modern society with odds that are perceived as virtually insurmountable for contact among individuals. Henley's starting point for the play was a crisis: her grandfather, lost for three days, was eventually found walking in the woods in Copiah County, Mississippi, after paratroopers had been called out to help with the search. Henley realized, "So I thought that would be a good idea for a play: a family crisis bringing everybody back home."[23] The setting of the play, five years after Hurricane Camille, reinforces the notion that Nature mirrors society: crises are not to be forgotten, even in normally sedate Hazlehurst, Mississippi. Civilization rears its ugly head to keep us from happiness as one crisis blends into another. We learn that Lenny's horse Billy Boy was killed the previous evening — struck by lightning. Babe, the youngest sister, has just shot her husband Zackery and is now facing a jail sentence; this crisis is the event that brings Meg home from California. Moreover, Lenny is facing a terribly tense situation as she virtually regards her thirtieth birthday as an important rite, albeit not one of celebration since she has no one with whom to share the event. As the play wears on, the crises are exacerbated. Old Granddaddy has a stroke and lies in a coma in the hospital. Zackery has come up with sexually explicit photos of Babe and Willie Jay that are so incriminating as to send his wife to jail for a long time or at best to an insane asylum, virtually negating Barnette Lloyd's legal work on her behalf and driving her literally to suicide. Even when the Magrath sisters hear the news that Zackery's liver has been saved, there is only momentary consolation, followed by the announcement that Peekay and Buck, Jr. have just eaten paint. Babe, upon hearing of the death of Billy Boy, sums up the neurotic condition: "Life sure can be miserable."[24] Babe's "insanity" is not atypical, for the modern neurosis cuts across all socioeconomic levels of the culture, as Meg assures her sister, "Why, you're just as perfectly sane as anyone walking the streets of Hazlehurst, Mississippi" (61).

Henley depicts the Magrath sisters as icons for the modern neurosis. Freud stated that the modern neurosis resulted when the happiness of oral gratification under the nurturance of the mother is replaced by the sanctioned behavior patterns of social institutions and their representatives. The father of the Magrath sisters abandoned them at an early age. At first, the mother turned to oral gratification to assuage the despair and loneliness: she sat smoking cigarettes on the back porch, slinging ashes on the insects below. As a result of the deep sense of loss and grief that the matriarch of the family experienced after her husband left her, she hanged herself in the fruit cellar of her home, along with the family cat, when her daughters were young and in need of guidance — Lenny was fourteen; Meg, eleven; and Babe only eight. Alan Clarke Shepard writes that the mother's suicide "is a curse as particular as any in Ibsen, Tennessee Williams, or Sam Shepard, and as general as post-classical Western culture itself...."[25] The mother's suicide suggests the modern existential condition, for she killed herself out of loneliness, despair, desperation in the Void, and face to face with the anomie and *angoisse* of modern civilization that condemns a life of isolation as meaningless. Exploring the nature of suicide in the play, Lana A. Whited astutely explains how the curse is related to the neurotic condition:

> Because for a woman the family is almost always the primary community, any woman's decision to commit suicide is, ultimately, also a statement about her perception of that community's value in her life. To continue to live is, then, to affirm one's life and relationship within the community. To commit suicide is to reject them, and to insist that we are fundamentally all alone.[26]

The absent father and the death of the mother has created a Void in the lives of the Magrath sisters; in other words, the curse, a significant absence resulting in loneliness and despair, has been passed from one generation to another. Billy J. Harbin notes that the mother's ties with her children were largely unemotional, having provided only shelter for her offspring but not offering nurturing, especially since her suicide has been perceived by the Magrath sisters as a sort of psychological abandonment.[27] Deserted by their father and mother, the Magrath sisters are alienated and isolated, divorced from familial nurturance. Babe muses that her mother had affections only for her old cat (19). However, Susanne Aflitsch writes that those affections must have been rather fleeting: "Thus, the mother is viewed by her daughter [Babe] as dysfunctional: unable to care for the cat, she was equally unable to provide a caring environment for her daughters."[28] Although Harbin relates this spiritual bankruptcy to lost American ideals in the tradition of Eugene O'Neill and Sam Shepard, who have lamented the shift from the stability of rural self-reliance and moral certitude to a sterile society and transient instability,[29] the problem seems, as Freud suggests, to be more universally widespread in modern society.

In any event, the curse of the existential despair has been passed down through the House of Magrath. The sense of loss and abandonment by the mother and father is now transmitted to the offspring in the form of "crimes of the heart." When asked to explain the title of the play, Henley confirmed, "I guess a lot of it is them [the Magrath sisters] coming to terms with their crimes and trying to unshackle themselves from the past."[30] The emotional "crimes" thus relate to the way these scarred sisters, cursed by the deeply rooted existential despair, end up hurting themselves, as well as other family members.

Exacerbating the modern neurosis are Chick and Old Granddaddy, who, as female and male, respectively, represent not so much the role that gender plays in the existential despair shared by the Magrath sisters, but rather the cultural inhibitions posed by societal restraint regardless of gender. After their father's abandonment, the Magrath sisters were torn from their Vicksburg home to live with their grandparents in Hazlehurst. Living in the shadows of the absent male and a mother who withdrew into her solitude, flicking ashes off her back porch while ignoring her offspring, the Magrath sisters were virtually raised by Old Granddaddy. The parental detachment is finalized four years after the move to Hazlehurst when the mother hanged herself and her cat. Old Granddaddy then began to script the lives of the Magrath sisters according to cultural norms; however, the happiness formerly attained through early nurturance by the mother is lost. The oral needs of the child are displaced once the mother dies, and Old Granddaddy's remedy for providing happiness was to stuff the three sisters with banana splits — the food source being a poor substitute for the nurturing the sisters needed. Meg remarks, "The thing about Old Granddaddy is he keeps trying to make us happy and we end up getting stom-

achaches and turning green and throwing up in the flower arrangements"
(39).

Rather than provide happiness that Freud depicts is the goal of
humanity, Old Granddaddy becomes the agent for cultural assimilation.
Billy J. Harbin notes, "Self-indulgence and the pursuit of material success
were his primary means of combating aches of the heart and soul; he
offered them to the sisters as substitutes for the familial nurturing."[31] As
an icon who reinforces the superficial yet permanently established cultural
notion of the American Dream, Old Granddaddy equates success or solidarity in society with money and fame. Babe was exhorted by the patriarch to marry Zackery Botrelle, for he was the richest and most powerful
man in Hazlehurst. Lenny recalls, "He remarked how Babe was gonna skyrocket right to the heights of Hazlehurst society. And how Zackery was
just the right man for her whether she knew it now or not" (14). Meg, the
second oldest sibling, was, at least in Lenny's view, Old Granddaddy's personal favorite of the three sisters: "She's the one who got singing and dancing lessons; and a store-bought dress to wear to her senior prom" (35).
Meg was also allowed to wear twelve jingle bells on her petticoats, while
Lenny and Babe were confined to only three. Meg is urged by Old Granddaddy to leave her siblings and pursue a singing career in Hollywood,
which would inevitably yield fame and fortune; Hollywood will give Meg
"exposure" (15), a chance of "getting [her] foot put in one of those blocks
of cement they've got out there" (15). Meg winds up living a life of lies
and illusions, even suggesting to Old Granddaddy that her career has
reached its zenith with her soon-to-be appearance on the *Johnny Carson
Show*. With regard to the lies Meg has been feeding Old Granddaddy, she
admits, "All I wanted was to see him smiling and happy" (37). On the
other hand, we feel the divisive nature of Meg's neurosis since she is
conflicted about her feelings for Old Granddaddy: "I hate myself when I
lie for that old man. I do. I feel so weak. And then I have to go and do at
least three or four things that I know he'd despise just to get even with that
miserable, old, bossy man!" (37). Lenny, the eldest sister, has probably
been the one who was most affected by Old Granddaddy's tutelage and
influence. While Babe and Meg have at least broken free from the household in favor of marriage and a career, respectively, Lenny has stayed at
home to act as a surrogate mother cum wife for Old Granddaddy. After
her grandmother's death, Lenny moved to a cot in the kitchen to be closer
to Old Granddaddy and attend to his whims and needs. In other words,
she has become completely acculturated according to Old Granddaddy's
norms and values. As Babe notes, "She's turning into Old Grandmama"
(20). As the voice of socialization, Old Granddaddy makes Lenny feel

unworthy because her shrunken ovary is unacceptable in a culture where the female is judged by her ability to produce offspring. Insisting that no man would marry a woman with a deformed ovary, Old Granddaddy forced Lenny to become overly self-conscious about her condition. After meeting Charlie Hill through a dating service, Lenny introduced him to Old Granddaddy. Lenny mistakenly assumed that Charlie refused to marry her because of her shrunken ovary, which we later learn is nonsense because Charlie does not like children and certainly wants none of his own. When Lenny laments that she will never be happy, Meg agrees: "Well, not if you keep living your life as Old Granddaddy's nursemaid—" (42). Minrose Gwin correctly infers that although Old Granddaddy's influence on the three sisters has not been abusive, his culturally ascripted values have certainly been oppressive.[32] In short, as Freud suggests, the assimilation process ascribed to modern civilization is depicted by Henley as creating a neurosis that interferes with happiness.

Unfortunately, the acculturation process as ascribed through Old Granddaddy's norms and values has gone awry, replaced by the modern neurosis. Meg's singing career that was supposed to be the ticket to a glamorous life has fizzled out; instead she is working in the most unglamorous role as a clerk for a dog food company. Babe's chance to skyrocket to the top of Hazlehurst society has brought her to the abyss—she will acquire notoriety only as Hazlehurst's most illustrious female criminal, forever infamously etched in the minds of this closely knit community. Finally, Lenny has lost her sense of self-worth to become a pathetic figure depressed and devoid of love. In short, Old Granddaddy leads the Magrath sisters to the Void of existential despair; he is best represented by his absence in the play.

Chick Boyle, the Magrath sisters' first cousin, is the other agent of acculturation or voice of public opinion. Looking like the stereotypical blonde Southern matron with rosy red lips, the type of social-climbing perhaps former debutante who might have sought to reign supreme as the town's Carnival Queen, Chick, as her name implies, informs the Magrath sisters how to act properly as females residing in a Southern community. Chick is overly concerned about her image, refusing to take the chance of being seen in town with holes in her stockings (5) or with her hair pooching out in the back (7). As the committee head of the Ladies' Social League, and consequently a major voice for the transmittal of acculturating norms and values in the community, Chick, who also has familial and social ties with the Magrath sisters' as their cousin and next-door neighbor, assumes responsibility for keeping the Magraths within social boundaries. Harbin correctly notes, "The ideal tradition of the charitable 'good neighbor,' or of the social organization devoted to the cultural enlightenment and well being of the village, finds no expression in the character of Chick. Her petty bitchery, ugly manners and gossip-laden harassment of the MaGrath [sic] sisters personify the spiritual bleakness of the community."[33] Chick despises the Magrath sisters chiefly because they do not conform to cultural expectations. She tells Lenny, "Why, I've had just about my fill of you trashy Magraths and your trashy ways; hanging yourselves in cellars; carrying on with married men; shooting your own husbands!" (57). Chick has had to endure the Magrath mother's suicide — a violation of community norms and values; rather than trying to maintain a sense of happiness for the Magrath sisters, Chick, as the voice of the acculturation process, exacerbates their neurotic condition. Chick has little concern for Babe's welfare but instead seems only interested in the negative publicity that Babe's crime has brought on Chick's social circles, lamenting to Lenny, "How I'm gonna continue holding my head up high in this community, I do not know" (5). Meg, however, the most rebellious of the three sisters and therefore the one least likely to accept social sanctions, most frequently incurs Chick's wrath. Meg, with her loose reputation in high school, was known in Copiah County as "cheap Christmas trash" (6). Meg's affair with Doc Porter, which left him a cripple, did not enhance her status in the community, a fact that Chick consistently conveys to Lenny. When Chick sanctions Meg for smoking, which may lead to cancer, Meg responds, "That's what I like about it, Chick — taking a drag off of death" (17). Meg then takes a long, deep puff of the cigarette and exclaims, "Mmm! Gives me a sense of controlling my own destiny" (17). Meg almost seems to be aware that Chick, the voice of civilization and public opinion, increases the sense of loneliness and despair while concomitantly reducing the subliminal desire for happiness. Meg calls Chick "Little Chicken," comparing her to Chicken Little, the alarmist of the Mother Goose story. Fairy tales provide an important means for the culture to be passed on from generation to generation, but Meg seems to be implying that the world will not fall if she fails to live up to Chick's expectations and her notions of acculturation. Strangely enough, Lenny, who has the most contact with Chick, chases her with a broom at the end of the play, in effect, exorcising the voice of community so as to relieve the source of the neurosis interfering with human happiness.

Meg's reaction to the modern neurosis has resulted in a narcissistic personality disorder. Freud characterized narcissism as libido withdrawn from the external world and directed to the ego.[34] Freud noted that narcissists seek to be loved rather than to love others; not being loved, insofar as it involves longing and deprivation, increases their self-regard.[35] In

The Culture of Narcissism: American Life in an Age of Diminishing Expectations, Christopher Lasch has expanded on Freud's study of narcissism. Lasch claims that emerging pathological disorders and neurotic behaviors in modern society clearly have their origins in cultural developments, including changing patterns of socialization, the cult of consumption, and delusions of grandeur that make us yearn for celebrity status or for fame and wealth while fearing old age and death.[36] Narcissism becomes a means for coping with the tensions and anxieties of modern life that produce feelings of emptiness and disturbances in self-esteem. Lasch defines this culture of narcissism as consisting of individuals who seek to remain at the center of attention, their self-interest negating any regard for others in their quest for immediate gratification. Lasch views the narcissistic personality as characterized by "dependence on the various warmth provided by others combined with a fear of dependence, a sense of inner emptiness, boundless repressed rage, and unsatisfied oral cravings."[37] Emotional titillation without involvement and dependence often makes narcissists sexually promiscuous as well. Plagued by a sense of anxiety and guilt, the narcissist is forever restless, constantly searching for the elusive meaning of life. Expanding on the work of clinical psychologists and psychiatrists who have studied narcissism, including Havelock Ellis, Freud, Heinz Kohut, Otto F. Kernberg, and Lasch, the American Psychiatric Association in 1994 posed diagnostic criteria for Narcissistic Personality Disorder. Narcissism can be designated by having five or more of the following personality traits: a grandiose sense of self-importance, a preoccupation with fantasies of success, belief in being unique with a sense of entitlement, the need for excessive admiration, exploitive of others, lack of empathy for others, envious of others, and arrogant or haughty behavior or attitudes.[38] In short, narcissists have a pervasive pattern of grandiosity, self-importance, and a need for admiration but lack empathy for others. Their self-esteem is very fragile, and thus criticism may leave them feeling humiliated or deflated. The American Psychiatric Association also concludes that narcissists "tend to form friendships or romantic relationships only if the other person seems likely to advance their purposes or otherwise enhance their self-esteem."[39]

At age eleven, Meg discovered her mother's suicide, obviously a traumatic experience for an adolescent. This sense of loss and guilt may have contributed to her narcissism, for Meg's life is a continuous failure to get close to anyone. In this early stage of narcissism, Meg seemed to believe that she was special, a unique person with a sense of entitlement who often showed arrogant behavior. Wanting to be accepted by others, Meg was promiscuous in high school, and her loose reputation was well known throughout Copiah County. Meg seemed to have her own agenda, with the result being that she was the center of attention without taking responsibility for her adolescent life. Lenny recalls, "Why, Meg's always run wild — she started smoking and drinking when she was fourteen years old, she never made good grades— never made her own bed! But somehow she always seemed to get what she wanted" (35). Meg was the favored offspring of her grandparents, the only one to get singing and dancing lessons and have the dubious status of wearing twelve jingle bells instead of three on her petticoats. Meg spent time reading *Diseases of the Skin* in the library and hour after hour would stare at a poster of crippled children; instead of giving her dime for the disabled, Meg would spend it on ice cream. This is the classic case of the narcissist refusing to show empathy for others; rather than donate the money for a noble cause, Meg spends it on herself, recalling Old Granddaddy's desire to eradicate the problems in the Magrath household through instant gratification or happiness by serving the sisters banana splits (in which, of course, ice cream is the chief ingredient). Meg disguises the lack of empathy for others by postulating that spending the dime on ice cream has hardened her to avoid being a weak person. Karen L. Laughlin remarks, "Although initially we might be tempted to characterize part of the particular image Meg has cultivated as 'masculine' (at several points in the play we hear of her attempts to avoid showing signs of weakness), this quest for strength really amounts to a refusal to care, a numbing rejection of her own powerful emotions; it is another dimension of the silencing of her own desires and inner being rather than a movement toward self-reliance."[40] By trying to block out the pain and *angoisse* of the trauma of discovering her mother's body, Meg has become unable to identify with anyone's else's pain or suffering. As Thomas P. Adler suggests, "Meg had found their mother hanging in the basement, and her defense against the trauma was to hide behind a defiant humor and harden herself to the misery of others, since to vent her feelings would have signaled weakness rather than strength."[41] This helps to explain her abandonment of Doc Porter during Hurricane Camille, five years earlier. When the roof caved in and crushed Doc's leg, Meg, although in love with him, lacked empathy, and, like most narcissists, thought primarily of herself first and foremost. Henley views this as Meg's main "crime of the heart": "Meg's crime was being so afraid of Doc she left him with his broken leg saying she would marry him and went off to Hollywood."[42] Meg's guilt is thus exacerbated because her refusal to identify with Doc's feelings left him emotionally, and obviously physically, crippled. When Doc asks Meg why she left, she initially responds, "It was my fault to leave you. I was crazy. I thought I was choking" (44) but then reveals, "I don't know why ... 'Cause I didn't want to care" (44).

Under the auspices of Old Granddaddy's tutelage, Meg went to Hollywood to pursue celebrity status through her potentially rewarding singing career. Like most narcissists, Meg had exaggerated her talents in a preoccupation with fantasies of fame and fortune. Believing that she is unique and special in Hollywood's fantasyland, Meg isolates herself from others, turning the narcissistic gaze upon herself. She takes the telephone off the hook and refuses to read mail from former acquaintances in the small-town Hazlehurst society that she left. Instead of immersing herself into blocks of cement for eternity (the perfect dream of any narcissist), Meg ironically winds up as a small-time clerk working for a dog food company. Her nightclub career as a singer cum femme fatale has long since been abandoned. During Christmas, Meg remained remorseful, staying inside her apartment. She recalls what degenerated into a mental breakdown due to her neurotic condition: "All I could do was sit around in chairs, chewing on my fingers. Then one afternoon I ran screaming out of the apartment with all my money and jewelry and valuables and tried to stuff it all into one of those March of Dimes collection boxes" (50–51). Meg was then confined to the psychiatric ward at L.A. County Hospital. As Nancy D. Hargrove realizes, Meg's mental breakdown has much to do with the guilt of someone who has become emotionally and geographically isolated from others, while hiding under the guise of refusing love because of the need to avoid being vulnerable or weak.[43] Moreover, as Lisa J. McDonnell notes, Meg's neurotic behavior helps to link her childhood trauma with her sense of loss and her unwillingness to get close to another human being despite the fact that she desperately stuffs the collection box as some sort of therapy for her deeply rooted alienation.[44]

Upon her return from California, Meg shows the effects of her neurotic behavior. She has "*sad, magic eyes*" and carries "*a worn-out suitcase,*" which only serves to reinforce her dishevelment. Lenny views Meg as lacking empathy, a true narcissist concerned only with a sense of her own entitlement: "I don't know; it's— it's— You have no respect for other people's property! You just take whatever you want. You just take it!" (41). Ganga Viswanath and Christine Gomez note that Meg's failure in Hollywood now results in a deep sense of guilt that she tries to hide under the guise of indifference.[45] These feelings of guilt force her to lie to Old Granddaddy about her career, making Meg feel even more insecure.

Lasch noted that narcissists, although often sexually promiscuous, "avoid close involvements, which might release intense feelings of rage. Their personalities consist largely of defenses against this rage and against feelings of oral deprivation that originate in the pre–Oedipal stage of psychic development."[46] To assuage their deep feelings of anxiety and despair due to a world in which they seek admiration through celebrity status that has replaced the happiness of the formative years, narcissists seek to regain the happiness of the nurturing lost in the "pre–Oedipal stage of psychic development" through oral cravings.[47] In writing about orality and identity in the play, Laura Morrow states, "Oral activities also reflect the need for or response to nurturing; an insatiable desire for sweets, for example, may indicate one is symbolically seeking food from a loving mother."[48] Meg's response to distress has been self-destructive behavior; during this family reunion, Meg eats, smokes, and drinks to drown out the modern neurosis, reduce her narcissistic lack of empathy for others, and return to a happier state of oral satisfaction that she had before her mother committed suicide.

The first example of Meg's lack of empathy for others through oral satisfaction is when Lenny tells her of Babe's shooting of Zackery, and Meg's response is to get a soda. When Lenny mentions that Billy Boy was struck by lightning, Meg lights a cigarette. The news of Old Granddaddy's three-month hospital stay has Meg reaching for the bourbon, and when she learns there is none, she settles for a Coke and Empirin, the latter to kill the pain of hearing news she would rather not have learned. We should recall that using food to avoid problems is a staple of the Magrath household ever since Old Granddaddy took the siblings out for banana splits to avoid familial grief. Thus, when Lenny reminds Meg of her potential as a singer and the hopes that Old Granddaddy had for her if she only received the requisite exposure, Meg grabs for the pecans, all the while reminding her sister that her ambitions have been repressed through her daily toil in the dog food company. Chick's entrance and her comment, "We keep looking for your picture in the movie magazines" (17), sends Meg for another cigarette. Chick admonishes Meg for smoking, but the latter responds that it gives her a sense of controlling her own destiny. Instead, as Laura Morrow informs us, Meg's smoking "unconsciously replicates her mother's repression of pain and anger,"[49] since it reminds us of her self-destructive behavior of withdrawing from life as she sat on the back porch flinging her ashes at the ants and insects. As the discussion centers around Lenny's loneliness because of her shrunken ovary, Meg bites into an apple and suggests that Lenny's desolation on her birthday can be best addressed if they order a birthday cake. When Meg begins to learn more than she needs to know about Babe's affair with Willie Jay, "that little kid we used to pay a nickel to, to run down to the drugstore and bring us back a cherry Coke" (27), she reaches for Lenny's box of candy and requests cold water to wash it down. Comments about Charlie Hill force Lenny to weep, but Meg's reaction is merely to down another drink with a cigarette. All of this oral activity is put into context when we recall that Meg's sole reaction to crippled children depicted in the March of Dimes posters was for her to down another double scoop ice cream cone. In short, Meg, like her sisters, feeds her stomach when actually it is the heart that is empty.

Lenny's response to the modern neurosis is what clinicians would call Depressive Personality Disorder, known to laymen as depression. The *Diagnostic and Statistical Manual of Mental Disorders* describes depression as behavior indicated by the following: moods of dejection, gloominess, and unhappiness; low self-esteem; brooding and worry; pessimism; and feelings of guilt or remorse.[50] The play opens with Lenny pathetically trying to stick a candle into a crumbling cookie she has substituted for a cake. Lenny is celebrating her thirtieth birthday alone, which is significant because she is terribly unhappy about growing old without a spouse to support her. Unlike Meg who has fled the nest to seek her fortune in Hollywood and Babe who has started a family of her own, Lenny has stayed close to home with the result that she now has no one there to ease her pain and suffering.[51] The birthday celebration, carefully orchestrated to include a solo rendition of "Happy Birthday," seems to mark Lenny as a martyr who chooses to suffer alone. When Doc enters and tells her of Billy Boy's death, Lenny, apparently crushed by Babe's plight and Old Granddaddy's deteriorating physical condition, begins to cry. Later in the play, when Lenny learns of Old Granddaddy's stroke, she becomes more gloomy and depressed, worrying that if Old Granddaddy dies, "I'm afraid of being here all by myself. All alone" (52). Although Old Granddaddy certainly contributed to Lenny's isolation, having favored Meg (the most talented) and Babe (the most beautiful) over her (the eldest, with a shrunken ovary), she certainly stood by him, virtually becoming a nursemaid for the old patriarch. Instead of living a life of her own, she became a surrogate for her grandmother (she even wears her grandmother's torn sunhat and lime-green gloves when gardening), and, after several years, as Meg reminds her sister, she wound up "living ... life as Old Granddaddy's nursemaid—" (42). Laura Morrow's observation about Lenny is particularly appropriate: "Despairing of any chance for appreciation as a woman because of her inability to bear children, she defeminizes her name, Lenora, to the masculine Lenny and resigns herself to tending the garden and Old Granddaddy."[52]

Lenny's guilt about her shrunken ovary and her low self-esteem because Old Granddaddy has made her feel conscious of her inadequacies, has made her depressed. Babe admits that after Old Granddaddy's second stay in the hospital, "Lenny was really in a state of deep depression" (21). Rather than brood all day and remain dejected and unhappy, Lenny turned to a dating service, aptly named Lonely Hearts of the South. Her only response was from Charlie Hill of Memphis. Babe suspects that Charlie's one trip to Hazlehurst resulted in the only time Lenny had ever had a sexual encounter. However, Lenny's loneliness and *angoisse* was only exacerbated after Charlie meets Old Granddaddy, who promptly refuses to sanction the love relationship because Lenny's deformed ovary precludes any chance of her having children. Meg, who has been in California while Lenny's guilt has been increasing and her depression has been getting worse, accurately assesses her sister's mental condition: "Poor Lenny. She needs some love in her life. All she does is work out at that brick yard and take care of Old Granddaddy" (20). Lenny has latched on to Old Granddaddy because she believes, "He doesn't want to see me rejected and humiliated" (42). Lenny has become overly self-critical and guilty about her shortcomings, refusing to seek love because she may be rejected, thus turning to her grandfather because he is the only person to provide what she believes is solace and comfort. Lenny says to Meg, "But I have this underdeveloped ovary and I can't have children and my hair is falling out in the comb — so what man can love me?" (42). Lenny also reveals that the real reason she could not establish a relationship with Charlie was because her feelings of inadequacy and low self-esteem put a damper on her passion before it could get ignited: "Because I just didn't want him not to want me —" (42). Thus, Lenny's crime of the heart is self-destructive guilt and remorse that forces her to abandon a possible relationship in favor of unhappiness and existential despair.

To assuage the depression attributed to the modern neurosis and redeem the happiness of the formative years, Lenny also turns to oral cravings. The play takes place in her living quarters— the kitchen — and opens with Lenny trying to celebrate over one of her favorite foods (the cookie) and closes with a food celebration (the birthday cake). Chick refers to Lenny as a "sweet potato" (7) who has "a sweet tooth" (7), and Doc calls her "Jello Face" (10). Lenny uses food, particularly sweets, to fill the void in her life, mistakenly assuming that the hunger of the stomach can substitute for hunger of the heart. Food becomes for her a temporary means of relieving the depression and spiritual emptiness of her daily existence. Like many depressed people, Lenny consumes food, not for nourishment, but for its value as a palliate for the pain of her loneliness. Billy J. Harbin explains how Lenny's oral cravings function as an opiate in her life: "Food is devoured not for sustenance, but as compensation for grievances of the heart; it has no relationship to the ideal tradition of family gatherings, a sharing with others or meal-time communion."[53] Lenny is particularly in need of oral satisfaction when her guilt and remorse are brought to the surface around other people. When Doc enters, Lenny has to have coffee (8); during conversation with Babe, Lenny reaches for her birthday candy (34), and while Meg poisons herself with bourbon and cigarettes, Lenny sips more coffee (36). Meg probably forces Lenny's guilt and depression to the surface more so than any other character in the play. Consequently, as Lou Thompson observes, when Lenny gets upset over Meg's biting into the box of assorted cremes given to her as a birthday gift, Lenny is expressing her grief at Meg's leaving the game of Hearts (with popcorn and hot chocolate) to be with Doc.[54] Lenny's overly hostile reaction to Meg's violation of her sister's oral satisfaction obviously reflects a more deeply rooted resentment of the fact that Meg has been successful with men and was favored by the grandparents while Lenny is left alone and was always made to feel inadequate. Lenny's oral cravings must be fairly well known, for her friends bring her food offerings, such as candy (from Chick) and pecans (from Doc), which certainly must have pleased her in the past.

Babe also represents the anxiety and *angoisse* that results from the deeply rooted existential despair of the modern neurosis. We know very little about Babe's life before her marriage to Zackery except that she among her sisters talks the most about her mother's suicide and tries to ponder its meaning. Babe's alienation and isolation seems to have increased since she married Zackery; there is no evidence that they ever loved each other. Instead, the marriage seems to have been sanctioned and arranged by Old Granddaddy, who, impressed with Zackery's credentials as a lawyer, saw him as Babe's ticket to skyrocket to the heights of Hazlehurst society. Babe thus entered into a marriage that, because of the nature of modern civilization, removed her from happiness. The Void that Zackery created in Babe's life is imminently discernible by his absence in the play,[55] much like the absent father, mother, and grandfather. Zackery abused her physically and mentally, forcing Babe to enter into a relationship with Willie Jay, a fifteen-year-old African-American male. Thus, the battered female, alone and trying to find a response to her despair, bonded with what seemed to her to be another outcast. When Meg questions the efficacy of Babe's relationship with a black boy deep in the South, the younger sister responds, "I was just lonely! I was so lonely" (28). When Zackery struck Willie Jay after learning about Babe's tryst with the young man, Babe attempted to shoot herself, imitating her mother, who had committed suicide years before. Babe's first reaction to the modern neurosis is therefore self-destructive, a trait that seems endemic to the Magrath household. Babe, however, cannot quite reconcile herself with her mother's suicide, so she rationalizes that the wiser decision would be to turn the gun on Zackery. Babe's shooting of Zackery because of his beating of the innocent boy is her "crime of the heart."

Babe's attempted murder of Zackery and her imminent jail sentence due to the callousness of her crime (making lemonade instead of calling the authorities) forces Lenny to question Babe's mental stability, deeming her sister "ill. I mean in-her-head-ill" (12). Babe's illness is due to suffering from existential despair, admitting, "Why, I feel so all alone" (31). Babe's neurosis increases when her support system vanishes—Willie Jay is sent north to be out of the way, Meg and Lenny are sufficiently preoccupied with their own neuroses, Chick taunts her about the crime, and Zackery has discovered revealing photos of Babe's affair with the black boy, thus making it difficult for Barnette, Babe's only hope for justice, to defend her. Babe also fears that confinement to a mental institution would permanently isolate her from family and friends. Babe, whom we have seen has already been prone to suicide, then tries to commit it twice, first by hanging herself and then by sticking her head in the oven. These suicide attempts gone awry bring Babe face to face with the modern neurosis, helping her to understand the existential despair that lies at the root of her loneliness. Although Babe admits that Meg was the one who found their mother's dead body, Babe seems to be the sibling who is most affected by the mother's suicide, constantly brings up the subject, and is the only daughter haunted by its repercussions. Babe's failed suicide attempts force her to understand why her mother hanged the cat with her: "It's 'cause she was afraid of dying all alone" (60). Babe begins to understand the effects of the modern neurosis. Assuming that angels would be present at the time of one's suicide, Babe realizes, "You'd be afraid to meet 'em all alone. So it wasn't like what people were saying about her hating that cat. Fact is, she loved that cat. She needed him with her 'cause she felt so all alone" (60–61).

Like Meg and Lenny, Babe's oral cravings help her to mitigate the modern neurosis that prevents human happiness. After her mother's suicide, Babe fell under Old Granddaddy's influence as his "Dancing Sugar Plum" (14), assuaging periods of loneliness with banana splits. Food and drink substituted for Babe's lack of bonding with others. Barnette recalls that he met Babe at a Christmas bazaar where she was selling cakes, cookies, and candy; Barnette trusted her wares, buying a pound cake from her. Babe trusts Barnette because she associates him with the pound cake, much in the same way that she associates Willie Jay, albeit subconsciously, as the person who brought her cherry cokes from the drugstore. Babe is also the one who insists that ordering the largest cake the bakery has will cure Lenny of her loneliness on her birthday. This infatuation with food and drink as a substitute for happiness explains why Babe's marriage fell apart at the dinner table where, as Laura Morrow asserts, Babe's attempts to nurture her husband through feeding failed miserably.[56] In particular, Zackery complained about the food served, and thus Babe's response was to ignore the man who refused the sustenance that Babe thought substituted for happiness: "I'd fall asleep just listening to him at the dinner table. He'd say, 'Hand me some of that gravy!' Or, 'This roast beef is too damn bloody.' And suddenly I'd be out cold like a light" (26). The marriage obviously was an inadequate substitute for Babe's oral gratification and probably never should have taken place, for Babe's only recollection of the wedding is viewed in relationship to orality: "Well, I was drunk on champagne punch. I remember that!" (38). Nevertheless, Babe tries to make amends for a loveless marriage by shooting Zackery in the heart, where the source of happiness is supposed to be located, but instead hitting him in the stomach. Henley is perhaps suggesting that Babe has missed the mark, much like her sisters who, as Lou Thompson observes, feed their stomachs when in reality it is their hearts that have been deprived.[57]

During intense periods of distress throughout the play, Babe seeks oral gratification either through eating, drinking, or playing the saxophone. When Babe complains that Chick, the voice of the community, blames the Magrath mother's suicide as a blight on the quiet town of Hazlehurst, she insists on having some lemonade. During the most intense moment of her life, her shooting of Zackery, Babe's response was to make herself a pitcher of lemonade and drink three glasses of it. When she is forced to recount the attempted murder to her lawyer, Babe relies on a bowl of oatmeal to get her through the ordeal. Moreover, Babe's new saxophone, another oral stimulus, is, as Henley herself admits, "more of a freeing image" for the youngest sibling.[58] Finally, when life becomes too stressful, Babe retreats to the sources of her oral cravings: rather than have Meg call her attorney, Babe puts the telephone in the refrigerator, and rather than face a jail sentence, Babe puts her head in the oven.

The anomie, existential despair, and *angoisse* produced by the spiritual bankruptcy of modern civilization can only be tempered by bonding through love. As the Magrath sisters prepare for Hearts, Lenny reminds them of how to play the game: "Hearts are bad, but the Black Sister is the worst of all —" (39). Sniping and quibbling with each other throughout the play and failing to come to terms with their past, the Magrath sisters have committed crimes of the heart, each of them more or less taking turns acting like the Black Sister. In response to a question about why she writes, Henley remarked that she tries to understand that ugliness is in everybody and that humans still seek love and kindness even though they are filled with dark, violent, primitive urges and desires.[59] In essence, *Crimes of the Heart* demonstrates the transition that the Black Sisters make, weighed

down by the neuroticism of the modern age, as they search for happiness
or love lost after the formative years.

Replacing the lost mother and the absent father, who represent the dis-
placement resulting from the neuroticism induced through modern civilization, the Black Sisters stop harassing each other to share in mutual
nurturance, allowing them to get through those really bad days. Bonding
through love and community (having a heart) produces happiness that we
long for but ultimately have difficulty in obtaining under the burden of daily
community norms and values. The bonding sustained by the Magrath sisters allows them each to experience their epiphanies. Henley implied to
Alexis Greene that the bonding of the three sisters enabled them to destroy
the secrets that cursed the House of Magrath: "Letting themselves be seen
for who they are to each other makes them closer, or a little more empowered to just be."[60] With the help of her sisters, Meg has found the capacity
to respond to the needs of others, which, as a narcissist, she has been unable
to do. Previously abandoning Doc and her singing career, Meg now develops a new sense of happiness and self-worth as a result of the bonding she
has received while confessing the sins of her past to her sisters. Meg tells Babe
that mutual confession is fundamental: "To talk about our lives. It's an
important human need" (26). Moreover, Meg now accepts the fact that her
singing career is a failure and admits her psychological breakdown to Doc.
After spending the evening with Doc, she acknowledges, "I'm happy. I realized I could care about someone. I could want someone. And I sang! I sang
all night long!" (50). Babe, haunted by her mother's death and faced with a
possible lengthy jail sentence, rejects suicide as a solution to the modern neurosis because she now realizes that she has two sisters who care deeply about
her feelings. Babe, lighting the birthday candles for Lenny and sharing with
her sisters in this communal celebration, begins to understand how bonding with others prevents the alienation and isolation precluding one's happiness in modern civilization. Babe realizes, "And I'm not like Mama. I'm
not so all alone," while Meg asserts, "You're not" (62). Furthermore, Babe,
having lifted the veil of secrecy over her affair with Willie Jay and the truth
about her tormented marriage, now feels empowered to greater understanding of the absurd condition. Finally, Lenny's epiphany comes when she
chases Chick out of her house, effectively exorcising the voice of community, and supported and encouraged by her sisters, simultaneously pursues
Charlie Hill, in essence ignoring Old Granddaddy's advice that her shrunken
ovary was the obstacle to her happiness. Lenny learns to come to terms with
her depression as she begins to understand that happiness derives from love
and sharing through communal support and that the voice of public opinion instead has produced for her nothing but worthlessness.

The last image in the play in which the Magrath sisters share in a communal celebration is in stark contrast to the opening scene in which Lenny, depressed and alone, is ineptly trying to celebrate her birthday by sticking a lone candle into a stale cookie that crumbles; then she begins to cry when Doc enters. At the end of the play, the communal sharing and outpouring of love produces a dramatically different effect. The overjoyed Lenny is no longer alone and even makes a birthday wish while blowing out the candles, now successfully mounted on the cake instead of falling off of the cookie. Lenny wishes that the moment of bonding will last, for she realizes that communal sharing is the key to happiness. The play ends in celebration with two oral images— the eating of the birthday cake and the notes of the saxophone — reminding us that alternatives to true happiness will always exist, but that the freeze frame moment of bonding in *"magical, golden, sparkling glimmer"* (63) offers the only fleeting joy of unity that can assuage the loneliness and despair of the otherwise modern neurosis.

5

The Miss Firecracker Contest and *The Debutante Ball*

Henley's next two plays, *The Miss Firecracker Contest* and *The Debutante Ball*, are linked by two important annual social events reflected in the titles of each play: the Fourth of July Miss Firecracker Contest and Hattiesburg, Mississippi's debutante ball. These two prominent social gatherings represent a crisis situation exacerbating the neurotic conditions of Henley's two protagonists, Carnelle Scott and Jen Turner, respectively.

Critics have mistakenly misconstrued *The Miss Firecracker Contest* as Henley's political or sociological indictment of how sexist institutions such as beauty pageants relegate females to the patriarchal gaze. For example, Sally Burke writes, "But Henley casts a cold eye on both beauty contests and the male gaze. Carnelle wants to win the contest so that she can 'leave [town] in a blaze of glory'; her belief in the contest does not stop Henley from satirizing it."[1] The potential is there for a diatribe decrying the stultifying effects that beauty pageants have on young women. Jonnie Guerra notes, "In *Miss Firecracker*, Henley never presents a satisfying portrayal of female interaction. In fact, the play's focus on a beauty pageant emphasizes the destructive effect of the politics of appearance on women's relationships: that the looking glass sets women against each other, makes them enemies and rivals."[2] Robert L. McDonald argues that Carnelle's identity is socially constructed through the confines of "static categories of small-town southern life"; therefore, Carnelle, who subjects herself to the pageant as a "community-sanctioned agency of confirmation" (ultimately of her reputation as Miss Hot Tamale), sets herself up for failure.[3] However, several other critics have realized that a reading of the play as a

86

sociological critique of how the male gaze empowers women to conform to certain expectations is not the focal point of the drama. Arguing that beauty pageants clearly reduce women to sexual objects and that male judgment and approval is important to Henley's protagonists, Lisa Merrill nevertheless concedes that Henley loses the opportunity to make a feminist statement: "Rather than merely presenting these regressive models, a feminist exploration of the beauty pageant might lead an audience to question women's complicity in a system where acceptance is dependent upon being reduced to a sexual object. Henley's play does not do this."[4] Laurin Porter, acknowledging that Henley had a perfect opportunity to offer a feminist critique of institutionalized rituals that offer women up for commodities of consumption, realizes that Carnelle is not an icon for the feminist cause. Porter notes that Carnelle wanted to win the contest, disagreeing with Elain, who insists that the pageant is ultimately meaningless: "Any possibility of exposing the pageant's inherent sexism is lost at this point. Carnelle never understands how being labeled 'Miss Hot Tamale' by the very men she gave her body to validates a system which insists that women are to be used and then discarded."[5] In an interview published in 1987, Henley stated that *The Miss Firecracker Contest* was not a sociological treatise: "It's a story about wanting to belong to the world. I didn't want to judge the contest. The contest is important to the character; winning it would make her feel like she is somebody."[6] Two years later, in an interview published in *Film Comment*, Henley was emphatic about her motivations for writing *The Miss Firecracker Contest*: "I don't claim to make any feminist or ideological statements. We all know what it's like as kids to watch Miss America pageants on television. I didn't write *Miss Firecracker* to criticize beauty contests, to show them as social problems. I just wanted to show how that contest becomes an opportunity for a girl to fulfill a dream of being beautiful and winning some recognition for it."[7]

Rather than focusing on a social indictment of the patriarchy,[8] *The Miss Firecracker Contest* presents a psychological portrait of the modern neurosis. Carnelle Scott's id is suppressed by the cultural ideals she has internalized as important to her, thus reducing her own chances of happiness in order to conform to social expectations. The result is that her neurotic condition closely resembles Borderline Personality Disorder, which also afflicted Marshael in *The Wake of Jamey Foster*. The *Diagnostic and Statistical Manual of Mental Disorders* depicts Borderline Personality Disorder as a pervasive pattern of instability in interpersonal relationships indicated by frantic efforts to avoid abandonment, behavior patterns characterized by extremes of idealization and devaluation, an unstable self-image, and chronic feelings of emptiness.[9]

Carnelle's life has been a tale of abandonment and rejection, leaving her feeling alienated, empty, isolated, and determined to prove her self-worth. Her mother passed away when Carnelle was barely a year old, again implying the mother's abandonment of her offspring, which is devastating for a young child. Carnelle remembers that her father treated her as an object before discarding her: "Then my daddy kinda drug me around with him till I was about nine and he couldn't stand me any longer; so he dropped me off to live with my Aunt Ronelle and Uncle George and their own two children: Elain and Delmount."[10] Moreover, Carnelle's father did not care for his daughter's hygiene, for she entered Aunt Ronelle's household in rags and suffering from ringworm. Thus, Carnelle was abandoned by both parents when she was in the formative years and was forced to live with her aunt, who undoubtedly would favor her own children over a child that is not hers and was dumped on her as excessive baggage. Aunt Ronelle assumed a matriarchal role for Carnelle, giving her nurturance, putting ointment on her ringworm sores, and providing her with a role model to emulate. Later, Uncle George was killed when he tried to pull a bird's nest from their chimney, which, for Carnelle, suggests further estrangement from her family. Her father came back to live with Aunt Ronelle for two years before dying of heart failure subsequent to running after an ice cream truck in the summer heat. Meanwhile, Aunt Ronelle, like Old Granddaddy in *Crimes of the Heart*, inculcated her family with her own stereotyped, warped values of womanhood, defining it in terms of beauty, which she believed determined one's chances at success and social grace in this small southern community. Thus, as an adolescent, Carnelle, trying to find a worthy self-image that Aunt Ronelle could accept and having to compete for attention with the more attractive Elain, became promiscuous (read carnal), much like Meg was in her adolescent years.[11] Delmount recalls, "Anyway, she never did attain any self-esteem. Had to sleep with every worthless soul in Brookhaven trying to prove she was attractive" (165–66). Carnelle's obsession with being popular caused her to suffer psychologically and physically: she developed an unwanted and, what to her appears to be an eternally damaging, reputation as Miss Hot Tamale while contracting syphilis as well. Laurilyn J. Harris perceptively infers, "In a society where virginity is a marketable commodity and virtue a bargaining chip, Carnelle has definitely devalued the 'merchandise.'"[12] Aunt Ronelle eventually developed cancer of the pituitary gland, which was treated by the medical authorities by replacing her gland with that of a monkey in an experimental attempt to save her life. This unusual treatment prolonged Aunt Ronelle's life for about a month longer than she might have lived otherwise, but the side effect, a rather gruesome vision but typical of what one comes to expect in a Henley black comedy, is that she grew black hairs all over her body, somewhat like an ape. During the Christmas before the Miss Firecracker Contest, Aunt Ronelle died, reinforcing Carnelle's sense of abandonment. Now faced with the deaths of her mother, father, aunt, and uncle, Carnelle develops the deeply rooted feelings of emptiness usually seen in neurotics suffering from Borderline Personality Disorder. Tracing her family history for Popeye, Carnelle even prefaces the saga with the comment, "It seems like people've been dying practically all my life, in one way or another" (152).

Meanwhile, Carnelle has been suffering from guilt about never having lived up to Aunt Ronelle's expectations. Like those suffering from Borderline Personality Disorder, Carnelle has mood swings alternating between idealization and devaluation. She earns a meager living working at Slater's Jewelry Shop but envisions herself moving up in the world by taking a modeling job in Memphis. Although she is guilt ridden about her past sexual transgressions, she tries to assuage the devaluation by an idealization that includes going to church and taking orphans to dinner or to a movie once a week; moreover, she subliminally seeks to transgress the negative image that Aunt Ronelle had of her by working on the local cancer drive, which, on the one hand, imitates what Elain, her idol, does in Natchez, and, on the other hand, would have pleased Aunt Ronelle, who died from the disease. Carnelle, suffering from a lack of self-esteem, rationalizes that these altruistic motives can assuage her past guilt: "My life has meaning. People aren't calling me, [*sic*] Miss Hot Tamale anymore like they used to" (158).

Now twenty-four years old, Carnelle enters Brookhaven, Mississippi's annual Fourth of July Miss Firecracker Contest partly because this is her last year to qualify, for next year she will be at the age limit. Moreover, Delmount is planning to sell his aunt's house, which has been Carnelle's residence for the past fifteen years, so she will be forced to move on.

Winning the Miss Firecracker Contest thus is a natural progression for Carnelle—the impetus for her to leave parochial Brookhaven in what she believes will be a "blaze of glory" (163, 179) and the means by which she can increase her low self-esteem and simultaneously eradicate the guilt caused by her loose promiscuous history as Miss Hot Tamale. The annual celebration therefore becomes a time of crisis for Carnelle, which she hopes will be her rite of passage or maturation of selfhood.

Keeping in tune with the Fourth of July celebration, Carnelle plans a patriotic display that she maintains is "noble" (148). Carnelle, who has dyed her hair red for the contest, practices a talent routine that consists of tap dancing, marching, and baton twirling while roman candles go off and sparklers blaze during accompaniment to the *Star-Spangled Banner*. Carnelle's red, silver, and blue outfit — patriotic yet ill conceived because she is out of white fabric — is an early indication of the disaster to come. Although her gyrations are somewhat uncoordinated, Carnelle gains renewed confidence when she places in the top five finalists who are allowed to compete for the title of Miss Firecracker.

As is typical of neurotics who suffer from Borderline Personality Disorder, Carnelle alternates between the extremes of idealism that aspires to a state of beauty inculcated into her persona by Aunt Ronelle and a devaluation of self accompanied by low self-esteem. This dialectic between the two emotional states affecting Carnelle forms the tension in the play, which Henley has described as a constant tug of war "about winning and losing, about the idea of beauty and ugliness, our need to be adored, and how we take the concept of our self-worth from everyone else."[13] Carnelle's environment is part of her estrangement, for she lives in Aunt Ronelle's house, which Henley describes as "*dreary*," "*suffocating*," and "*frightening*" (146); moreover, Carnelle, as a foster child, does not belong in the same way that Elain and Delmount, Aunt Ronelle's offspring, might feel comfortably at home. Carnelle is defensive about her self-esteem, so when Popeye admits to designing clothes for bullfrogs, Carnelle interjects with, "Well, I certainly hope you don't think of me as any bullfrog," and then elaborates: "I mean, think I'm ugly like one of those dumb bullfrogs of yours" (150). Carnelle desperately needs the recognition of winning the contest to raise her self-esteem. When Elain, Carnelle's idol, mentions her estrangement from her husband Franklin, Carnelle cannot fathom leaving someone who might dote on a woman, admitting to her cousin, "It seemed like Franklin loved you so much. I thought I wanted a man to love me that much" (159). When Carnelle fears that she will not be one of the five finalists in the contest, she laments to Popeye, "I'm ugly, Popeye! My thighs are fat! No one loves me!" (172). Carnelle views the contest as her chance to belong, a means to evade the rejection she has had to live with in Brookhaven, the "visible proof" (168) of her acceptance into the community, measured by the response to the crowd if she rides in the winner's circle on the float, waving to her admirers. When named as one of the five finalists, Carnelle's idealism is at its peak, and she exclaims, "They're — they're gonna be taking my picture for the newspaper at ten o'clock in the morning at the Courthouse square. I'll be famous!" (174). Her idealization is bolstered by the fact that since the contest has become integrated, the quality of the contestants has declined, elevating her chances of winning. Tessy Mahoney, the contest coordinator, assures Carnelle that her only real contender for the title of Miss Firecracker is Caroline Jeffers, the girl with the yellow teeth. Carnelle's idealization provides her with confidence that she can defeat the other three finalists. She tells Delmount, "I know I'll beat Saphire Mendoza just 'cause she's the token Negro and Mexican. I'm not trying to be mean about it, but it's the truth" (179). Frank Jacob's sister is "a shrimp" and Missy Mahoney, Tess's sister, is reported to be the ugliest girl in Brookhaven. When Carnelle comes in last place, the conflicting demands of idealization and devaluation are too much for her to bear; she is confused and dejected, and the stage directions indicate, "*She looks at herself in the mirror, then she bravely turns to face her family and friends, hoping for acceptance*" (196).

The Miss Firecracker Contest depicts how cultural norms and values preclude any chance of happiness, thus contributing to the modern neurosis. Carnelle becomes obsessed with "mean" Aunt Ronelle's warped view of beauty as an avenue to fortune, which will eventually establish one's self-worth in the community. Carnelle's obsession with winning the contest to establish a saving sense of self-worth and recognition in Brookhaven merely serves to set her up for failure. On stage, Carnelle trips over her red skirt and falls flat on her face. She is further humiliated as the citizens, refusing to forget her past reputation as a loose woman, yell, "Miss Hot Tamale! Miss Hot Tamale." Instead of having the winning banner draped over her, Carnelle is inundated with peanuts, trash, and ice. Elain's seductive red dress is reduced to looking like a whore's outfit on Carnelle. Although Carnelle's tap dancing routine is a big success, the citizens cannot let her forget the ghosts of her dismal past, and as Laurilyn J. Harris reminds us, as long as Carnelle accepts their standards, she is at their mercy.[14] Ranting at Elain, Carnelle takes out her wrath on the ideology that duped her into believing that happiness was possible in this absurd universe: "I can't believe I ever wanted to be like you or that mean old monkey either" (197).

The tension associated with the Fourth of July celebration is further exacerbated by the return of Elain Rutledge, turning what typically would be a festive occasion into a family reunion and thus a crisis of sorts for Carnelle. Elain has bought into Aunt Ronelle's concept of female self-worth through beauty; Elain's mother ignored her until she started winning beauty pageants, resulting in gaining the title in the Miss Firecracker Contest when she was merely seventeen years old. As her mother predicted, after being accepted as a beauty queen, she would get a rich husband, have children, and own a mansion in Natchez replete with material possessions that she adores, including beautiful clocks; she is like Meg, who believed in Old Granddaddy's myth of fame and fortune yet found it ultimately to be shallow. Elain is described in the cast list as "a beauty"

(145), and at age thirty-two, she is still glamorous, *"but her looks are now more strained and anxious than they once were"* (154). With Elain returning to Brookhaven, Carnelle must once again live up to Aunt Ronelle's standards of beauty and perfection. Carnelle describes her cousin as "perfectly perfect" (155) and "my ideal" (152), admiring Elain as having everything "just like a queen in a castle" (159), seconded by Delmount's assessment of his sister as "the beautiful, the sweet, the perfect, Elain Rutledge" (161). Moreover, Elain's purpose for attending the Fourth of July reunion is to present a speech titled "My Life as a Beauty" to the citizens of Brookhaven, thus cementing the idea in Carnelle's mind that Elain is an honored guest because she has the right words of wisdom to convey. Furthermore, Elain's mere presence forces Carnelle, perhaps subliminally, to want to compete with the aging beauty, her idol, and do well in the contest to follow in her mentor's footsteps as an icon of beauty and glamour, thus also sustaining respectability for herself in the community.[15]

Elain can offer no support to Carnelle because the aging beauty queen herself seems to suffer from her own anxiety disorder — Narcissistic Personality Disorder, the same condition with which Meg was afflicted. As was discussed in chapter 4, narcissists, according to the *Diagnostic and Statistical Manual of Mental Disorders*, have a grandiose sense of self-importance, are preoccupied with fantasies of unlimited power or beauty, require excessive admiration, exhibit haughty behavior, and lack empathy for others.[16] As the former winner of the Miss Firecracker Contest, Elain has parlayed her beauty into an acquired status in the community, which she believes commands respect and admiration. Her Southern Belle facade forever serves to exemplify a persona consisting of graciousness, kindness, and gentility that provides her with a grandiose sense of self-esteem. Adhering to Aunt Ronelle's standards, Elain has been the only one in the family to attain success, which, in her mind and in her grandiose view of the world, warrants homage from the peons in the community. She basks in the spotlight of the Fourth of July celebration, which seems to be about her rather than about Carnelle: "It's amazing but everyone recognizes me. They say I'm still exactly the same as I was. 'Just in full bloom like a rose!' That's what one dear man said. I wish Mama were here" (181).

Like most narcissists, Elain has no empathy for anyone except herself. Elain's personality disorder prevents her from providing solace to Carnelle during the stressful time of the contest, which is unusual because Elain has already won the beauty pageant and therefore knows what to expect; moreover, Carnelle would readily accept advice from her cousin, whom she considers to be her mentor. Elain downplays the importance of the contest and exhorts Carnelle not to get excited because she may not even place in the five finalists. When Carnelle expresses disappointment in Elain's lack of faith in her, Elain, quite the egotist, snaps at her cousin, "And I wish you would stop fishing for compliments—'cause I'm sick and worn out with giving people compliments about themselves!" (158). More-over, Carnelle recognizes the true spirit of Elain's gift of a Mardi Gras mask that ostensibly would add mystery and elegance to her demeanor: "You never wanted me to win! You think I'm ugly, that's why you told me to wear that stupid mask over my face!" (197). Elain has left Franklin and her two sons, professing no love for her family (169); when Carnelle won-ders how the two youngsters will manage without a mother, Elain selfishly resents only having to give up her beautiful clocks (159). Delmount is also affected by his sister's narcissism and sarcastically confronts her: "She could never tell that the beautiful, the sweet, the perfect, Elain Rutledge refused to help her own brother get out of a dirty lunatic asylum!" (161). Elain, in turn, complains to Delmount that he needs no empathy because "Mama always loved you ten times better than me" (167); she realizes that Ronelle left the house, its furniture, and even the quilts to her brother, which, in the mind of a narcissist, is enough rationale to deny her empa-thy to someone that she believed received more love than she did from her own mother. Even the earrings that Elain gives to Popeye seemingly out of her own graciousness reflect more of her lack of empathy, for she later acknowledges, "I hated the damn things. They pinched my ears. I was glad to get rid of them" (199). In a 1991 interview, Henley delved into the psy-chology behind Elain's altruism toward Popeye:

> I don't know if it's just in the South — this happened to me in Hawaii as well — but people give you things because they have such a desperate need to be liked. Later in the play, the character reveals that she hated those ear-rings; they pinched her ears, and she was glad to get rid of them. Some-thing that appears to be a generous act — I'm trying to make myself look good by giving you something that I really don't like — the duplicity of that act, I think, reveals something later about Elain.[17]

In short, Elain demonstrates that she cares little about her family and friends, and when she does make a gesture of goodwill, such as the gifts to Carnelle and Popeye, we discover that she has ulterior motives. As Hen-ley stated, "Elain has this wonderful way of trying to be nice, but it really winds up being about herself...."[18]

Elain's narcissistic sense of self-importance, her fantasies of beauty, her need for excessive admiration, and her arrogant, haughty behavior typifying elitism all serve to fuel a neurosis that prevents her from shar-ing happiness.[19] She suffers from the modern *angoisse*, candidly admitting,

"The abundance of treasures merely serves to underline the desperate futility of life" (159). Elain's marriage had deteriorated, not because she is treated as an objet d'art, which would provide a sociological reading as some critics prefer, but because she is so egocentric that she has no empathy for her family. Elain will never be able to cope socially and recognizes the source of her frustration when she tells Popeye, "It's such a burden trying to live up to a beautiful face. I'm afraid I'm missing everything in the world" (169). She is stuck with being the eternal beauty, Miss Firecracker, until the day she dies, a dangerous ideology that forces her to shut out everything in life that is dreary or ugly. However, because of her narcissism, Elain displays none of the charm of the stereotyped Southern Belle: her egocentricity and lack of empathy for others belies the facade of southern gentility she is forced to exude for her admirers. The facade has admittedly caused Elain much distress, even anger that lies dormant most of the time. The frustration and wrath is due primarily to a neurotic need to pose as the eternal, grandiose beauty she consciously yearns to emulate, rather than due to any deeply rooted reaction to a system that forces her to conform and surrender to patriarchal values.[20] Elain's fundamental problem is having to live up to a facade of beauty that was inculcated in her from childhood, which has become part of her neurosis that she cannot evade. Henley states, "Elain can't really be loved in the purest sense of the word because she won't let anybody know her.... She's just not what she wished she were."[21] Elain thus feels that if Carnelle wins the contest, coupled with Aunt Ronelle's tutelage, the damage will turn her cousin into the narcissist that she herself has become with no chance of egress. Elain, in speaking of Carnelle's fate, is actually describing her own neurosis: "Poor Carnation. She wants to be beautiful without understanding the limitations it brings" (194).

Elain allows Carnelle to believe that she understands her neurosis and is coming to terms with her existential despair by starting anew, away from her husband and children, and no longer the narcissistic beauty queen. She boasts to Popeye and Carnelle, "Neither of you is starting life all over again, feeling nothing but terror and fear and loneliness!" (173). Elain is truly frightened by the notion that she could live without her admirers who fawn over her as a former pampered beauty queen: "I don't know what to do! I don't know what I can do!" (173). Delmount has high hopes for his sister, prognosticating that her decision to leave her family is the impetus for a new start in life: "You're free. You're finally gonna find out just why you're alive" (194). However, Elain never finds out why she is alive and thus turns out to be a poor role model for Carnelle, for the elder sibling can never become aware of the absurd condition, like Sisyphus, who endures; instead, she succumbs to it. After trying to realize that life away from her husband will mean no more roses that he sends her to accentuate the fact that she is an icon of beauty, she relents. The narcissistic desire to be loved is too much for Elain to bear, so she decides to return to her husband, explaining, "And he adores me. I need someone who adores me" (194). Moreover, those clocks, which signify her wealthy status and grandiose self-importance worthy of someone who seeks unlimited success, beckon her. Elain even refuses to be alone for any social occasion, so she must make a date with Mac Sam, the physically pathetic yet charismatic carnie, so as to avoid watching the fireworks by herself. After this reckless fling, Elain returns to her "dreary, dreary life" (199) with her family, where she can reign as the narcissistic beauty queen in perpetuity.

Neither can Carnelle expect any psychological support from Delmount, for he himself has been in a mental institution, like Meg in *Crimes of the Heart*; even his own sister considers him to be "insane" (161). Although Delmount has delusions about studying at a university to be a philosopher so he will be trained to "let everyone know why we're living" (200), the reality is that he is more suited to his present toil scraping up dead dogs from the road after "working at disgusting job after disgusting job" (161). First, Delmount has a problem controlling his violent temper, which seems to match his wild, unkempt hair. After having hit a man in the face with a bottle, Delmount was looking at a jail sentence when confinement to a mental institution turned out to be the preferable solution arranged by his lawyer. Prior to his criminal offense, Delmount attempted to murder Carnelle's father by choking him because, in Delmount's own words, "he was boring me to death!" (162). Indeed, Carnelle views Delmount's violence first-hand when he smashes Ronnie Wayne's head after he threw peanuts and trash at her during the contest. Second, Delmount has a problem with women, which obviously does not bode well for him to be Carnelle's confidant.[22] He prefers women who have at least one classically beautiful characteristic, which is probably why he is initially nonchalant toward the homely Popeye. However, Delmount also took advantage of the ugly Mahoney sisters in their attic, robbing them of their virginity because he admits, "Well, I felt sorry for those two ugly daughters with their deformed box of cats" (163). Delmount has had dreams about mutilated and bloody women's bodies, making him a prime candidate for psychoanalysis. Finally, Carnelle would be wary of Delmount for attacking what she cherishes the most. Although Delmount gets caught up in Carnelle's desire for transcendence by winning the Miss Firecracker Contest, he criticizes the beauty pageant as "nothing but a garish display of painted-up-prancing pigs!" (168). Moreover, he resents Elain, considered by Carnelle to be the ideal to which she is striving, because she let him founder in a mental asylum. Whereas Carnelle views Elain's life as a beauty queen as perfection, to Delmount, "perfect is dull!" (167). Furthermore, Delmount, although he winds up going to see the fireworks with Popeye, through his idiosyncrasies, eccentricities, and delusions of grandeur, makes Popeye, Carnelle's naive yet down-to-earth friend, feel estranged or stupid (172).

Although Carnelle can receive no support from psychologically disturbed Elain or Delmount, she is somewhat bolstered in her confidence by the physically deteriorating Mac Sam, the balloon hawker. Although he is only in his mid-thirties, Mac Sam is slowly dying. In agony from the acute effects of tuberculosis, syphilis, and alcoholism, Mac Sam suffers interminably, as he says, "sitting here rotting away in the July sun" (193), while occasionally coughing up clots of blood. Mac Sam, Carnelle's former lover, is a quiet inspiration to the aspiring beauty queen that life can be endured without grandiose dreams of success and idealization. Larry G. Mapp intimates that Mac Sam becomes a type of role model for Carnelle: "Mac Sam intrigues us because he seems almost Christ-like as he takes on the diseased condition of human life and bears it uncomplainingly."[23] Mac Sam, perhaps somewhat foolishly, even laughs in the face of life's afflictions: for his coughing spells, he smokes cigars; for his rotting stomach, he drinks alcohol. With regard to the syphilis that Carnelle provided him with, he merely brushes it off, saying, "I'm having fun taking bets on which part of me'll decay first: the liver, the lungs, the stomach, or the brain" (202). Although the play is full of images of debilities, such as deformed kittens, tuberculosis, cancer, heartbreak, venereal disease, and mental illness, Mac Sam is an enduring presence. Miriam M. Chirico's argument that Mac Sam, comfortable with the grotesqueries of his body, serves as an inspiration to Carnelle is perhaps a bit of a stretch, but her remark that Mac Sam's sanguine attitude, in contrast to the hardened, selfish, and emotionally withdrawn behavior of some of Henley's other protagonists, incites Carnelle's potential spiritual transformation is certainly accurate.[24] As is true in Henley's canon, the characters who are the most impoverished or who have the most to regret are the least likely to complain and are more apt to maintain sympathy from the audience. Indeed, in the stage directions, Mac Sam is described as "*sensual*" and "*magnetic*" (175). He is the epitome of what he sees as the stoical potential that Carnelle has, the ability of someone "who can take it right slap on the chin" (186).

Popeye Jackson, the seamstress who is just one year younger than Carnelle, is the visible proof to the aspiring beauty contest winner that some females can "take it right slap on the chin." Popeye can be compared to Elain; whereas Elain is described as "a beauty" in the stage directions, Popeye is homely in her thick glasses yet radiant in her own way, a "*glowing person*" (147). While Popeye was growing up destitute, her family was unable to afford dolls for her, so she managed by designing clothes for bullfrogs that lived in her backyard;[25] in contrast, Elain's beauty was an avenue for success and wealth. Elain at least graduated from junior college; Popeye has had little formal education. Elain considers women to be potential rivals, while Popeye sees them as potential friends; as such, Elain's narcissism precludes her from encouraging Carnelle's chances of success in the contest, but Popeye is always empathetic of Carnelle and genuinely in awe of her talent routine. Popeye's gift to Carnelle, a frog in a pink outfit, is from her heart; Elain thinks it is horrifying. Elain complains that she does not want to be with her family any longer; Popeye would love to be married with children. Elain has known love, but Popeye has never been in a relationship. Elain views her brother with the disdain of someone who wants nothing to do with a person who has been in a lunatic asylum and is now picking up road kill for a living; Popeye chooses instead to focus on Delmount's uniqueness, admiring his ability to write poetry and wiggle his ears. Finally, Elain views marriage as a means to be admired as a glamour goddess showered with roses and exquisite clocks as a queen in her castle. On the other hand, Popeye seeks someone to accept her as she is; Laurilyn J. Harris aptly notes, "Most improbably of all, Popeye finds romance, not with a dream prince, but with a human being — neurotic but real — who accepts and loves her as she is and who in turn is accepted and loved by her on the same terms."[26] This comment is echoed by Linda Rohrer Paige, who notes that Popeye earns Cinderella status finding her Prince Charming by presenting herself as a compassionate princess who is "not repelled by the frog-prince, Delmount, made ugly by his checkered past."[27]

Popeye has endured throughout her life, being able to "take it right slap on the chin" and recover. When her brother Lucky threw a handful of gravel in her eyes and then gave her eardrops to remedy the situation, she developed the bulging eyes of her namesake. However, rather than be vengeful, Popeye sees the good in a bad situation, rationalizing that "the fortunate part is I can now hear voices through my eyes" (160). After being fired from her job at Miss Lily's Dress Shop[28] for giving a child a sea-shelled compact case, Popeye simply refuses to be bitter or vengeful. Coupled with her eternal grace is an imaginative vision, a sense of wonder about the world that allows her to appreciate special moments in life. Joel Colodner, in his review of the play at the Krannert Center in Urbana, described

Popeye as "Sleeping Beauty, pretending that she pricks her finger on evil Ronelle's antique spinning wheel, and her kiss almost transforms the poetic Delmount."[29] Like so many of Henley's ugly or seemingly impoverished protagonists who have so little, such as Pixrose in *The Wake of Jamey Foster*, Popeye is glad to be alive and ignores life's brutalities, instead choosing to focus on its burning poetic visions much like a child, devoid of cynicism, might first view the world in wonder. After all, Popeye is goal-oriented, hoping one day to travel to the Elysian fields; when Delmount explains to her that this mythological image of heaven is fictitious, Popeye, never discouraged, states, "Oh. Well, shoot. Guess I won't be going there" (200). Never to worry — there is always the beauty of sharing the fireworks display with Delmount.

By the end of the play, Carnelle has learned from Popeye's (and perhaps from Mac Sam's) sense of stoical acceptance the need to endure in an absurd universe. After being pelted with ice, trash, and peanuts by the denizens of Brookhaven and then having gone through the humiliation of coming in last in the contest, Carnelle reassesses her desire to resemble Elain, the ideal, the icon of beauty. Carnelle, looking at herself in the mirror, begins a process of self-examination. She literally drops the mask Elain asked her to wear during the contest, thus beginning to accept herself as she is, like Popeye has done. Moreover, she realizes that the red hair has to go, and Carnelle is now able to remind herself, "It used to be brown. I had brown hair. Brown" (203). When told that she does not have to follow the Grand Float while carrying an American flag, Carnelle insists on doing so: "Look, if you come in last, you follow that float. I took a chance and I came in last; so, by God, I'm gonna follow that float" (197). Like Sisyphus, condemned to push the rock up the hill, Carnelle chooses to endure the labors of life stoically and willingly; "her rock is her thing," and thus, like Popeye also, she will try to find bright moments amidst the existential despair. The Miss Firecracker Contest is similar to a rite of passage for Carnelle, who has learned that her indomitable spirit as one who "can take it right slap on the chin" is a more viable way of approaching life than trying to emulate beauty and find happiness in her own fantasy of the Elysian fields. Carnelle chooses to face the *angoisse* directly and then move on; Elain, on the other hand, is stuck eternally in the fantasy world of Miss Firecracker.

Near the end of the play, Carnelle sighs, "Anyway, I just don't know what you can, well, reasonably hope for in life" (201). Mac Sam replies, "Not much, Baby, not too damn much" (202). Mac Sam mentions to Carnelle the possibility of eternal grace, but in a world where the modern *angoisse* is ubiquitous, we can only expect isolated moments of solace amidst the existential despair. Carnelle then joins Popeye and Delmount to watch the fireworks display, and she exclaims, "Gosh, it's a nice night" (204). In an interview that I conducted with Henley on 29 June 2002 in Los Angeles, she explained what she meant by eternal grace in this context of the play: "It seems to be a spiritual life, a connection to other people in a spiritual way, just that we're all graced by being human. A state of grace can occur at any moment in any given day in your consciousness."[30] This moment of silent bonding with others is similar to the solidarity displayed by the Magrath sisters during the denouement of *Crimes of the Heart*, again suggesting that Henley is not making a feminist statement per se. Instead, these epiphanies provide Henley's protagonists with a deeper understanding of the anomie and angst of modern civilization — similar to Sisyphus's revelation as he assesses the absurd condition when he arrives at the top of the hill and reconsiders his labor. The fireworks suggest the hope and glow of Carnelle's revelation of her independence from the norms and cultural values that have contributed to her *angoisse*, much like the manner in which Sisyphus was caught in his moment of awareness of the absurd condition. Robert J. Andreach realizes, "Though Carnelle has not left town and still must contend with her reputation, she has a new sense of herself and her possibilities."[31] The fireworks, coupled with Carnelle's awareness that the source of her neurosis is the need to be loved to the point where she felt that she had to win the contest or to wear the facade of Miss Hot Tamale, provide a festive moment of eternal grace that can assuage the modern neurosis only temporarily. This moment of eternal grace at least gives Carnelle a sense of empowerment, and, like Sisyphus, the awareness of the overpowering *angoisse* at least helps to stifle its burden momentarily. Unlike Sartrean existentialism in which existence is determined by actions and deeds, Henley's protagonists seem more closely to follow the tenets of Camusian existentialism. Billy J. Harbin astutely perceives, "Perhaps for Carnelle, as for so many of Henley's characters, the redemptive grace that comes through self-knowledge, spiritual enlightenment or nourishing bonds with others can be but dimly glimpsed and only partially realized."[32]

Just as *The Miss Firecracker Contest* can be misconstrued to be a politicized attack on beauty pageants that make spectacles of women, *The Debutante Ball* can be given a limited perspective as a play that challenges the tropes of femininity validated by the traditional Southern ritual of the coming-out party. For example, Janet L. Gupton argues that in *The Debutante Ball*, "Henley repeatedly parades these women's grotesque bodies as material flesh and blood rather than as a fetish or object of the white patriarch's desire, and thus destabilizes the idealization of a certain type of beauty validated by the debutante tradition."[33] Miriam M. Chirico maintains that *The Debutante Ball* uses the grotesque to vilify traditional social rites of the Southern aristocracy: "The debutante ball — like the earlier beauty contest — is a public forum where women are transformed into objects of visual pleasure. It is the quintessential symbol of southern patriarchy, because it is the symbolic moment when the family displays their daughters as wares for the purchase of some male suitor."[34] However, when Alexis Greene virtually baited Henley into admitting that the play must somehow be a vilification of the "American beauty ritual," the debutante ball, Henley refused to take the hint, all but denying any feminist intent:

> Well, I think everybody wants to be beautiful. I think we envy beauty. People get better seats in restaurants if they're beautiful. I'd love to be beautiful. I know it has its problems, but beauty is an asset. Just as intelligence is an asset. I've become more in awe of beauty the older I've gotten. I just love to look at somebody who's beautiful.[35]

Instead of politicizing the play, I want to universalize its content as a means of coping with the absurd condition, much like Camus discussed in *The Myth of Sisyphus*.

The Debutante Ball centers around the neuroticism of Jen Dugan Parker Turner, who, with enough names to establish her claim to Southern gentility, believes in noblesse oblige. Well into her fifties and her second marriage, Jen, like Elain and Meg, suffers from what appears to be the classic symptoms of Narcissistic Personality Disorder. As was discussed in chapter 4 and earlier in this chapter, narcissists have a grandiose sense of self-importance, are preoccupied with fantasies of success and beauty, display arrogant or haughty behavior, believe that they are unique and should thus associate with persons of high status, devalue or try to control people, and lack empathy with the feelings or needs of others. Narcissists display delusions of grandeur in their attempt to remain at the center of attention; beneath the artificial exterior, narcissists have an inner feeling of emptiness and, fearing that they will not be loved, they often display boundless repressed rage. Moreover, narcissists fear criticism and defeat, which leaves them humiliated, degraded, and hollow.[36]

Jen Turner suffers from deep *angoisse*, having been tried for the murder of her first husband and found not guilty. However, the humiliation that she suffered in the Southern community of Hattiesburg has been overwhelming for her. In order to assuage the guilt and clear her good name, Jen lives vicariously through her daughter, Teddy, whose debut at the debutante ball will offer her the salvation she has longed for during the many years she has suffered silently. Jen's infatuation with Teddy's debut becomes an obsession for her — a narcissist's delusion of grandeur of wanting to be accepted in the community. When *The Debutante Ball* was about to be staged at the Manhattan Theatre Club in New York City during 1988, Henley stated that the play concerned how the need for love can actually be crippling.[37] Jen came from a family that had difficulty expressing any love, and although we do not know very much about her parents, she recalls, ""Why, my father never even once gave me a gift or a remembrance of any kind."[38] During Christmas, she would invent pets that her father might have given her, and then, in order to save face from the neglect, she would tell her friends that the pet had died. Jen's first husband, Theodore, was a fruit picker that Jen admits never having loved, perhaps because his life of embezzlement and fraud coupled with isolated periods of rage, one in which he smashed Teddy's thumb and poured chili over Jen's head, was enough to embarrass his wife in the community. When Theodore found out that Jen filed for divorce, he went on a rampage, pulling out a switchblade knife. Before Jen could step in the door, Teddy hit her father with a skillet to allow her mother the chance to escape. Jen then finished off her husband by crowning him seven more times with the same skillet. Although Teddy's blow was the one that killed her father, Teddy lied during the trial to protect her mother, claiming that Jen reacted to Theodore in self-defense, even though the jury saw that there were no marks on her body; nevertheless, Jen was forced to do time in jail.

While in jail, Jen met Hank Turner, a wealthy attorney who defended her in court, saving her from a long prison term. Hank was very generous to Jen, giving her gifts and admitting his love to her. Jen, out of desperate fear of not being loved now that she was without a husband, married Hank. Although Hank was brilliant and was attracted to Jen's despair, Jen never loved him, admitting that she married him because of his wealth. Jen desperately tried to remake Hank in her own image by providing him with a new wardrobe, acquiring a toupee for him to wear, getting him fancy manicures, and changing his toothpaste and deodorant. However, nothing seemed to alter his image as a bumbling oaf to Jen, outwardly manifested by his ability to knock over vases of flowers (287), upset an urn of party favors (295), or break a woman's toe while waltzing with her (299). To no avail, Hank has been constantly trying to prove his worth to his wife. Instead of relying on her husband for salvation, Jen turns to her daughter's debutante ball, now being held three years after the murder, which Jen insists is the first and perhaps only viable opportunity to redeem her reputation.

In her attempt to secure love from the community, which has previously been denied her, thus exacerbating her feelings of emptiness, Jen displays the typical narcissistic need to acquire a grandiose sense of self-worth. Stephen Tobolowsky, who directed *The Debutante Ball* at South Coast Repertory, stated, "It's a black comedy about what people will do for love, and during the course of a mother and a daughter coming to terms, a lot of hates and terrible secrets surface."[39] Like many narcissists, Jen, lacking the empathy to feel for the needs of others, selfishly tries to control people in order to nurture her own grandiose sense of self-importance. Jen views the debutante ball as a high-stakes game, a fantasy of success and beauty, a "coming-out" or renewal of sorts that can extirpate the "terrible secrets" that typically leave her degraded and hollow. In an interview with Alexis Greene, Henley explained how the debutante ball becomes a facade to cover up family secrets:

> The more secrets you have the more facade you need. They think that nobody will have to know Teddy killed her father, and the family will be accepted again. If they have the right boy and the right dress and the right presentation, then they will be seen as the mask they put on. They can't be seen as they are, because it's too horrifying.[40]

Jen wants revenge on "Everyone in this town who ever shunned or ostracized us" (276). Hank, without adequate expertise to recognize Jen's narcissism as a type of neuroticism, describes her preparation for the debutante ball as turning her "into a crazy woman" (285); Brighton, Jen's nephew, corroborates the diagnosis, and from a lay point of view, deems his aunt "insane" (303). Even Jen's maids and cooks, realizing Jen's frenzy, have had enough sense to flee their obsessed employer. Jen herself is aware of the underlying *angoisse* of her neuroticism and admits to Hank, "I guess there's just some blackness buried so deep inside my chest you never could have pulled it out with a pair of pliers" (313).

The debutante ball is the penultimate event for Jen, the narcissist, to associate with people of high status, thus displaying the narcissist's need to feel unique, wallow in delusions of grandeur, and remain at the center of attention in high society. Jen is deteriorating mentally and physically. She has resorted to smoking and drinking; she is also in need of psychological help because of her perpetual desire to demean others so as to remain the focal point of attention. The spreading of psoriasis is a constant reminder of her physical decay. She acknowledges to Teddy, "God, look how the ravages of time have conquered me. All these cracks and sores and ugliness. I hate it so much. Being trapped inside this—body" (314). When she looks at herself in the mirror, she is despondent: "Ah. Hmm, why'd you have to get to be such an old bag of bones?" (275). Henley discussed Jen's physical deterioration: "Her literal body is decaying as much as her secrets have decayed her insides, because her insides are becoming harder to mask. Everything that has been internalized and hidden is now coming through."[41] Thus, Jen, psychologically maimed as a pariah in the community and ravaged by the decay of time, puts all her hopes in the youth of her daughter, whose entrance into high society presents her with the vicarious thrill of a rejuvenated life. Early in the play, Jen coaches Teddy on how to prepare for her entrance into the world of haute couture decked out in a jeweled cape, a diamond tiara, and comforted by "corrective makeup": "Now turn majestically toward the audience, filling the room with your stunningly youthful presence. Remember your eye contact. Keep the chin up. Now let's see an elegant shimmer of a smile. Yes! Oh Yes! Now for your grand bow" (269). Jen has spent the last year making sure everything will be perfect for the coming-out party — forcing the florist to prepare nine different rose bouquets before she agreed on the ideal one for her daughter's ensemble, approving of Teddy's escort, and coordinating the events down to the last detail. Jen has prepared for years for this reemergence into high society: she reminds Teddy both that she married Hank for money and that when Teddy tried to help with the family's financial situation by taking a job in the school cafeteria, Jen refused to allow her to do so, claiming, "You'd never have gotten into a proper sorority" (294). Teddy understands the importance that the debutante ball has for her neurotic mother: ""Everyone has high hopes about my entrance into society. It's gonna turn everything around for us. I look divine in my gown" (274). Jen agrees, assuring herself of her ascension into the good graces of the community: "Tonight's going to be all you ever dreamed! I promise you! I promise!" (276). Henley ascribes exclamation points to Jen's statements because Jen is emphatic that the debutante ball will forever alter her persona in the eyes of others, confirming her narcissistic desire to be loved eternally. Jen fantasizes about the event to come, decked out in her display of grandeur: "We'll all drive out to the ball — together again! Theadora Parker's going to enter my new house and shake my dirty hand which will be dripping with jewels and gold" (276). She envisions that her wardrobe, which to a narcissist is an outward display of a grandiose sense of self-esteem, is an essential component to her redemption, boasting to her husband, "I want to appear enormously enriched! I want them all to be speechless with envy" (287).

For Jen to assume that her social, physical, and psychological rehabilitation will occur through her daughter's debutante ball is patently absurd; narcissism is a debilitating form of neuroticism that cannot be treated through the artificial veneer of a social event. She is essentially living out her delusions of grandeur. Henley stated that the play was "about facades and secrets and suppressions and longings and ... I wanted my characters to be seen as animals fighting to pluck and spray and shave away their true natures—adorning themselves with lies."[42] Since Jen's life is essentially disingenuous since she lives it as a lie, we are not surprised when the debutante ball goes awry and her aspirations to be worthy of love go unfulfilled. Underneath the lie of the debonair, aristocratic noblesse oblige vision of "Miss Theadora Jenniquade Parker" is the reality of a young woman terribly insecure about the significance her mother has placed on the precise coordination of events and her responsibility to ensure that she uphold appearances in Hattiesburg's high society. When Jen's escort is forced to bail out because of broken bones due to an accident, Jen, ever the self-centered egotist lacking empathy with anyone but herself, responds, "He can't back out on us at the last minute. Get me his number, Teddy. Goddamnit, the little bastard's not gonna ditch us like dirt" (280). Jen merely sees the disaster as being "snake-bit" but insists, "I won't be stepped on anymore. No one is ruining this night! No one!" (280). Jen, out of desperation upon realizing that nothing can possibly taint the penultimate momentous occasion of her life, forces her husband to be Teddy's escort, even though Brighton warns her that this is a serious breach of decorum: "This is ridiculous. The escort is supposed to be a young, eligible man, not some ancient old goat who's married to the debutante's mother" (282). As Henley stated, Jen adorns herself with lies, pleading with Teddy to accept Hank as her escort in what is seen as an empathetic plea for Teddy's happiness, which is actually Jen's underlying obsession to be loved through the success of her daughter's coming-out party: "I know I can never change the past. But please, please don't deny me this ferocious dream I have of giving you a future" (283).

When the events of the debutante ball go awry — Teddy embarrassing herself after taking lewd bows with her gown pulled up over her head, crawling under the table to smear cream cheese on people's shoes, and then finally fleeing the scene after Hank started a brawl resulting in her hairpiece being deposited in the punch bowl and her expensive wardrobe covered with dirt and vomit — Jen, now forever condemned to be mocked rather than loved, is enraged. Like most narcissists, Jen must be the center of attention — there is no empathy or sympathy for anyone else. The other debutantes are merely chattel to Jen, and she reminds Teddy before the ball, "You are one hundred times more beautiful and alive than any of the jackasses sitting out in that banquet hall. You're a goddess and they're all swine" (269). Frances, Hank's deaf niece, goes unescorted to the ball because Jen, embarrassed that Frances's physical deformity would taint the evening of its glamour, refused to find a date for her.[43] After the fiasco, when Jen realizes that her dream of vicariously living a new life of acceptance through her daughter is forever lost, she bursts into uncontrollable anger directed at everyone but herself. When narcissists realize that they are not loved, the inner feeling of emptiness and *angoisse* degenerates into boundless rage. Reminiscent of Meg losing control of herself before being committed to a mental asylum, Jen calls her daughter Bliss a whore (302), reveals to Hank that she loved him only for his money (303), and slaps the pregnant Teddy until she has a miscarriage (308). As Hank, Bliss, and Teddy leave to go their separate ways after their one chance of family unity has gone awry, Jen can only lament the need to flee from a debilitating condition: "I want to move away from here for good. God, I just wish I knew — I just wish I knew where we'd — fit in" (303).

Jen can expect no psychological support from her daughter because Bliss suffers from the same debilitating Narcissistic Personality Disorder as her mother. Like Jen, Bliss desperately wants to fit in, but she was a pariah even at the start of her life, having been illegitimate. Jen married Theodore when she was four months pregnant with Bliss, so Bliss never knew her father, and Jen, living a life riddled with guilt, pretended that the fruit picker was Bliss's father. Bliss reminds Teddy that Jen "hates me for being born" (273). Bliss remembers her foster father as "an abusive drug addict as well as an embezzler and thief" (291). After Jen killed him with the skillet, she was forced to stand trial, which meant that Bliss's debut was cancelled. Thus, the ultimate fantasy of success and beauty for a narcissist — the debutante ball — is denied Bliss. She reminds Teddy of the bitterness she has suffered after being deprived of what might have been the penultimate moment of her life: "Why, I could burst into hysterical tears thinking about how I was never ever allowed to be a debutante. Oh God, never to be allowed. Not allowed. The agony" (288). Moreover, Bliss is one of the few people who realizes the secrets behind Jen's life of lies, especially the truth about Theodore's murder. Thus, she is resented by her mother, who has what seems to be an unconscious desire to deny her daughter, the narcissist, love. Although she was beautiful, young Bliss, desperate for love, married Tommy, a repulsively overweight man, and had a child by him, appropriately named Butterball. During their marriage, Bliss, with her narcissism extending virtually to nymphomania, slept with virtually all of Tommy's friends before leaving the state. Tommy forced her to leave after her infidelity, realizing that Bliss was difficult to live with on a daily basis. She went to New Orleans, where she developed a relationship with a dog trainer. Like most narcissists who lack empathy for the feelings of others, Bliss neglected Butterball throughout her fling in New Orleans, refusing even to send gifts to her daughter. Her relationship with the dog trainer eventually failed also, culminating in her boyfriend depositing her belongings on the sidewalk, thereby exacerbating the feelings of emptiness brought on in narcissists who insist that they are unique persons who must be at the center of attention. Bliss laments to Teddy, "I'm destitute, penniless, deserted, and alone. No one wants me. No one can stand me" (273).

At home in Hattiesburg after a long hiatus, Bliss obviously has mixed feelings about herself. On the one hand, she is guilt-ridden about never seeing her daughter, thus forcing her to be self-destructive; Bliss thus resorts to smoking cigarettes, drinking alcohol, and popping pills, and when the latter activity is accompanied by champagne, Jen chides her: "You just keep on taking those pills, but they're going to kill you just like they killed Judy Garland. Only you won't have any fame, or money to show for it!" (290). Bliss also intuitively understands that Jen, also a narcissist who must be at the center of attention, is jealous of her daughter's angelic beauty. Bliss has come to believe and accept the idea that she shares her mother's elegance, which is the source for competition between the two self-centered women, causing Jen to neglect Bliss. Jen, frustrated about the disastrous turn of events during Teddy's coming-out party, takes out her anger on Bliss for neglecting Butterball. In order to distinguish clearly between what she believes to be her own elegance and Bliss's perceived sense of her own attractiveness, Jen demeans her daughter by calling her a cheap "Southern strumpet whore" (302) returning to town, not to attend the debut of her sister, but instead selfishly "here to intrude on my life" (302). With regard to Bliss's fantasy of becoming a ballerina, Jen sarcastically notes, "She's always been such an awkward dancer" (289). The truth is that Jen cannot live vicariously through Bliss because she realizes that her eldest daughter, often mirroring her own narcissistic behavior, is nothing but a miserable failure.

Thus, Bliss, feeling neglected by her family and in turn neglecting her own daughter, overcompensates, like most narcissists, in an attempt to achieve a grandiose sense of self-importance while being preoccupied with fantasies of success and beauty. Bliss is arrogant and haughty in her constant efforts to associate with the upper class. Upon entering a room, she drenches herself in lilac perfume as if to separate herself from the filth of the degenerates with whom she is forced to associate. When Frances remarks that Bliss is so beautiful, the latter sprays herself with perfume, as if to corroborate the matter of fact statement. Even when Frances complains of being covered in filth, Bliss's solution is to spray her with perfume, as if to blot out the stench of others that she so abhors. She speaks French — the language of the elite — to what she considers to be peons like

Frances, and then revealing her arrogance, sarcastically wonders, "Why was I speaking *Français*! Good gracious! Silly me" (284). She envisions herself as a ballerina doll spinning herself on top of a jeweled music box. When the corsages arrive for the ball, Bliss receives the biggest one, sent to her by the person who adores her the most — herself. Moreover, Bliss is forever covering herself with more makeup as if to suggest that mascara is an elitist method of covering up life's grime while simultaneously bringing beauty to the forefront.

Underneath the artificial exterior of a woman who speaks eloquent French and hides behind perfume and mascara is the stench of a lonely, guilt-ridden narcissist who desperately seeks love but instead suffers from neglect, which results in her own lack of empathy for others and concomitant boundless rage and frustration. Bliss admits, "I don't mean to be cruel. I just have this sort of hole inside me. This desperate longing to love and be loved. Somehow it cripples me. It makes me be cruel" (306). Her cruelty is visibly demonstrated when the frustration of having to wear a mask of elitism becomes too much to bear; underneath the facade is a seething individual, which becomes readily apparent when Jen mocks Bliss's dancing abilities, and her daughter reacts by scratching a record then kicking and punching a wall. Bliss's neurosis also surfaces in the way she treats anyone with whom she is forced to interact. She is aloof from her half-sister's moment of glory, tending to focus on herself rather than on Teddy's psychological needs during the most important event of her life. She lacks empathy with her mother, wishing that she had stayed in jail; Jen, in turn, sees her daughter as an intrusion (302), tossing her out of the house. When Bliss telephones Tommy, imploring him to reconsider their former relationship and perhaps start anew, she is again rejected, rationalizing it as "a fleeting fancy" yet one that leaves her further removed from Butterball. Bliss's desperate need to be loved and wanted even degenerates to a brief lesbian relationship with deaf Frances, whom Bliss previously demeaned as "deformed" (280).[44] Bliss takes advantage of Frances; realizing that one reason Frances has come to the debutante ball is to find a husband, some contact in her life, Bliss uses Frances for her own selfish need to be loved. Although she resents Frances for being unsophisticated as well as disabled, Bliss does not hesitate to demean her while simultaneously using her when she realizes that Frances is in awe of her beauty and elegance. Frances, who herself was feeling like an outcast after receiving no offers to dance at the ball while constantly in agony because her mother was being ravaged by cancer, is being taken advantage of by Bliss, who seems to sense Frances's despair. Meanwhile, Bliss has no empathy for Frances and treats her merely as an object, calling her an "ugly, ugly thing" (302) ostensibly for having green food between her teeth but actually in order to transfer the guilt after being admonished as a whore by her own mother. Even Brighton, Teddy's wealthy, pompous cousin, can see that Bliss is "festering with secrets and lies" (290), yet she demeans him just like she does to the others, not because he snorts when he laughs, but because he reveals her hypocrisy. Bliss throws a glass of champagne in his face, but afterwards he responds, "I always knew you were never really part of my family. Your mannerisms are different. They're affected and coarse. The older you get, the more apparent it becomes" (290). Upon leaving her mother's residence at the end of the play, Bliss hands Teddy her princess's crown to give to Butterball. In short, coinciding with the lack of empathy that Bliss feels for virtually everyone she comes into contact with is the guilt with which she is haunted and fails to address adequately; her narcissism rears its ugly head even in a relationship with her own kin.

The irony underlying Jen's neurosis is that she lives vicariously through another neurotic, Teddy, her twenty-year-old daughter. Like Marshael in *The Wake of Jamey Foster* and Carnelle in *The Miss Firecracker Contest*, Teddy appears to suffer from Borderline Personality Disorder, which, according to the *Diagnostic and Statistical Manual of Mental Disorders*, is characterized by a frantic effort to avoid real or imagined abandonment, unstable interpersonal relationships as a result of alternating moods between extremes of idealization and devaluation, recurrent self-mutilating behavior, and chronic feelings of emptiness.[45] Teddy's angst is due to the fact that her id — the innate desire for happiness— is suppressed by a strong superego in the form of a cultural ideal that supposedly will break the curse on the family and restore its honor in the community. In short, as Brighton reminds Teddy, the debutante ball is the long-awaited social event that will lift the household from its dark secrets: "I mean, the whole purpose of tonight was to enhance the Parker family image, not to disgrace it further" (282).

Teddy, forced to lie during the trial to protect her mother after murdering her own father with a skillet, has to live with the guilt of patricide and the pent-up feelings of hostility due to her own disingenuousness. Moreover, Teddy, who years ago smashed her father's skull after he had thrown a sugar bowl at her chest and was threatening to harm Jen, is not apologetic for her past recrimination, admitting to Hank, "I cry sometimes thinking how little I miss him" (312). Instead, Teddy has been molded into the image her mother has of her, which is a phoenix rising from the ashes to resurrect the crumbling family. Teddy, then, has been groomed for her debut at the ball by a narcissist. She has become neurotic essentially because her family provides no love for her; instead, Jen preys upon Teddy's superego, using her daughter for her own selfish purposes. Henley also described *The Debutante Ball* as a play that focuses both on how individuals cover up the pent-up rage within themselves and on what the consequences are of acting on that anger.[46] Teddy needs love so much that it cripples her; instead of receiving nurturance from the mother, which is the means for our early state of happiness, Teddy is put on trial by her mother in order to resurrect the family image. The long-term preparation for the debutante ball becomes an unusual civilizing process that interferes with the id's natural desire for happiness. Teddy is thus conflicted to the point of becoming neurotic.

Teddy has also gradually become socially maladjusted. She has been put on probation at the University of Mississippi, and her sorority sisters at the university have threatened to expel her, as Jen states, "for idiosyncratic behavior" (277); being expelled from a sorority at a southern school where membership in the Greek system is a matter of status suggests being ostracized from your peers. Bliss, in speaking to Jen about her half-sister, admits, "Well, frankly, her social skills do need a good deal of refining. She went out today wearing socks on her hands instead of mittens. She's just trying to get attention. It's repulsive" (277). Bliss does not realize the truth of her statement, for Teddy desperately seeks love and attention, especially from her family; however, they view her as merely an icon for their own selfish ego-fulfillment. Teddy has started smoking again, perhaps in part because she seeks that subliminal oral gratification she is denied by her mother. Brighton even senses Teddy's neuroticism, and in his unofficial diagnosis of her mental condition, he offers his cousin a chance at respite: "Grandmother wants you to come live with her. She wants to give you a chance to get away from your mother and regain your, well, your sanity" (299). Conflicted by a real or imagined sense of abandonment from a mother that refuses to nurture but can respond to her daughter only through a narcissistic need for ego support, as well as a father who, like many of Henley's paternal figures, has abandoned his daughter through an early death or desertion, Teddy's Borderline Personality Disorder results in self-mutilating behavior. Forced to live up to an unrealistic ideal of perfection at the debutante ball, Teddy takes the tweezers and violently scratches her face (272). She also pulls out her hair, thinking that it contains rats (293). Jen fears that Teddy is having "a breakdown" (293); indeed, she is terribly conflicted with guilt about her ambivalent feelings toward her father. Although she despised him and remembers his violent temper, capable of smashing her thumb and then pouring chili over her mother's head, she also feels abandoned by his death, especially during this time of extreme angst when she is forced to carry the weight of the world as her burden. She laments to Jen, "I wish Daddy were here. See, otherwise, they'll all look at me and it'll just remind them of how he died and how he can't be here tonight" (293). When the events of the debutante ball go awry, Teddy resorts to self-mutilating behavior that she cannot control. Although having her gown pulled up over her head was an accident, smearing cream cheese on the guests' shoes was merely adding insult to injury, as was leaving her hairpiece floating in the punch bowl and then running off into the night. The self-inflicted wounds culminate when Teddy, well after the damage to the family's self-esteem has been done, continues to mutilate herself by pulling up her skirt and cutting her leg with a cheese knife (306).

Teddy suffers from *angoisse* that is realized by her Borderline Personality Disorder's manifestation of unstable behavior characterized through extremes of idealization and devaluation. Described as *"a thin and strange-looking girl with large, frightened eyes"* (269), she is physically compromised because of her conflicted values. On the one hand, Teddy has bought into her mother's self-centered values and adopts a persona to fit her mother's needs and whims. Teddy is faced with idealizing herself as an icon of perfection, the daughter who has been groomed for years to be a princess with all of the required social graces necessary for her grand debut. She has been kept out of trouble so she could attend the right sorority at Ole Miss. Hairpieces and plenty of makeup hide any potential physical deformities. However, the truth is that this sense of grace is tainted by a deeply rooted guilt that seems to outweigh the idealization. When Brighton asks Teddy to bare her soul to Hank, thus cleansing herself through catharsis of pent-up hostilities, Teddy instead rushes to the bathroom to hide by covering herself with massive amounts of makeup as she protests the psychological probing: "I don't know anything. You're a liar. There's nothing that I know. Shut up. Just shut up! Oh, I need some more makeup. On my face. My face" (290). Moreover, Teddy's guilt is exacerbated when she realizes that she killed a man that her mother never loved but ostensibly married for money so that Teddy would not have to take a job working in a cafeteria, which would have precluded her getting into a proper sorority. Teddy's reaction to this revelation is similar to her denial of guilt when accused by Brighton. She cries, "Oh, my face. My face" (294) and then runs again to the toilet, only this time to vomit. These same feelings of guilt and devaluation have forced Teddy to seek love elsewhere. One evening, while she was staying at a hotel in Oxford, Teddy rode up the elevator to her room with a man who was missing half his face and part of his left arm. Teddy reveals to Violet, the maid, that, in a moment of existential despair, she had intercourse with this deformed man. Teddy explained to Violet why she would have sex with a stranger: "I was at a point, you see, where I couldn't take on any more, ah, bad feelings, guilt. Just no more" (298). The sexual interlude, however, did little to assuage the guilt. Instead, Teddy recalls that the anonymous stranger treated her like an object, nothing more than a piece of eye candy, reflected by his parting comment, "Mm-mm good," which Violet clarifies as "Kinda like you was M&M's or somptin'" (298). Moreover, Teddy is so full of guilt over the pregnancy that she refuses to tell Jen the truth about the man in the elevator, allowing Jen to mistakenly assume that the father is David Brickman, Teddy's fabricated lover from Atlanta. Teddy's neurotic personality fully blossoms during the debutante ball, which, on the one hand, should function as the pinnacle of her idealization, but, on the other hand, serves to complement her devaluation. On the eve of the debutante ball, Teddy seemed to have a premonition of disaster, and, white with fear, she had serious doubts about attending. After the debacle, Bliss confirms that Teddy, dashing Jen's hopes for her own overwhelming need to be loved and accepted by the community, deserves to be guilty: "She's mad at you. You're nothing but a disappointment. She hates the sight of you" (301). In short, Teddy's id has been suppressed by the cultural demands placed on her by Jen—a classic Freudian case of the mother unable to nurture effectively, turning her child into a weapon for her own dreams and aspirations. Teddy makes it clear that she is unable to flee from the guilt, and when Jen asks what she is afraid of, Teddy replies, "Afraid of you" (307).

The title of the play reflects a ritual in Southern culture known as the coming-out party, which suggests that the grim secrets and guilt that can be attributed to the modern neurosis will somehow be exorcised. Tish Dace reads the denouement as a type of exorcism: "By the play's end, the debutante appears bound for happiness, as does her neglected half-sister, who heads into the sunset with her step-father's deaf-mute niece."[47] The denouement in a Henley play is not that sanguine. The last scene in the play is a beautiful tour de force and a fitting way to put some calm into a social event that has become a fiasco. After the family members disperse, Jen is left alone with Teddy. Jen, for the first time in the play, appears vulnerable; the stage directions state, "*Jen enters the bathroom nude with a large towel wrapped around her shoulders. She is trembling like a newborn bird*" (314). Teddy enters and calmly rubs salve over Jen's body to heal the effects of the psoriasis. They share a cigarette together, which becomes a type of catharsis since mother and daughter have also both been lying about their smoking. In essence, this scene become one of physical and emotional healing. Henley stated, "I wanted the image to be a peeling off, a renewal, a washing off, an applying ointment to the wounds."[48] Both Jen and Teddy have so many scars, suffer from so much guilt, and have hurt themselves or others in such a way that they have lost what it means to love each other in a pure way. The modern neurosis can never be quashed; the best we can hope for in this absurd universe is for momentary relief. Teddy has a brief moment of reconciliation with her mother, an interlude that suggests that pure moments of love are possible during the existential despair. Teddy dreams of a brighter future amidst the neuroticism: "I don't have a feeling anymore like it's never gonna get better" (315). The moment of spiritual grace is equivalent to the effect that the fireworks display has on Carnelle or that Sisyphus has when he watches the rock roll down the hill. Teddy understands the need to endure in the face of the absurd condition created by the dichotomy between the demands placed upon us by modern civilization and our eternal quest to adhere to the desires of our id. The best that we can hope for amidst the *angoisse* is a Sisyphuslike understanding of our absurd condition. Teddy achieves this sort of epiphany at the end of the play as she momentarily engages in the healing process with her mother, the source of her guilt. Teddy frames the moment of enlightenment in terms of a new spirit marked by the approaching rain and thunder, which will temporarily wash away the detritus of life: "Yeah, and that ole snapping turtle's gonna let loose and I'll just be standing there in the rain and in the thunder, and these arms will want to hold onto somebody and have their arms holding onto me" (315). For a brief moment, Teddy, while helping her vulnerable mother heal the ravages of time and assuage the guilt of a life spent hurting themselves or others, can stop to smell the roses through an awareness of their shared neuroses, and as Carnelle learns, that is all one can hope for in life.

6

The Lucky Spot and Abundance

The next two plays, *The Lucky Spot* and *Abundance*, mark a sudden departure for Henley, who now moves the locale farther west of the deep South and further back in time. *The Lucky Spot* occurs in Pigeon, Louisiana, a rural area approximately sixty miles west of New Orleans and nearly twenty-five miles southwest of Baton Rouge[1]; *Abundance* is set in the Wyoming Territory and St. Louis. For the first time, Henley moves the action away from the immediate past, the former play occurring during 1934, at the end of the Depression, and the latter spanning twenty-five years beginning in the late 1860s. The time spans for these two plays are significant and reflect Henley's depiction of how the modern neurosis evolved from its nascent stages in the nineteenth century into full blossoming during the twentieth century.

The Lucky Spot is structured as two acts—a long expository first act and a second act containing three scenes occurring early during Christmas Eve, later than night, and Christmas morning, respectively; the second act thus is choreographed to personify the various changing moods one sustains during the Christmas holiday. Although the structure of the play is not Chekhovian, Henley's motifs are once again derived from her mentor's use of failed relationships and unrequited love to personify the absurd condition. *The Lucky Spot*'s Christmas setting suggests a festive occasion — a moment when joy to the world even extends to those most afflicted by the modern neurosis. Moreover, setting the play in 1934, when the United States was emerging from the Great Depression, reinforces the overall sanguine spirit of cooperation. Reed Hooker, a down-and-out gambler who has converted an old Victorian farmhouse into a taxi dance hall, expects the Christmas Eve opening to be the first step toward his road to financial recovery. Moreover, Hooker's hired help, including Cassidy Smith, Turnip Moss, and Lacey Rollins, all suffering from unrequited love, hope that Hooker's venture into fame and fortune in a remote area of southeastern Louisiana will also be the impetus to turn their lives around from spiritual bankruptcy to love and acceptance in the community. However, in Henley's black comedy, the setting and time are ironic. Christmas is frequently a traumatic time of the year for lonely individuals, which only serves to exacerbate the modern neurosis, especially when we recall the Freudian notion that love or contact with friends and family is a source of pleasure to negate the neurotic condition; thus, at Christmas, social isolation creates further ontological insecurity. The setting suggests the glory of pipe dreams amidst pathos: Hooker's dream is noble yet ludicrous; although the taxi dance hall is located along the main road, hence its name, the Lucky Spot, its chances of success among the rural poor of Louisiana who can hardly afford the luxury of a night on the town are nil. Carol Kane, who starred in a production of the play, noted that the director, Norman René, told the cast in rehearsals, "Beth's characters are filled with hope. Insane, unstoppable hope against all reason."[2] Moreover, the notion of taxi dancing seems perfect for Henley's depiction of Chekhov's unrequited love as a manifestation of the modern *angoisse*. In the Introduction to the play, Henley stated, "Ever since I heard Ruth Etting sing 'Ten Cents a Dance' I have been fascinated by the idea of Taxi Dancers. There seems to be something heartbreaking and wondrous about a human being paying another human being for the short pleasure and romance of a dance."[3] Taxi dancing, a brief interlude during which lonely and despairing individuals seek contact and nurturance with strangers, becomes a metaphor for the human condition, mirroring Ashbe's search for dignity in *Am I Blue* and thus reinforcing the motif that Henley consistently returns to in virtually all of her plays.

Reed Hooker, the owner of the Lucky Spot Dance Hall, epitomizes the existential madness of modern society. Reed, in his mid-forties, has great hopes that the Christmas Eve opening of the Lucky Spot will change the previous poor luck that has been endemic to his life as a gambler. Henley described the pathos that she had for Hooker:

> After some thought I devised the idea that Hooker was opening up his dance hall in an isolated rural area. Who would start a business so obviously doomed to fail? A man seeking to rebuild a life from the fractured images of the past. A man that would become the blustering, passionate, much flawed dreamer, Reed Hooker.[4]

Hooker, a sly and street-smart character, seems to live in his own fantasy dream world in which he maintains a cheerful, grandiose sense of over-confidence despite the ubiquitous modern neurosis that impinges on his daily existence. Hooker lives his life on a wing and a prayer, which, he fails to realize, is no way to mitigate the absurd condition. Hooker won the Lucky Spot in a card game with Davenport Fletcher, who used the farmhouse as collateral for a three-hundred-and-fifty-dollar debt that he owed to his cousin, Whitt Carmichael. Thus, the Lucky Spot becomes a liability when Hooker cannot come up with the money he now owes to Carmichael to resolve Fletcher's debt. Ironically, the Lucky Spot now must show a profit between Christmas Eve and January 1; otherwise, Carmichael will have it closed down. Moreover, Carmichael has gone out of his way to create negative publicity for the taxi dance hall. Furthermore, Hooker must be a poor gambler as well, for he owes money to several of the local residents, who almost murder him, turning the idealist into a bloody mess. Hoping to make a fortune despite the reality of broken dreams and an unfulfilled life, Hooker, on the eve of the Lucky Spot's opening night, fantasizes about success: "Hey, look, it's Christmas Eve. People are so lonely out there you can smell it rotting on 'em. Here at the Lucky Spot we'll be selling hot music, fine dancing, and sweet solace of kindhearted women."[5] By the end of the play, however, Hooker is forced to abandon his pipe dream as he sells the Lucky Spot to Carmichael to cover his debts.

Hooker's luck with cards also causes misfortune in his love relationships. His is a classic case of unrequited love since his marriage to Sue Jack Tiller creates sexual frustration for the overreaching gambler simply because his wife is physically separated from him, occupying a cell in Angola Penitentiary. Besides, although Sue Jack loves her husband, the only physical relationship they ever have is constant fighting and bickering rather than love making. The relationship between Sue Jack and Hooker is worse that the classic Chekhovian scenario of unrequited love, for Hooker admits to loving his wife (252), although the couple are clearly incompatible. As Freud indicated, love and nurture provide the means to assuage the modern neurosis. In a love-starved relationship, Hooker turns to Cassidy Smith, a fifteen-year-old orphan that he won in a poker game in Gulfport. Cassidy is a liability for Hooker, for she is underage and therefore "jail bait"; moreover, since Hooker is still legally married to Sue Jack, he cannot wed Cassidy. Nevertheless, perhaps because of a deeply rooted need for contact, the love-starved Hooker, trying to use sexual contact as a means of nurture to stave off the spiritual bankruptcy that he hopes would not accompany his ever-threatening financial bankruptcy, has sex with Cassidy. Hooker, who is worldly, idealistic, intelligent, and somewhat cultured, cannot fathom a relationship with an unkempt, uneducated, semi-literate, unrefined teenager. Thus, there is no chance, even as a gambler, that he would marry Cassidy even though she is pregnant with his child; besides, bigamy is outlawed in Louisiana. In short, as Freud noted, the dichotomy between individual happiness and the socializing norms of civilization produce despair and *angoisse*. Hooker understands that he is a victim of broken dreams and an unfulfilled life, especially in the way he has treated Cassidy: "Hey, I'm not a blind man. I know how I've treated her. I know I'm a bilge bag. I hate my own goddamn guts" (237).

Cassidy is the personification of how the need for love and nurturance becomes a means to assuage the modern neurosis. Cassidy was denied the love that Freud claims is a source of pleasure when her mother died of diphtheria when Cassidy was five years old. However, she remembers that her mother would give her an orange and a peppermint every Christmas morning — again reinforcing the idea that oral gratification has replaced maternal nurturing. Cassidy admits that she has never known her father, who left her before she was born, but fantasizes that he might be either a bum standing in the breadlines or a wealthy lord living in a castle. Without a family — her siblings having died from diphtheria as well — and then witnessing her house burned down because the authorities feared it was contaminated, Cassidy, faced with a mother that abandoned her and an absent father figure, intuitively understands the modern *angoisse* as an isolated and ontologically insecure person. Apprenticed to "Mr. Pete," whose brand of nurturance for her consisted of a diet of cow feed, Cassidy became nothing more than an object. Rebecca King associates Mr. Pete's treatment of Cassidy with the commodification of animals: "Represented through animal imagery, she was Mr. Pete's pack animal, and also the 'kitty' in the poker game that places her with Hooker."[6] Treated as a social inferior by the self-proclaimed minister of religious holiness, Cassidy recalls that Mr. Pete branded her with a holy cross to sanctify her otherwise presence as "a godless bag a' stench" (245). Cassidy claims that her life changed for the better when Hooker won her in a card game with Mr. Pete. Hooker impregnated Cassidy, while still treating her as an object or animal, keeping her locked in the attic at night only to unlatch the door in the morning.

The Cassidy-Hooker-Sue Jack relationship is the typical Racinian ladder now elevated to the Chekhovian unrequited love triangle that Henley depicts so often to indicate spiritual bankruptcy. Cassidy, now eight months pregnant, has contacted Angola Penitentiary to initiate Sue Jack's early release, hoping that Hooker's wife's physical presence at the Lucky Spot will lead to Hooker filing divorce papers. Cassidy, alone without friends to provide love to negate the despair and *angoisse*, has turned to an imaginary furry animal who, only in her dreams, said it loved her. Realizing that such a fantasy is inadequate, Cassidy has formed a bond with Hooker, whose purchase of her as a commodity in a poker game has the teenager believing that she has been accepted, and will be nurtured, as part of Hooker's family. Cassidy readily acknowledges, "But here, well, we have supper together every night. It's the most I ever felt like a family" (245). Cassidy hopes that by divorcing Sue Jack, Hooker will marry her, providing love to assuage the existential madness. Moreover, Cassidy fears that her child will grow up as an unwanted and unloved bastard, repeating the feelings of nothingness that she experienced by her absent father and a mother that abandoned her psychologically. Thus, Cassidy has begun to wear an engagement ring made out of rope, firmly believing that she plans to marry Hooker, whom she insists also loves her (250). Cassidy is convinced that Hooker promised to divorce Sue Jack, acknowledging to Turnip, "But I don't think he cares much for her" (210). In reality, Hooker loves Sue Jack and mocks Cassidy as a physical deformity with six toes (211) and an unkempt woman bereft of personal hygiene (214). Hooker reveals that he actually dislikes Cassidy: "Maybe I just got fed up with the way she kept rolling herself down the staircase and eating boxes of match heads and banging at her belly with a two-by-four" (213). Nevertheless, Cassidy, comparing herself to Hooker's more intelligent and more worldly wife, finds it difficult to accept that she is unworthy of Hooker's love: "Still all an' all, I bet she's not one whit better 'n me" (223). Cassidy's plan to initiate the early Christmas release from prison for Sue Jack actually backfires on her, as Hooker and his wife, ill suited as a happily married couple because of Sue Jack's violent temper, now are able to demonstrate the passion for each other that failed to materialize between Hooker and Cassidy. Cassidy finally resigns herself to the existential despair, admitting to Sue Jack, "The thing is I can't never awaken no love in him for me — 'cause, well, he's got you in his blood; you're his partner" (259). Cassidy's quest for meaning and dignity amidst the *angoisse* remains elusive until Christmas day, when she, like the others who work at the Lucky Spot dance hall, experiences the sharing of a brief moment of happiness that temporarily mitigates the absurd condition.

Lacey Rollins, a taxi dancer in her thirties who works at the Lucky Spot, is another of Henley's desperate neurotics whose passion for romance and happiness in life has been seared by social norms and expectations that cannot be fulfilled. Although there is no mention of Lacey's father, we do know that Lacey's mother provided her with an inferiority complex, constantly reminding her that she was swivel-hipped and thus unsuitable for marriage — like Lenny, her worth being defined by adherence to

cultural norms. Refusing to talk any longer with her mother, Lacey's raison d'être has been to find dignity amidst the broken dreams. Coinciding
with the physical disability of swiveled hips is the weak bones she has in
her ankles, forcing her to stumble and fall, often at inopportune times.
Lacey's physical deformities thus recall several of Henley's physically challenged neurotics, such as Popeye and Frances Walker. Although Lacey tries
to mask the disability by peroxiding her hair while wearing heavy makeup
and high heels to attract men, this rather short woman comes across as
clownish rather than elegant when she awkwardly stumbles in the dance
hall. Moreover, because Lacey's id is suppressed by the cultural norms
expected of her, her chances of happiness are reduced while her despair
continues to increase. Lacey describes how her one chance at marriage
went awry:

> I've never been married. But I did get left at the church once. Well, actu-
> ally, it was a home wedding. Oh, we had the house all decorated with col-
> orful flowers and garlands and candlelight. I don't think they'll ever invent
> anything more romantic than candlelight. Anyway, it's a very funny
> story — all about how he never came by the house. I guess it makes me out
> t'look a little foolish. Afterwards, everyone remarked how I took it really
> well, coming down and joining the party like I did [230].

Lacey, looking for love in all the wrong places, has made a living for herself by romancing men in taxi dance halls from New Orleans to Pigeon,
Louisiana, which, going from the glitz and glamour of New Orleans to
Pigeon, seemingly is itself a sort of descent. With all of her material possessions in a pawn shop, Lacey has wound up indigent and unloved. She
admits to Turnip, "Gosh, the main thing I wanted outta life was fame,
wealth, and adoration. Instead I'm poor and broke and nobody likes me"
(260). Lacey has tried too hard to buy into cultural expectations, and the
result is that the dichotomy between individual happiness and the socializing norms of civilization have led her to despair. Her notion of success
is tied to the norms and values of society, which imply that a woman's
worth is linked to marriage and money. Lacey, weighed down by the alba-
tross of the psychological burdens placed upon her coupled with her physical disability, can only lament, "I just don't understand, people always
despise me, no matter where I go!" (258). Her condition is exacerbated
during Christmas Eve, as she realizes that she must celebrate the holiday
alone, without anyone to give her a present, in the backwoods town of
Pigeon, without a nickel to her name.

    Nevertheless, despite the inequities that inexorably tie us to the absurd
condition, Lacey, somewhat like Pixrose, stoically accepts life's miseries.

Although her relationships with men have all gone awry, including the most recent in which her last potential beau tried to drown her in the bathtub, Lacey admits, "Since then, it's been hard t'let myself trust a man. But I still keep trying. I still believe in love" (224). Lacey's fall, then, figuratively depicted by her lack of financial and personal success while literally demonstrated by the result of her weak ankles, is also personified by her profession: the taxi dancer who tries to find love in all the wrong places. Moreover, Lacey's plight is even further aggravated by another of Henley's unrequited love relationships. Lacey seems to be attracted to the younger Turnip, although she probably is confused by his philosophical rantings. Similar to the self-styled Delmount, the metaphysically inclined Turnip preaches about the existential madness, the *angoisse* that Lacey intuitively understands but cannot express as lyrically as can Turnip, who sees life as a gamble, an absurd game of chance:

> What a low-down, rutty, rotten, little game we're all playing. It ain't like checkers. In checkers somebody wins and somebody loses. It's clear-cut. But playing this other — we're all big-time losers; every one of us. No ringing in the cold deck, no aces up the sleeves, no hold-outs. Just stacking up piles and piles of chips, t' give 'em all away. All losers! Every one of us—Christ, what a racket [240].

Turnip, who works daily with Lacey, never sees her as a suitable companion, preferring instead the younger Cassidy, who, intent on marrying Hooker, views Turnip with contempt, reducing him to merely "some nitwit" (250) likely to fall off the truck.

Sue Jack Tiller forms the third and most significant member of he female triad, for the play centers around her release from prison on Christmas Eve, just in time for her to return to her former profession as taxi dancer in order to allow her husband to keep his pipe dreams for the Lucky Spot alive. As subordinate characters, Cassidy and Lacey only provide us with brief glimpses of their past lives—certainly not enough data to make a diagnosis about their psychoanalytic conditions; besides, a fifteen-year-old can hardly be diagnosed as neurotic. Sue Jack, however, as the charismatic focal point of the drama, has quite an onstage presence and, either through her own voice or through the gossip of Hooker or Carmichael, furnishes us with enough information to make a reliable assessment of her neurotic condition. Sue Jack suffers from Antisocial Personality Disorder, a sociopathological condition essentially consisting of a pervasive pattern of disregard for, and violation of, the rights of others. The *Diagnostic and Statistical Manual of Mental Disorders* states that the specific behavior characteristics of Antisocial Personality Disorder fall into any of these four categories: aggression to people and animals, destruction of property, deceitfulness or theft, or serious violation of rules.[7] The patterns of antisocial behavior usually begin in adolescence and continue into adulthood. Neurotics suffering from Antisocial Personality Disorder repeatedly, and without regard for the feelings of others, perform acts that are grounds for arrest, such as destroying someone's possessions, stealing, or pursuing illegal occupations.[8] They may also lie to con others, engage in sexual behavior or substance abuse with a high risk of harmful consequences, and neglect to care for a child in a way that puts the youngster in danger. Moreover, those suffering from Antisocial Personality Disorder are often highly callous, cynical, impulsive, irritable, and aggressive, the latter indicated by repeated physical fights or assaults.[9]

Although we do not have evidence that Sue Jack's Antisocial Personality Disorder began as an adolescent, the neurosis is certainly full blown as an adult. Again, the seeds of Sue Jack's neurosis can be found in childhood, where individual happiness was not allowed to flourish because of the absent father and the mother who abandoned her. Sue Jack reveals, "Well, I never met my daddy but if I did, I'd like nothing better than t'spit straight at him" (229). Her mother, who "went insane due to religious troubles" (229), eventually committed suicide while looking in a full-length mirror. The abandonment by the mother is reminiscent of the plight of the neurotic Magrath sisters, now represented by Sue Jack's low self-esteem anytime she is forced to look at herself in a mirror. As a former taxi dancer at the Glitter Dance Palace in New Orleans, Sue Jack began her life of illicit behavior. Possessing beauty, charm, and wit, Sue Jack was able to converse with the clients at the dance hall while all the time trying to manipulate them in order to milk the guys for gifts, such as silk gowns and mink furs; Reed Hooker was likely one of her clients. Sue Jack was also hot-tempered, and, Lola Dove, one of the former taxi dancers who worked in New Orleans, even recalls the time when Sue Jack hit her with a brick just to see if she would bleed (228).

Sue Jack's Antisocial Personality Disorder fully blossomed during her marriage to Hooker. As is true of many women who suffer from Antisocial Personality Disorder, Sue Jack engages in harmful sexual behavior and substance abuse. She intimates to her own husband that she had been promiscuous throughout her life, probably beginning as a taxi dancer cum whore and even continuing her sexual escapades during their marriage (257). Gambling with cards was her forte, even to the point of wearing fine lace gloves to avoid damaging the delicate touch she required for such illegal activity. During her marriage to Hooker, Sue Jack recalls that her gambling habit was responsible for their financial ruin: "Look, I lost most of our stinking money playing the horses and dogs and roosters. As I remember, I was always pretty good with cards" (255). The substance abuse also included excessive drinking, which gave her unwanted notoriety; even Turnip is aware of Sue Jack's reputation for destructive behavior once drunk: "See, she's very touchy. 'Specially when she drinks. Meanest damn drunk I ever heard of or saw" (210). When Hooker began writing poems to Caroline Carmichael, Sue Jack's neurosis was aggravated to the point where the drinking, gambling, and promiscuity were fully accentuated. Complaining about his wife's five-week binge drinking in a "trash can shack" while having sex with her cousin no less, Hooker recalls that he was fed up with, and unable to adjust to, Sue Jack's neurotic condition: "And what the hell was I gonna do when you shut me out with you drinking for weeks on end, staying binged out of your goddamned mind, gambling away every nickel we ever had?!" (234).

Certainly the single most significant act that occurred during Sue Jack's marriage to indicate how serious she suffered from the sociopathological disorder was the death of toddler Andy, her only child. For years, everyone believed that Andy's death was an accident because he ostensibly pulled away from Sue Jack on the street and was hit by an automobile while he was trying to chase a hummingbird. Sue Jack breaks down to tell Hooker the truth: "Jesus Christ, don't you get it? There was no goddamn hummingbird. I went into a speak t' get a drink. I left him standing there on the porch. He ran off, a car hit him and I was sitting there in the bar, slinging back a shot of whiskey" (254). This traumatic episode indicates several symptoms of the Antisocial Personality Disorder from which Sue Jack suffers: her total disregard for the feelings of others (in this case, her own son), her addictive substance abuse behavior that certainly led to harmful consequences on this occasion, her neglect and care for a child that would put the youngster in serious danger, and her insistence on the lie to con others of her innocence. Moreover, Hooker recalls how callous his wife was after the death of their child, another characteristic of Sue Jack's Antisocial Personality Disorder: "The night after they laid my kid in the ground she went out to a cockfight in a red tasseled dress and squandered away her wedding ring. She went on boozing and brawling and lavishing away everything decent we ever had together" (213).

Sue Jack receives early Christmas release from Angola State Penitentiary after being confined there for three years for throwing Caroline Carmichael over a balcony railing when Whitt's sister was found in bed with Hooker. Upon receiving news of Sue Jack's return, all of the taxi dancers leave the premises in fear of what Whitt refers to as the arrival of "Hooker's outlaw wife" (227). Now in her thirties, Sue Jack, with the "*jar-*

ring presence of a ravaged beauty" (224), acknowledges that her wild transgressions have cost her "the bloom of youth" (253) in which sadness has sunk deeply into her face. Prison has not provided any therapy for her neurosis, and although she does not have the ability or expertise to engage in self-diagnosis, she seemingly understands that her disability, rather than being palliated, has worsened; she tells Hooker, "I — I got sick in prison" (253). Moreover, her pervasive pattern of behavior disorder consisting of a disregard for the rights of others, which ostensibly was why she was sent to prison, has not been assuaged. She is callous toward others, as she boasts of her aggressive behavior without regard for social norms: "I'm glad I threw Caroline Carmichael over that balcony rail. I'm glad she broke both her arms and gashed up her face" (235). Sue Jack also displays the deeply rooted cynicism often associated with those suffering from Antisocial Personality Disorder, particularly when she mocks Hooker's dream of getting lucky with the Lucky Spot: "Come on, Reed, the whole world's a joke. Consider yourself a real sucker when being taken seriously becomes any sort of goal at all" (246). Returning to her husband with the hope of making a good impression on him after her long absence, Sue Jack tries to convince Hooker that she is not the same person as in the photograph of herself she maintained while incarcerated. Her whine, "I guess I'm not sure who I am" (231), falls on deaf ears, for Hooker realizes that although her outward appearance has changed noticeably, her persona has not. She pleads, "I'm not the same one who kept on hurting you by drinking, and brawling and gambling it all away" (231). However, the reality of an aggressive, impulsive, and irritable neurotic suffering from Antisocial Personality Disorder is revealed by Sue Jack's destruction of property and hostility to individuals who threaten her, resulting in physical fights or assaults. When Cassidy reveals her love for Hooker, Sue Jack proceeds to fire a shotgun, shattering a mirror, and destroying light fixtures and her husband's juke box — the means by which he makes his living; then she threatens to turn the gun on Cassidy. When Hooker enters, the stage directions indicate, "*What follows is an all-out, low-down, and rutty brawl*" (234) that leaves the Lucky Spot in total shambles while Sue Jack swings the rifle at her husband. Act 1 ends with Sue Jack and Hooker strangling each other before the wrestling match ends on the floor. Act 2, on Christmas morning, concludes with Sue Jack's understatement that she realizes that she is not compatible with her husband. To compensate for a relationship gone awry, Sue Jack, ever the sick individual, offers a fitting gesture to make amends at the expense of others: she suggests stealing a neighbor's pumpkins to make the taxi dancers a Christmas pumpkin pie. Henley, in commenting on Sue Jack's neurotic behavior, stated in the Introduction to the play, "That Sue Jack would be capable of such violence and destruction informed me tremendously about the despair and rage that lived inside her — unrepentant and unresolved."[10] In short, the despair and rage, now even more fully accentuated by her inability to bear children (thus increasing her guilt) due to sickness she developed while in prison, are manifestations of an ontologically insecure individual faced with a disability of one form of the modern *angoisse*.

Sue Jack's presence is an unwanted interference for Hooker, Cassidy, and Lacey, whose hopes for a successful opening of the Lucky Spot dance hall are actually a quest for dignity and meaning in an otherwise absurd universe. Of course, although Henley's protagonists are dreamers, their long-term hopes of assuaging the modern *angoisse* always go unfulfilled. The only paying customer to frequent the dance hall is Sam, a man in his sixties forced to spend Christmas Eve alone after the recent death of his wife. In a moment of pathos that speaks volumes about the human condition, Sam, who now realizes how lucky he had been to take care of his blind wife for so many years, chooses to pay for a taxi dance with fifteen-year-old Cassidy, who, figuratively blind herself, has eyes only for Hooker, a married man. Hooker's virtually barren dance floor on Christmas Eve becomes a metaphor for the quest for dignity amidst the absurd human condition, suggesting the broken dreams and spiritual bankruptcy of modern society.

The play ends with a moment of happiness that can be shared in order to provide a brief respite during the search for human dignity in an absurd universe. Reminiscent of the bath scene subsequent to the fiasco of Teddy's debutante ball, the shared moment of happiness between Carnelle and Mac Sam after the former had failed to place in the Miss Firecracker Contest, the reconciliation of the Magrath sisters after Old Granddaddy's coma, or the soothing communion between Brocker and Marshael after the wake of Jamey Foster, the Christmas day aftermath of the failed opening of the Lucky Spot provides that moment of eternal grace necessary to get through the existential madness of daily life. The spirit of Christmas gift giving overwhelms Hooker and his taxi dancers, and although they are too poor to give lavish presents, the disposition of the moment imbues a sense of collective happiness. In what appears to be the calm after the storm, the spirit of Christmas altruism seems to subdue the modern neurosis momentarily. Mary Stuart Masterson, who played Cassidy in the 1987 Manhattan Theatre Club production, noted, "The first act is about taking, for survival. The second act is about learning how to give."[11] Cassidy comes to accept the fact that she will not marry Hooker, a wish she had hoped for so that her child would not be raised without a father. During the gift giving and calm resignation of Christmas morning, Cassidy tears off the engagement ring made of rope and bonds with her rival Sue Jack, giving her a gift of a paper hat. Cassidy, perhaps flattered by the fact that Sam chose her to dance with rather than the other girls in the lineup, is willing to accept the fact that love is something that one must earn and deserve; indeed, the gifts that Hooker brings— peppermint candies and oranges— serve to remind Cassidy of her first Christmas, a joyous time when her family was united in harmony. Lacey forms a bond with Turnip, who admits that he enjoys talking with her because she pays attention to him during their conversations. Lacey reciprocates the gift giving by allowing her colleagues to accept four sprays of her genuine French perfume. Hooker hands out oranges to all, and Sam displays his generosity by dispensing peppermint candy canes. Even Sue Jack and Hooker briefly dispense with the past to embrace under the mistletoe while the festive atmosphere continues with music and dancing. As Charles S. Watson notes, for one brief moment, all the denizens of the Lucky Spot dance hall share in the joy, like one big, happy family.[12] Tish Dace suggests that the denouement of the play indicates that happiness need not elude us: "These are losers, but — without any of O'Neill's irony in *The Iceman Cometh*— hopeful losers, still, appropriately, looking at life through rose-colored glasses."[13] Thus, the Christmas spirit of gift giving and reflection in this play becomes Henley's version of the consciousness that temporarily mitigates, and helps us revolt against, the absurd condition or the modern neurosis, endemic to all of civilized society.

In an interview with Mary Dellasega, Henley revealed that her next play, *Abundance*, was inspired by her reading of Michael Lesy's 1973 book, *Wisconsin Death Trap*,[14] which became the source for director James Marsh's British Broadcasting Company Film with the same title. Lesy's book was based upon a historical account of the bizarre disasters that befell the town of Black River Falls, Wisconsin, during the last decade of the nineteenth century, including suicides, murders, and violence due to the town's outlaws and arsonists. Henley stated, "I saw this book, and I was just stunned because of the harsh reality of the West it showed, which was not portrayed in the cowboy movies or the westerns of the time. I was fascinated with the specifics of everyday life and how brutal they were. They triggered my imagination, who these people actually were and their madness."[15] The West in the cowboy films usually symbolized expansiveness, freedom, and the American Dream of hope for the future amidst the lure of the glitz and glamour of far-away places (similar to Willy Loman's desire to remain in the city while his brother Ben made his fortune in the wilderness of Alaska). Henley, however, takes Lesy's book and uses it as a starting point for her revisionist play,[16] which seeks to demythologize the

West and its appeal to those individuals inculcated by the American Dream. However, rather than focusing on demythologizing the West, I will argue that *Abundance* is mainly concerned with exploring how the seeds of the modern neurosis germinated in the nineteenth century.

Abundance is an important transitional play for Henley. Set in the Wyoming territories (Wyoming was not admitted as a state until 1890) and St. Louis, *Abundance* moves Henley's sense of place farther west and out of the deep South, which was the locale for her previous six plays. Whereas most of her early plays followed unity of time, *Abundance*, in epic-style fashion, spans twenty-five years beginning in the late 1860s. *Abundance* is the only play in Henley's canon set in the nineteenth century, which fundamentally alters the content of the play. Instead of protagonists who suffer full-fledged from angst and *angoisse* due to the cultural ideals that conflict with the id's libidinal desires, the characters in *Abundance* reveal how the modern neurosis developed through its genesis at the end of the nineteenth century. Bess and Macon come west with youthful optimism; we know nothing about the possibility that they have lived sordid lives, as we do with most of Henley's protagonists. The frontier 1880s setting also allowed Henley to maintain poetic license in her use of language: "You can be more poetic, use stranger twists of phrase, which is what I always liked about the South."[17]

Abundance begins during an early spring morning in a Wyoming stagecoach ranché in the late 1860s, where two mail-order brides, Bess Johnson and Macon Hill, are anxiously awaiting husbands they have never met. Unsure of what to expect during their first trip out West, Bess and Macon immediately seem to bond together in a spirit of starry-eyed optimism as they share the wondrous possibility of starting a new life in a territory filled with limitless possibilities. Bess has been waiting at the stagecoach ranché ten days for her husband, a man she knows only through correspondence with him. Bess is one of Henley's cherished protagonists — a woman without marketable skills yet someone consumed by the overwhelming need to be loved for who she is and the passion she has for life. Although Macon shatters Bess's hopes that her future husband will be a dashing prince like in the love stories she has been enamored with, Bess still is idealistic: "I don't know. I — well, I bet he's gonna like me some."[18] Bess, with dreams of being domesticated in familial bliss, hopes that her singing skills, the one talent that she demonstrates, will be enough to captivate her future husband: "Oh, I'm betting we're gonna be a match made in heaven, if only I ain't left stranded" (7). In contrast to Bess as the poetic-spouting wallflower, Macon, in green goggles and a cape covered in road dust, has come west to savor the boundlessness, the wild flavor, the excitement of new territory. She tells Bess, "I want to discover gold and be rich. I want to erect an ice palace and kill an Indian with a hot bullet. I'm ready for some sweeping changes" (6). Considered to be the runt of the family back home, Macon sees the frontier as her opportunity to start life anew free from the old stereotypes people had of her. The West represents the lure of the unknown to her, a chance to "see the elephant" (5) and perhaps even write a novel about her daring adventures. This brief moment of happiness between two starry-eyed women who are so different yet share a common bond will never be duplicated again during their lives. The remainder of the play demythologizes the American Dream, demonstrating the Freudian notion that the push and pull of the socialization process felt directly on the ego and superego interfere with the id's libidinal desires, thus creating the angst manifested by the absurd condition.

The hint of the downward trajectory in the lives of Bess and Macon occurs at the stagecoach ranché, when the two idealists actually meet their husbands for the first time. Upon learning that Michael Flan, the man with whom she corresponded, was killed in an accident, the distraught Bess realizes that her pipe dreams of a happy marriage have dissipated: "'I do, I do.' I worked on saying them words the whole way here. Over cliffs, across streams, in the rain, in the dust. 'I do, I do.' Every dream I ever had I said in them words. 'I do, I do, I do, I do...'" (8). Michael's brother Jack, a brusque man whose initial response to Bess's agony is toward violence (he threatens to knock Bess down, and when Macon tries to intervene, her grabs her by the hair and slings her to the ground), reluctantly agrees to marry her as long as she refrains from crying. Meanwhile, Macon's sense of wondrous anticipation is dashed as she meets her beau, William Curtis. Unlike Macon's rough and tumble demeanor and dress, Curtis, *"neatly dressed"* (8), seems to be out of kilter with the type of adventurous man she sought to spend the rest of her life with; moreover, the scar down his face and the patch over his left eye suggest that he is not the handsome, debonair man of her dreams.

Bess's marriage to her husband begins precariously, with Jack, unaccustomed to being around women, finding it difficult to adjust to married life. Jack was perfectly happy living in filth, being inundated with fleas, ticks, and lice, while Bess finds it unbearable. Moreover, Jack, a gun-toting violent man, has no desire to hear Bess sing and even decides to tear up what Bess considers to be Michael's love letters when he believes Bess is patronizing his illiteracy as she reads the letter aloud. Even worse, Jack is lazy and shiftless, refusing to engage in any meaningful work ethic; instead, he tries to make a living by falling into get-rich-quick schemes, such as buying a worthless mine that he thinks will yield gold. Jack, however, is handsome with an air of wild danger about him, so despite the fact that he is not a good provider and treats his wife like chattel, Bess is attracted to him. When Macon suggests that Bess abandon Jack because she cannot change his demeanor, Bess agrees to make the best of the situation by staying with the man she agreed to marry. When Henley was asked why Bess would prefer sexy yet abusive Jack, she replied

> He represents that affliction women have with the wrong guy. Both women fall in love with him. You see it in life all the time. There's this wonderful guy who only has one eye whom nobody wants. And then there's this horrible guy. He's totally lazy, totally deranged, totally sexy, and everybody wants him. I've seen it over and over. "You should go for the guy without the eye." "I know. But I want that other one."[19]

Macon, on the other hand, is married to a man who is judicious, stable, and a good provider. Although Will Curtis is humble, hard working, loyal, good natured, and makes for a worthy husband, Macon finds him clumsy, dull, and unattractive, the latter largely because of him missing an eye due to a mining accident. Will's first gesture is to give Macon his late wife's wedding ring as a gift of his appreciation. Will has known his share of misfortune in life, his eye having been put out by a pickax and his wife having died by his side as she "coughed up both her lungs" (11) after losing three fingers in a sheep-shearing accident. Even after Macon refuses to accept the ring because of fear of contamination, Will insists on getting her another one, even if it means the indigent rancher has to make a temporary one out of tin before he can afford a real ring with a stone in it. Although Will orders a glass eye to assuage Macon's repulsiveness to him, she acknowledges to Bess, "I know he does try; but, well, frankly, I'm allergic to him physically" (13).

As the seasons pass, Bess and Macon prostitute themselves as demands of the ego and superego outweigh the id's desire for happiness. Bess enters into an abusive, rather than caring, relationship with her husband while adhering to the vows of marriage yet struggling to be loved. Macon's desire to expand her horizons and "see the elephant" become subordinate to a sense of place — she acquires more land. Both Bess and Macon accept the cultural norms of society and therefore become frustrated or conflicted about not achieving their libidinal desires. Moreover, as Freud indicated, love relationships cannot assuage the modern neurosis because humans tend to be aggressive rather than caring toward each other. This is certainly the case in the marriage of Bess and Jack, whereas Macon's situation is the classic Chekhovian unrequited love. Jack shows no sexual interest in Bess, always finding fault with the way her eyes are too close together, but is passionate about Macon, who shares an attraction for him but cannot do anything about it since she is married and also does not want to hurt her friend Bess. The play thus presents the absurd condition Freud described in which humans find themselves conflicted when they cannot live their own dreams and must adopt the dreams of others.

Over the years, the lives of Bess and Macon take unexpected twists and turns, exacerbating the neuroses. Bess became pregnant but lost the infant baby; wolves dug up the buried child and ate it. Bess then dressed up a prairie dog in a calico bonnet and shawl and then proceeded to rock it to sleep on the porch while murmuring softly to the animal. Will makes his own diagnosis of what he deems to be Bess's "strange and gruesome behavior": "Look, I've observed in her strong symptoms of derangement that just ain't healthy" (17). Bess and Jack celebrate one awful Christmas, which typically should be a time of joy, with the news that the prairie dog was killed by a vagabond. Starving to the point of being forced to eat wheat out of their mattress, Bess tries to cheer up her husband by baking bread from the cornmeal she has been saving as a Christmas gift for him. Jack, claiming that his brother Mike died from choking on cornbread, lacks empathy for his wife, instead accusing her of selfishness and an instinct for killing off her loved ones: "First Mike, then the baby, next Prairie Dog, now me. You want us all dead, don't you? You like things dead. You want it all for yourself" (19). Jack throws the cornmeal in her face, and Bess can only lament how her dreams of love have dissipated: "I wanted this to be good. I wanted to be your true one" (19). That evening, Jack sets the cabin on fire, leaving him and his wife homeless. Bess describes her despair about lack of love and contact to Macon: "I been so lonely. I been going outside and hugging icy trees, clinging to them like they was alive and could hold me back. I feel so empty sometimes I eat warm mud, trying to fill up the craving" (22). Meanwhile, Macon, the adventuress, has become more domesticated as the ranch prospers. She buys copper kettles to improve the cheerfulness of her home, judges the local baking contest in which she won first prize the previous year, becomes enamored with ordering rainbow-colored petticoats and wearing different hairpieces, and tries out the latest fashions, such as waterfall curls, from Boston. When Bess exhorts Macon to flee their husbands and seek their fortunes farther west, it is Macon, in a reversal of roles, who now refuses to "see the elephant," claiming that she has household obligations to fulfill.

Tensions become heightened when Bess and Jack move in with Macon and Will, as the tight quarters produce animosity between friends. Selfish Jack has no desire to rebuild his cabin, and his only plans for making a living include ridiculous gambling schemes. Meanwhile, he has no qualms about sponging off his neighbors, for example, devouring the last piece of cake that Macon made for her husband. During the years the two couples share the cabin together, the sexual tensions remain high. Jack remains disdainful of his wife yet has searing passion for Macon. On the day of the second anniversary of Macon and Will, which was supposed to be the deadline for Jack and Bess to evict themselves from the cabin voluntarily, the celebration turns awry. When Bess takes a spill while dancing, Jack can only be critical of his wife, who is trying to enjoy herself; "Try to be more ladylike. Everyone saw all your things under there" (28). Bess's singing is marred when she forgets some of the lines, leaving Jack to remark with disdain, "I don't know a thing about singing, but it seems to me, if you're gonna sing a song, you need to know the words to the song you pick" (29). These insults become the impetus for Bess to evade the household tensions by wandering by herself outside. Bess is kidnapped by Indians, the event that ends act 1, which is the peripeteia that drastically alters the lives of these two women.

After a five-year absence, Bess is released by Chief Ottawa, who sells her to the military for two horses, three blankets, a box of bullets, and a sack of glass beads. Bess returns home barefoot, with sun-bleached hair, burnt skin, and a tattooed chin. She finds it difficult to adjust to her previous environment. Ironically, Macon, the daredevil who came west to experience adventure, is now fully domesticated and, believing that she would never see her friend again, is now fully engrossed in an affair with Jack. Macon's attraction to Jack is fully understandable because "Mr. Curtis," which is how Macon addresses her husband, is too formal, unable to express his feelings directly. For example, at Christmas, the self-effacing Will gives his wife a Christmas card from Brown Spot, the cow. Nevertheless, despite the fact that Macon admits to despising Jack because, as she tells him, "You're mean and selfish and a liar and a snake…" (31), there remains a sexual attraction between them. Bess, however, who wanted only love in her quest to come west, has now experienced first-hand the adventure that Macon so keenly sought. *Abundance* thus reaffirms the absurd condition that results in frustration when we realize how difficult it is to fulfill our own dreams and ambitions. With regard to one of her major intentions for writing the play, Henley noted, "It really is about how insidiously people's dreams are taken away from them."[20] Like theater of the absurd, whose purpose, Esslin stated, was to make audiences aware of their precarious positions in the universe, *Abundance* presents us with the metaphysical Absence, the existential madness, and the difficulty of maintaining dignity in an absurd world in which our dreams and aspirations are often negated by chance. In an interview with Alexis Greene, Henley discussed the absurd condition behind the turn of events that forced Bess and Macon to exchange personae: "And another frightening element is how tangents just take some people. These people end up with things they didn't even want. They destroy their lives for things they don't want. I do feel sorry for human beings, because they start off wanting things simply and innocently and truthfully, and getting through life can be so treacherous."[21] The absurd condition becomes more painfully obvious when the once-prosperous household of Macon and Will is now reduced to penury because wheat prices have dropped, the drought has affected the ranch's output, and demand has been decreased because of the rerouting of the railroad. When Professor Elmore Crome, a Ned Buntline-type opportunist, convinces Bess to cowrite a book with him about her survival among the Oglala (the western Sioux) Indians, the once-starving duo of Bess and Jack ironically now begin to prosper.

The essence of the play revolves around the motif of belonging—feeling a sense of self-worth or establishing one's dignity—in a world of existential madness, which was the initial premise of Lesy's book about the harsh reality of life in the West. At the beginning of the play, the libidinal desires of Bess and Macon forced them to seek happiness in different ways: Bess to find love and Macon to seek adventure; the strong bond of friendship the two women established was initially a means to assuage the neurosis. However, in Freudian terms, the push and pull of social and cultural obligations, particularly the desire to have power through ownership of property and by acquiring capital, become all too consuming for Bess and Macon. Consequently, Bess and Macon prostitute themselves by failing to adhere to their own libidinal desires as they adopt each other's dreams and thus change their personae. Bess begins to sound like Macon as she tells Crome, "It's true, I've suffered. But I come out here drunk with western fever. I wanted to see the elephant. To hunt down the elephant. Bang! Bang! Bang! I savor the boundlessness of it all! The wild flavor!" (43). Macon, the domesticated homebody, has become like Bess, whereas the latter has experienced the brutality of the West first-hand because she was transformed into a savage by the Indians. Bess and Macon become jealous of the fact that they have stepped into each other's shoes. Macon even suggests to Crome that she accompany him on the lecture circuit to discuss the Oglalas—to talk about an experience that was not even hers: "Just imagine Bess on a big stage in front of a whole room full of people. Such a shy little thing. She'd die of fright. You need somebody who's got a real knack for that sort of thing. Ya know, I once played the Virgin Mary in a Christmas pageant. I had such a saintly face, an unearthly glow" (43). Bess, on the other hand, is jealous that Macon was able to steal her husband while she was with the Indians. She also feels betrayed by Ottawa, who sold her for trinkets. When Mary Dellasega asked Henley why Bess, by selling her story of her abduction to Crome, gave her approval to the idea of genocide of the Indians, she replied, "That to me shows how far she has gone away from her dream of true love because I feel that she did love Ottawa [*sic*] and her children. But she feels *he* betrayed *her*, and so that's her revenge."[22] Thus, as Richard Wattenberg notes, Bess, in cooperating with Crome, "who embodies the commercial imperative underlying Eastern civilization," accepts a culture that manufactures lies and illusions; by doing so, Bess prostitutes herself by adopting a persona that she picked up from her friend Macon's sense of adventure, the need to "see the elephant."[23] Robert J. Andreach reminds us that in the first scene of the play, when Bess and Macon meet at the ranché, Macon notes, "You're like me" (5), which suggests that the two are doubles capable of mirroring each other.[24] Indeed, Macon ironically becomes the savage — not the wilderness savage that she initially sought to emulate, but the civilized savage who steals her best friend's husband in an attempt to have love and power simultaneously. As Bess's book becomes enormously successful, especially since it reminds Macon that she was once going to write a novel herself about her adventures, the jealousy between the two women exacerbates, further altering their personae. Bess, once the timid wallflower physically and verbally abused by her husband, now gives orders to Jack, treating him like a lackey. Macon, who exhorted Bess to flee with her because she could not bear to be with her dull, ugly husband, now is abandoned by him after her land and house are repossessed.

What originally began as a bond of friendship between two women who promised to remain lifelong friends now degenerates into a play of power to dominate the other. When asked about the power play between Bess and Macon, Henley stated, "I think nobody in my plays basically feels they're empowered. I think they're all struggling with that issue and doing cruel things to empower themselves, or get what they feel would be empowerment."[25] For years, Macon was flirting with Jack in a subliminal quest to become the most powerful woman of the household; when Bess becomes a national celebrity, she takes revenge on Macon, refusing to help her hold on to her husband or her household. Moreover, Bess boasts about her newly won fame and fortune, rubbing Macon's misfortune in her face, using her power to humiliate her friend:

> Because, maybe you would like to be ... remarkable. But you're not. You look forward to things by decades. You're settled, staid, and dreamless. I see it haunts you how ya just can't compare t'me. To Bess Johnson, the

woman who survived five adventurous years of Indian captivity. Who returned to write the book of the century and be adored by throngs all over the globe [47].

By calling Macon "dreamless," Bess hits a nerve that awakens Macon's romanticized vision of going west to achieve her version of the American Dream. Macon fires back at Bess in a pitiful attempt to reclaim power by momentarily assuming her old persona:

> You don't fool me. I know how ya done it all. You pictured me. You stole from me. You stole me. I showed you how to walk and speak and fight and dream. I should have written that book. People should be clamoring t'meet me, t'talk t'me. I'm the real thing; you're just a watered down milquetoast version. Them Indians stole the wrong woman [47].

Bess, acknowledging that she has resented Macon for all the years they lived together, refuses to lend her friend the fifty dollars necessary for her to avoid bankruptcy. Bess has become selfish and egotistical, admitting to Macon, "Honey, I'd rip the wings off an angel if I thought they'd help me fly" (48). Bess even signs a contract that demands that she advocate the immediate extermination of the Indians; she will thus exploit others in order to gain fame and fortune.

The last two scenes of the play are set in St. Louis fifteen years later. Bess, now worn out traveling the lecture circuit, faces the reality that because her novel has become a tired melodrama, she must end her business venture with Crome. Bess, the family breadwinner, gives orders to Jack, who seems to obey dutifully so long as he can ride his wife's coattails. The love relationship that she sought obviously went awry since Bess is childless and refers to Ottawa as her husband. Meanwhile, Macon has descended upon hard times working in St. Louis dispensing whiskey, tobacco, and raisins. She was prospering for a while selling an Indian remedy for those addicted to drugs, alcohol, and tobacco, but when she contracted syphilis, which forced her to break out in sores, her business was ruined. Will, her estranged husband, met a disastrous end when he bled to death after his leg was cut off by a threshing machine. Macon, acutely aware of pains in her chest, realizes her imminent death. Bess and Macon can only share the fact that their dreams went awry. The love that they shared for each other twenty-five years earlier upon meeting for the first time at the ranché can never be recaptured. Karen L. Laughlin claims that the reunion of Bess and Macon is a moment of sisterly bonding reminiscent of the birthday party at the end of *Crimes of the Heart*.[26] Instead, the reunion appears to be merely a lament of lost opportunities in which the two women are glad they have each other to listen to their confession, and when Macon acknowledges, "There ain't much t'tell," Bess, in appreciation of Macon's former attempt at true friendship, confides, "Maybe not, but I'm glad you looked my way" (53). Setting the latter portion of the play in St. Louis, the gateway to the West, is a stroke of brilliance on Henley's part, for the sense of place reinforces the sarcasm associated with the motif of how romanticized ideals of civilization go awry. St. Louis thus brings the title of the play fully into its ironic resonance; as James S. Torrens notes, "The elephant, the vast promise of the West, abundance, has proved illusory."[27]

Abundance, Henley's first play to be distanced from the rest of her canon in time and place, is thus not easily pigeon-holed, yet critics have made rather unconvincing attempts to paint the play as feminist or "gothic." Frank Rich argued that the play is a parable for women who sell out their identities to patriarchal entrepreneurship, thereby leaving them less humane (as ultimately tent-show freaks) and more likely to forsake sexual pleasure, love, friendship, and children.[28] Another feminist approach to the play has Bess and Macon embracing the patriarchal values that enslave them and eventually destroy their friendship for each other.[29] Karen L. Laughlin adopts a similar reading of the play: "In her story of two mail-order brides who come west to seek their fortune, Henley looks at the West through the lens of romance, a romance based largely on women's desires and ambitions. In so doing, she proposes a postmodern feminist reworking of the Western myth."[30] In addition to the attempt to paint Henley as a feminist playwright, critics have tried to pigeon-hole *Abundance* in the gothic tradition, reminding us of images such as Bess's scalping by the Indians, Will's tossing of his glass eye, his wife's loss of three fingers in a sheep-shearing accident, Jack shooting a gun at Macon's feet, the pet prairie dog, wolves eating a baby's corpse, Will's Christmas card to his wife from Brown Spot, Ottawa drinking a lantern of kerosene upon his capture, Will's demise via a threshing machine, and side-show freaks (armless boy, electric girl, skeleton "dude"), with Macon ultimately reduced merely to another tent-show freak ravaged by sores from syphilis. However, these readings fail to do justice to the central issues Henley explores in the play. *Abundance* is somewhat confusing to critics because unlike Henley's other plays, she begins with the moment of consciousness that mitigates the absurd condition. This moment of shared recognition, which is typically manifested by a bond of trust or friendship, usually occurs at the end of the play; in other words, Henley's dramas present the absurd condition and then offer a means to confront the neurosis. *Abundance*, however, begins with the moment of consciousness and becomes a parable of what happens when the bonds of friendship are abandoned. Henley stated, 'It [*Abundance*] is a cautionary tale. How not to live your life.'[31] The moment of consciousness occurred in the first scene set in the Wyoming ranché, a brief bond of friendship that became the pinnacle of Bess and Macon's trek west. The remainder of the play follows their descent from this moment of consciousness to their realization of lost dreams.[32] Thus, although, on the surface, *Abundance* is concerned with demythologizing the romanticized view of the West and the glamorized notion of the American Dream, the play is similar to Henley's other dramas in depicting how the id's libidinal desire for happiness is derailed by the acculturation process that directly affects the ego and superego. In betraying their own dreams, Bess and Macon eventually destroy themselves; unfortunately, there is no moment of consciousness to prevent the spirit of disfigured dreams from ruining their lives. Moreover, because the play is set in the nineteenth century, when the civilized demands of frontier life were not as overwhelming as in modern society, the psychopathology is rather benign compared to the full-blown neuroses that Henley typically depicts in her plays. *Abundance*, then, while depicting the absurd condition in which society imposes cultural ideals on us that force us to abandon our dreams and bonds of friendship as we betray ourselves and others, demonstrates how life at the end of the nineteenth century in America firmly planted the seeds for the growth of the modern neurosis.

7

Signature and *Control Freaks*

In quick succession, Henley finished *Signature* (consisting of eighteen scenes in two acts) and *Control Freaks* (a long one-act drama of approximately ninety minutes in duration), two plays that can be examined together not only because they can be paired chronologically, but also because they share the same setting. *Signature* is set in future Los Angeles, in 2052, while *Control Freaks* occurs during present-day Los Angeles. The fact that Henley is now moving westward (*The Lucky Spot* was set in Pigeon, Louisiana, whereas *Abundance* moved even farther west to the Wyoming Territories) indicates that she was perhaps unconsciously abandoning the stereotyped notion of herself as a Southern playwright with regional roots. Henley admitted that *Signature* and *Control Freaks* allowed her "...to write more about now than about my nostalgic past."[1] *Control Freaks* depicts the detritus of the modern wasteland, with Los Angeles as the nexus of a civilization that pits humans violently against each other; the result of the neurosis is manifested, for example, in Sister's acute schizophrenia. Slightly more than half a century later, the Los Angeles of *Signature* has degenerated into a nightmarish vision of the modern neurosis where unrequited love is the norm and euthanasia is only a telephone call away.

Signature's 2052 date is, oddly enough, significant, since Henley was born in 1952, exactly one hundred years earlier. *Signature* thus allows Henley to postulate about what society will be like near the end of her lifetime. Set in Los Angeles of the future, the play provides Henley with license both to be creative by virtually fashioning a new lingo and to be imaginative with her vision of an apocalyptic society populated by neurotic individuals. Jim McGrath, who directed the Passage Theater Company's

1996 production of the play in Trenton, New Jersey, aptly characterizes Henley's nightmarish vision for Los Angeles 2052:

> The characters of *Signature* live in the future at a time when the forces of death would seem to have won. Many citizens die young from an omnipresent plague. The government has conquered individual liberty and severely hampered free will. Addictions abound, the strongest being to the Warhol fifteen minutes. The Springer cult has turned every breakup of every personal relationship into a televised event. A tar-like substance is eating the environment alive. Every man is a Job, every woman a Joan of Arc. In such a world, hearts have reason to be heavy.[2]

In the stage directions, Henley describes her vision of futuristic Los Angeles in a tone somewhat reminiscent of what Ridley Scott depicted in *Blade Runner*: "The effect is a strange, chaotically horrifying, deathly beautiful, sadly silly world."[3] Henley presents a pathetic society in which even so-called creative personae, such as art philosophers, are forced to take in government wards in hopes of attaining money, the almighty "K." Image has replaced direct discourse to the point where when one person wants to talk with another, the point of contact is through a television image. To secure a government subsidy, one is required to maintain some type of image. The purity of seeing the natural world is now reduced to viewing the sky or moon on a video screen or a portable TVP; natural acts, such as sex, are reduced to super-safe sex kits. Since image is everything, icons are now fantasy puppets, who "look sin" (61), and discussion degenerates into which of the fantasy puppets—for example, Pansy Martin, Chee Chee Kitty, or Moe Zoe Beam — is the hottest star of the moment, worthy of having their paraphernalia worshipped as collectibles. Adults in this society are actually happiest when imitating these fad fantasy puppets, for celebrity status is the ultimate thrill, and tearing off the arms of one's Chee Chee Kitty doll is tantamount to ultimate warfare. As Alvin Klein noted in his review of *Signature*, Henley purposefully set the play in Hollywood to accentuate the idea that this is a land without mind or heart ruled instead by celebrity status.[4] Marriages break down so often that they are handled through Video Divorce. Homelessness is typical of many, and street urchins, dressed in rags and uneducated, now contribute to the urban blight; the government supplies the urchins with food boxes, but they have no shelters in which they can eat them. The society is typified by isolation, estrangement, and lack of compassion, to the extent that brothers are alienated from brothers, husbands from wives, and parents from offspring (Boswell even calls his daughter, whom he initially cannot even recognize, one of his "swarmy brats"); parents who can no longer afford their children put them in deep freeze until their finances improve. For parents who worry about raising troublesome adolescents or teenagers, Toss 'Em Toddlers are the way to go; their life span is only three years, so they are guaranteed to remain cute, and the parents do not have to worry about the high cost of their child's education. The death instinct is so prevalent that an individual's fate is forecasted on the Up and Coming Obits. Drugs, commonly in the form of ear fuel (similar to a snort of cocaine to the brain), emotional equalizers, blue dots, soul sedatives, and pain executioners, are ubiquitous. The environment serves to reflect the neglect in this society, as splatterers and other laborers toil daily to clean up the detritus of earthquakes, spills, and fires that inundate the denizens of this horrid underworld with a black undercoat of soot and grime.

Signature presents a microcosm of a society that is directly responsible for human misery. In Freudian terminology, Henley's futuristic civilization depicts the extent to which our libidinal desires—the id—have been diminished by social norms and values. This futuristic civilization is what contemporary society is moving toward—a unity of individuals who are under pressure to conform to the notion of image and celebrity. Henley is again working with the Chekhovian motif of unrequited love in which the characters in the play ignore the natural desire of a loving relationship in favor of seeking to attain what they cannot have. Meanwhile, because natural desires are suppressed in favor of the collective mentality, the individual becomes conflicted, which leads to neurosis. Commenting on the denizens of this futuristic nightmare, Miriam M. Chirico notes, "Their desires and behavior are suffused with the grotesque and this futuristic setting warns the audience that human nature will progressively become more greedy and self-centered the more fads and media attention preclude human relationships."[5] Henley poses the question of whether individuals can find dignity and meaning—their signature—in an absurd universe. With regard to her underlying thesis of the play, Henley stated, "It's really about what is your signature, what do you leave in life, what's important that you've done or haven't done—or is anything important?"[6] Can the existential despair caused by the modern neurosis be negated? Can we assume a sense of individual dignity, or signature, in a world in which the modern neurosis leads to impaired social contacts and an inability to work or love? Can work, family, or love be salvaged in this type of malaise, or are we destined to succumb to the death instinct? Henley acknowledged that she chose the most appropriate milieu to examine these philosophical issues: "And L.A. seemed the perfect town where people are looking to leave a signature."[7]

Signature is unique in Henley's canon, for this is the first time in the plays where the focus is not on female protagonists, which obviously makes it difficult to ascribe any feminist interpretation to the play. The focus of the drama centers around a contrast in the lives of Boswell and Maxwell — two brothers, ironically named Boz and Max who obviously are not doing "well." Maxwell loses his wife L-Tip to the lure of celebrity status and thus chooses suicide, the Freudian death instinct. Boswell suffers from unrequited love for William Smit,[8] but instead of finding a suitable relationship in his own household where William is living, he chooses art to assuage the neurotic condition. Ironically, Boswell seeks advice from Reader, a graphologist whose own condition can best be described as mental illness.

Maxwell T-Thorp, Boswell's younger brother, is a poet and Tank Bureau worker in his thirties living with his brother in the Eighth Box on Garbage Bag Row. Although living in what amounts to be this pitifully decaying metropolis, Maxwell seemed content when he was married to L-Tip, a woman he truly loved ever since they were childhood sweethearts. Maxwell becomes uncontrollably depressed when L-Tip divorces him for the fast-paced world of fame and fortune, which Maxwell cannot provide. Maxwell is like so many of Henley's protagonists who become neurotic and suicidal when they feel abandoned and unworthy of love. L-Tip, speaking of herself in third person, rationalizes her decision to divorce her husband: "You always pogoed around. You forgot her birthday eleven times. You ignored her at parties. You complained about the meals she clicked. You tore the arms off her Chee Chee Kitty" (95). Maxwell admits that he was not the ideal husband, yet he insists that they should try to salvage their marriage. Max believes that love is fundamental to life, so he refuses to allow his shortcomings to interfere with human happiness. He tells L-Tip, "You see, I'm not one of your twenty-first century use and cruisers who disposes of love like it was last meal's fuel frock" (95). L-Tip's resignation to a better life of fame and fortune, rejecting love in the process, is typical of the Freudian notion that modern society is responsible for human misery as the id's desires for gratification are reduced through social norms and values. When L-Tip buys into the Hollywood vernacular that success is equated with celebrity status, she effectively accepts the media-induced notion that creates a unity out of individual human beings; the result is that L-Tip and Maxwell become conflicted or neurotic.

Maxwell becomes overly obsessed with the divorce, believing that he has lost a vital part of his persona. He shares his affliction with Boswell: "Because, you see, I love her so much. Oh, why can't she love me?! What made her stop loving me?!" (59). Henley notes the emphatic tone in Maxwell's voice by punctuating his sentences here with the unusual combination of a question mark and an exclamation point, suggesting that he is passionate about his confusion. Maxwell is so disturbed about the divorce that at first he can only react with hostility, calling his former wife a traitor and hoodlum (61) and urging his brother to fire her as his manager (61). As Freud implied, neurosis leads to impaired social contacts and an inability to work or love, so Maxwell quits his job and commits himself to euthanasia. He puts the blame for his homelessness squarely on the shoulders of L-Tip: "She did it. It's her fault. She divorced me" (70). At a loss about what to do, Maxwell completely loses touch with reality and insults his former wife, calling her a fat pig. Only after she leaves does he realize that he insulted the only person who can assuage his neurotic condition: "Oh, why did I call her a pig? What a mistake. What a misguided blunder! (*He slaps himself in the face.*) What now? What now?" (74).

Maxwell's despair leads him to the euthanasia hotline. Once the media learn that he is committing suicide because of a broken heart, they begin publishing his poems. Max states, "I'm the very first person to be euthed for love. I'll be remembered as the most romantic figure of the twenty-first century. I'll make history. It's part of the marketing" (85). When William urges him to cancel the death wish, Max retorts, "Look, before I was gonna get euthed I had nothing to live for. Now that I'm getting euthed, everything's going my way. Why rock the shuttle?" (85). Maxwell even gets to make an appearance as an icon on Celeb Bites, where he is interviewed by L-Tip the Hip Lip. Ironically, modern society ultimately becomes responsible for Max's fate as he succumbs to celebrity status as the poet euthed for love. Maxwell's quest for dignity in modern society thus becomes a literal death wish as civilization's pressure on the ego and super-ego to conform to social expectations of fame and fortune overwhelms libidinal desires that cannot be met. Maxwell thus opts for suicide, the Freudian death instinct, rationalized by Max to be endemic to the need to find his signature in society. Thus, when L-Tip correctly refers to the suicide as distorted masochistic indulgence, Maxwell rationalizes it as his personal quest for dignity in this absurd universe: "I believe by dying I'm tipping my hat to life and the grand effect it can have on the living" (95).

L-Tip, as a woman who lacks spiritual enlightenment about her own precarious position in the universe, descends from a line of Henley females that includes Katty in *The Wake of Jamey Foster* and Elain in *The Miss Firecracker Contest*, who feel that their only raison d'être is to be loved and admired by others. L-Tip uses her fourteen-year marriage to Maxwell as a stepping stone to better things; for her, love is nothing more than a weapon. Like Katty and Elain, L-Tip feels that she is the center of the universe, and other people are merely objects that exist to glorify her self-esteem. Once L-Tip grasps the idea that she is becoming successful as Boswell's manager (a quantum leap from her former job working at a noodle stand), she dumps Maxwell as if he were yesterday's garbage; in short, she sees love as a commodity. Described as "*a tall, striking woman in her thirties*" (60), L-Tip is young and attractive enough to realize that opportunities await, and Maxwell's acute depression because of the divorce is no longer her problem.

Social acceptance is the norm that immerses L-Tip in ego or selfhood, which leads her away from the id's desire for personal happiness in her relationship with Maxwell. L-Tip seeks the gaze of the Other; she has bought into the hype of media fantasy that glitz and glamour create a sense of dignity and self-worth. In order to be noticed, she adorns herself with ghastly colored flowers and weird antennae poking out of her headdress; at other opportunities, she is scantily clad but stands out in a crowd because of green stripes painted up the back of her legs. We also catch a glimpse of her wearing a trendy dress covered with packages of food and vials of drugs, not only drawing attention to herself, but also encouraging friends to be drawn to her out of a need for sustenance. Even Maxwell acknowledges that his former wife is trendy, for she cries blue tears. L-Tip admits that she lives for celebrity status or stardom: "I ultimately realized, what I really wanted to be doing was all the things the real Chee Chee Kitty was doing on Celeb Bites—wearing outfits made of sugar stars, lapping up the limelight, dancing at Café Who's Who with Count Tidbit" (78). Immersed in her own dream of a fantasy existence, L-Tip models herself on Chee Chee Kitty and passionately collects the fantasy puppet's accessories, including fashion attire and appropriate toiletries.

Sharing Katty's need to be well liked and Elain's narcissistic sense of self-importance, L-Tip also lacks the spiritual enlightenment of the absurd condition; she refuses to recognize that human happiness is not found in the social need for excessive admiration. She uses men as commodities to enhance her career further in the eyes of the public. Her relationship with Boswell is explained by the fact that he is making a comeback after his trendy box theory had fallen out of public favor. She is also going to manage K.Y. Von Ludwig, "the Big Splash of the season" (73). Ludwig and others like him realize that L-Tip is trendy and is therefore admirable. She begins to be known as L-Tip the Hip Lip and even develops her own signature that she believes will live as legend: "Trend is life" (77). Maxwell views her as a prostitute, selling herself to the public gaze: "You are out there hawking yourself like meat wrapped in tin foil down by the fucking bay?" (74). When Boswell fires her as his manager, she shifts the blame to him rather than look inward. Boswell is treated as a commodity, a has-been whose theory of boxdom is long past its prime: "Oh, it had its day. It lived for about as long as a fish can breathe in cement. But it's over, it's zapped, it's glue rot. He's not in step" (77). Instead, L-Tip turns her attention to K.Y. Von Ludwig, who is now "sin" because of his appearance on the cover of countless videozines. L-Tip admits that the love relationship is strictly a means to improve her status as a celebrity star, acknowledging that despite the fact that Ludwig is "conceited and self-sucking," he is the ticket for her social mobility: "Anyway, this time I don't expect my marriage to work out. It's more like a career move. I'll do anything to get out ahead. 'Cause that's what I believe in. I mean, you gotta believe in something, right? Otherwise, what's the point?" (78). After the short-lived marriage to Ludwig inevitably fails, Maxwell meets L-Tip while she is waiting for her tranquilizers after a night of partying at Café Who's Who. L-Tip is confused about why her priorities, her goals in life, have gone awry:

> I've tried my best. I study what to wear. I'm up on trends in music and restaurants, drugs and entertainment. I have all the up-to-date kitchen equipment. I thought if I got hold of all that, then other people wouldn't be mean to me. In fact, maybe I might even have this imperceivable right to be mean to them, just for not knowing or doing the things people who are worthwhile know and do [88–89].

Like Elain, who accepts the idea of living up to a facade of beauty and elegance she has been inculcated with since childhood and with which she has willingly accepted, L-Tip feels that the pressure of the socialization process has made her unhappy, even though she does not have the spiritual awareness to understand why. She laments to Maxwell, "Oh God, I'm so wretched and worthless—so swollen in salted, tormenting misery!" (89). However, L-Tip is not capable of self-introspection, so she continues to use others as objects for her own gratification. After her marriages break down, she opts for a low-maintenance Toss 'Em Toddler, adorable during the formative years yet disposable when she becomes a nuisance three years later. The Toss 'Em Toddler reflects Henley's sarcasm in reference to a world in which humans are used as commodities and "trend is life." L-Tip's attitude toward her child is typical of what is important to her:

> See, I don't have time for a full-term child. I mean, I'm competing in a world where fantasy puppets set the step. They never take time out for children or family, ultra surgery or even rehab. They're completely consumed with constructing careers. The pressure gets to be devastating. Of course, I'm terrifically unhappy. Before I started going to my therochief I

never even suspected how unhappy I was. Now I'm totally aware of my
misery. It's a big improvement [106–107].

When L-Tip sees Maxwell dead at the Euthanasia Gardens, she realizes
that her life has been spent pursuing the goals of others. Her libidinal happiness has been sacrificed by a steadfast adherence to the socializing norms
of civilization. L-Tip breaks down in tears, sighing, "Max. Dear Max. God.
How can I live without him? How can I ever live without him?" (108). Her
unrequited love became lost in society's acculturation process.

In contrast to the pairing of Maxwell and L-Tip is the relationship
between Boswell and his twenty-something-year-old government tenant,
William Smit. William is an unattractive, dim-witted, uneducated splatterer from the CDZ whose job it is to wipe away the tar that has "splat-
tered" urban wildlife. William, decked out in her orange splatter's suit,
helmet, and boots, which she proudly displays ad infinitum, seems to have
found her niche in life. Although Boswell views William's work of picking lethal stickem off of dying plants and animals to be "a mindless job,
unglamorous, unrewarding, unbearably dull and useless" (71), to William
the daily grind represents a sense of commitment to helping the needy.
William has another reason to be goal-oriented: if she can get the Worker
of the Year Award, she will be allowed a quarter cubicle and will thus be
able to start the defrost on her two children, who are currently in the
Frozen Dorm. William appears to be an idealist who expresses a concrete
vision of what her life can become: "I want a home to live in and I want
my kids out of F.D. Then I want us all to learn to read and write and clap
to music" (80). Although William's vision of life is simplistic, it is endearing to Henley, who probably would classify her with the other similar
females in her canon, such as Babe, Pixrose, Popeye, and Macon, whose
lack of education does not stand in the way of their fiery poetic vision and
zest for life.

William's life is conflicted because her sense of compassion is con-
trasted to an indelibly etched vision of her youth when she murdered animals out of a need to demonstrate power and authority over them. Since
then, however, she has been able to devote her life's work to caring for
blighted animals, sometimes even caressing them, as well as delivering her
children from the deep freeze. Living with an art philosopher, who, at
twenty years her senior, represents a sort of educated professional that she
could never be, William develops a fondness for Boswell. However, the
relationship is based on unrequited love that further exacerbates her
conflicted persona, for Boswell insults and demeans William as nothing
more than an uneducated, nonskilled worker — a splatterer, nomenclature

that, even by today's standards, sounds crude and offensive. William is forced to turn inward, hugging herself when Boswell, even sitting next to her, virtually ignores her (66, 72). Boswell is incapable of understanding that his own roommate is the only person who cares about his imminent death due to his terminal illness. Although her attitude toward life is simplistic and idealistic amidst the despair that she suffers, William is forever sanguine about maintaining her dignity in a naive sort of way:

> They say the sun is orange. My suit is orange. My favorite food is an orange. I give myself an orange every Holiday Day. Maybe that sounds strange to you, someone giving their own selves a present. But I believe on occasions it's worthwhile to do nice things for one's self. For instance, I always try and keep my shoes nice and buffed. That way I know I always got something shiny to look at as I'm walking down strange roads that may not be going my way [86].

Whereas Boswell is dying slowly, his uneducated ward has a burning vision of living. Henley thus has a particular passion for William, admitting, "Still, I think as a person, she has a clearer sense of self than many of the characters I write."[9]

Whereas L-Tip divorced her true love Maxwell in order to seek a more exciting life of glitz and glamour, Boswell T-Thorp spends his life on a quest for meaning in an absurd universe, virtually ignoring William, the one person who cares about him. Although Maxwell's suicide is a means of surrendering to what Freud referred to as the death instinct, in contrast, Boswell emulates Sisyphus in his refusal to succumb to the absurd condition; Henley admires him for his perseverance in struggling with his art and in seeking to find love, both of which she sees as worthy battles. Henley has compassion for Boswell, and when asked by Cynthia Wimmer-Moul which of her characters she most admires, she singled out Popeye and Boswell, thus further deflating any notion that her fundamental concerns are feminist.[10]

Boswell is an over-the-hill art philosopher still committed to Boxdom, the now vastly outdated fad that he created years ago. Boswell explains the Box Theory to L-Tip: "The whole thesis is that one may put a box around anything: a circle, a rectangle, a triangle, a moving spill! If only the box is big enough, everything will fit. It's all so—so freeing!" (62). Boswell is deeply passionate about Boxdom, adorning himself with square boxes on his chest and forehead while wearing box apparel, including box ties, shoes, wigs, shirts, and belts. The Box Theory enabled Boswell to have his Andy Warhollike moment of fame, as he was formerly awarded the Grand Poster Prize when Boxdom became a phenomenon; he was even emblazoned on buttons. Boswell was treated as a highly sought-after celebrity invited to all sorts of appointments and dinners, making posters of himself, doing ads for box perfume, and selling souvenir boxes. Boswell refuses to see himself as outdated, the inventor of a fad that has long gone out of fashion. He criticizes the competition in the form of K.Y. Von Ludwig, the up and coming celebrity whose octagons and zigzags are now the current trendy fashion. Moreover, he is insulted when L-Tip invites him as a guest on "The Whatever Happened To Show"—and even then only, along with "vulture hairdos," as an alternate if the other celebrities fail to appear. Boswell is appalled at the suggestion that someone of his stature should lower himself to appear as a has-been: "This is an insult. Why, I'm not some out-fad Fantasy Puppet. I'm an art philosopher" (63). Instead, Boswell is thinking more in terms of a salute to Boxdom along the lines of a Grand Memorial Dinner in which trendy L-Tip the Hip Lip hosts V.I.P. guests who will pay an exorbitant fee to renew Boxdom before Boswell's death.

Boswell's refusal to recognize a lasting relationship with William in favor of his adamant insistence on the relevance of Boxdom is an example of how social constrictions overwhelm our libidinal desires for happiness. Boswell's obsession with the Warhollike fifteen minutes of fame has made him conflicted, or essentially, neurotic. As Freud mentioned, art cannot assuage the neurotic condition—it is merely a temporary diversion. Boswell is simply on the wrong track, figuratively boxed in by his own art, which has become his raison d'être. Henley explained Boswell's state of mind to Alexis Greene:

> Boxdom means a reduced way of thinking, in which you can put a box around anything. If you make a box big enough, it will fit around anything. If you make this truism big enough, it's a fear of the unknown, a fear of the mysterious and the spontaneous— it is what Boswell has. That's what this philosophy connotes.[11]

Boswell gets too caught up in his work and thus forgets how to live. Through his fear of professional failure, Boswell ignores potential love at his own doorstep and spontaneity, in the form of C-Boy, who is living with him as well.

Despite Boswell's shortcomings, Henley seems to admire him because he engages in an overwhelmingly difficult quest for dignity in an absurd universe, rather than taking the easy way out, succumbing to suicide as did his brother. Boswell has some unidentified terminal illness that will probably claim his life in less than one year. His problem is that he must learn to "think outside the box" if he is to imprint a lasting signature, his legacy, onto society. Boswell fears dying without being loved or remembered, admitting to William his innermost fears:

> Oblivion. I'll be in oblivion, where I'm sure I'll be perfectly dead and won't be plagued with any cares or woes. It's now, however, that's concerning me. It's now that's the problem. This time now when I'm alive and living with the burden of a mind, an imagination, and a trembling heart. Now, when I can lie awake nights picturing eons and eons of vast, dark deadness; where I'll be eternally alone, lost in nothingness without a book or a magazine or a smile from some stranger's child [72].

As Boswell's disease gets worse, graphically depicted by the gray sores daubing his body, his neurosis concomitantly increases, suggesting the interdependence of the mental and physical. Boswell's intense need to find his signature before he dies, an urge that is essentially socially driven by civilization's impetus to create a collective unity, produces neurosis as he becomes conflicted between his libidinal desires for happiness and socially accepted avenues of success. The art philosopher finds it increasingly difficult to work or love because his neurosis leads to further impaired social contact. Boswell brushes off a visit from one of his daughters who heard about his terminal illness in the Up and Coming Obits. He dismisses her as "One of my swarmy brats" (75), who interrupted him from perusing his memorabilia and glorifying in the fact that someone who admired his box theory years ago asked for his autograph — his signature. Boswell does not realize that his daughter, whom he rejects, is also part of his signature, his legacy. He becomes adept at insulting those that care for him, especially William, whom he tells to lower her face guard because he "can no longer tolerate the sight of [her] face" (75). Boswell even gives poor advice to his brother about love: "What do you think love is? Why, it's nothing more than an archaic form of egotism. A tawdry reflection of all the holes in your own shredded soul. Be a human being. Forget about love" (60). As Boswell waxes philosophic, we realize that the art philosopher has lost his perspective on life and is in no position to give advice to others.

After Boswell fires his manager L-Tip, he has no one to love or provide advice for him. Wandering in solace at the beach, he stumbles on Reader, a graphologist for hire. Reader seems to perceive Boswell's depressed, neurotic condition and claims that she can tell his future through his signature. After writing two sentences for her, Reader tells Boswell, "You're shallow, self-absorbed, antisocial, conceited, cruel, and cowardly. You let a minute early success paralyze you into doing, holding, and believing nothing. You're going to die unloved and unremembered" (82). Boswell, who desperately wants to leave his signature in life, now becomes obsessed with the idea that if he can change his life and be a different person, he can change his signature as well.

Reader is obviously a scam artist whom Boswell initially refers to upon first sight as a "filthy arrangement of molecules" (81). In an interview with Alexis Greene, Henley discussed her vision of this fortune teller/artist: "The Reader is a mysterious character. She's hard to pin down, because she is a lunatic and a poet. And a criminal. All of those things that make people creative, that they struggle with."[12] As Reader gets more comfortable with Boswell, she begins to develop an infatuation for him. In an interview that I conducted with her, Henley discussed the reasons for Reader's attraction to Boswell: "I think money is the reason. It's not without avarice. And also a sense of control, the power and enchantment of being able to control someone's moods. She actually does become physically attractive to him, so they have a sexual connection as well."[13] Reader even tries to eliminate her competition, discrediting William as "an unattractive, uneducated, dimwitted splatterer from the CTZ with frozen children" that are not even Boswell's offspring (100). In other words, Boswell has befriended not only a charlatan for worldly advice on how to live his life, but also a self-centered person as well.

The need to establish one's signature in life is not innate, and, as such, animals could care less about it, but is instead a social norm inspired by civilizations. In short, Boswell ignores his libidinal desires in favor of serving ego and superego. His quest for dignity in modern society is pathetic because it is guided by the will of a collective unity, but Henley certainly has compassion for misguided souls such as Boswell. Boswell, exhausted by Reader's charge that he must learn all he can about the universe before he dies, is frantically clicking images of objects onto the TVP screen, which he uses as a learning tool. Maxwell describes the neurosis as a mental aberration: "I'm afraid he's gone completely mad" (85). Also told that he must reach out to humanity, Boswell adopts C-Boy as his ward. In a subsequent visit to his mentor, Boswell is told by Reader to study the pickle, write its name ten thousand times, and become one with its spirit. Now walking with a cane and obviously getting closer to becoming disabled, Boswell decides to replace Boxdom, which he begins to equate with "puerile dribble" (90), with a poster of a pickle — a masterpiece that he can leave behind as his legacy.

Reader, unimpressed with the idea of a poster of the pickle, asks Boswell to write the name of his beloved one hundred times. Boswell, who admitted that he is socially inept (59) and has no beloved, now realizes that Reader's advice must be sound, for one's social life must be balanced with one's fully recognized creative spirit. On the spur of the moment, Boswell proposes marriage to William, arguing for a wedding because she could be wealthy when his poster is a success, she is already living with him, super safe sex kits make the relationship less risky, and finally, even if the marriage is a failure, he will soon be dead anyway. The relationship might be ideal, certainly the means to resolve a situation based upon unrequited love, except for the fact that Boswell asks William to marry him, not out of the innate libidinal desire for love, but instead because he believes that Reader's advice to seek a beloved is the legitimate way to establish a legacy under the constraints and guidelines of social norms and values. As his sores change from gray to red, Boswell becomes more desperate, realizing that time is fading. When he seeks further advice from Reader, she tells him, out of personal jealousy, that William is not right for him. Boswell, now totally confused, abandons C-Boy, evicts William from his apartment, and explains that he has no intention of marrying her, for he wants to devote all of his attention to the pickle.

Boswell, standing with two canes, covered with sores that have turned black, and having lost most of his hair to this strange malady, appears on Celeb Bites to unveil his poster of the pickle — the last opportunity to present his legacy before his death. Unfortunately, the public rejects his chez d'oeuvre by throwing fruit cores, chairs, and mudballs at the poster. Boswell is despondent that his vision of the value of art is not universally accepted: "I wanted the people, I wanted them to understand my pickles. Their thoughts, their feelings, their predicament. What it was like for them inside that jar. Oh, why can't they see what I see?" (104).

The full irony of Boswell's misguided quest for dignity in an absurd universe occurs in the last scene of the play, which takes place in the Euthanasia Gardens. Boswell receives first-hand knowledge of what death is like when he sees his brother's body laid out for display. Maxwell's body is capsulized so that he remains a tiny shell of his former self. Boswell hardly recognizes Reader in the Euthanasia Gardens, for she has changed her appearance. She has also received brain fiber treatments for her mental illness; her profession was nothing but a sham. She admits to Boswell, "I was malignantly insane. I thought I could read people's lives through their handwriting. I'd take people's K. and spin deluded tales. I made one pathetic man write the word pickle ten thousand times. But I'm much better now" (108). Upon hearing this, Boswell becomes unraveled. As his fortune now takes a turn for the worse, he learns that William's life is on the upswing: she has received the Worker of the Year Award, has taken in C-Boy as her new ward, has her children in final thaw, and is about to embark on a vacation, hoping to be far removed from Boswell, never to see him again. Boswell, now face to face with death — what his brother so willingly resigned himself to— and having understood that the only true value was happiness in the deeply rooted affection he had for William, realizes that his futile quest for dignity, his chance to create an eternal signature in society, will end the same way that it did for his brother. The play concludes with Boswell's deep lamentation of unrequited love: "William! My beloved! William!" (108).

Signature demonstrates the Freudian notion that the modern neurosis leads to impaired social development, including an inability to work or love. Reader, whose generic name suggests the anono-mass of modern civilization, similar to the typed characters in expressionist dramas written first by Strindberg and then later by German and American playwrights from approximately 1913 to 1925, represents for Boswell the sanity of socially ascribed norms and values. In short, Boswell looks to her to learn how to leave his mark — his signature — on society. The irony is that she is mentally ill; in effect, this person who gives advice, the spokesperson acting as an icon for socially ascribed behavior, does nothing more than create misery in Boswell's life.

To reinforce the relationship between social constraints and libidinal desires in the play, we can compare the characters of Reader and C-Boy K-Trill. Although Reader is much older and more jaded by society than is C-Boy, perhaps even in her fifties, C-Boy, at age eleven, is still in his formative years. Reader, in the business of taking people's money for dispensing tales about how they should live their lives, is corrupted by artificial values; C-Boy is not tainted by social mores or institutional norms, even though he is a government ward. Reader has ulterior motives for helping Boswell; C-Boy has not yet learned what ulterior motives represent. When Reader speaks, she mouths inanities about pickles or about how to succeed in life; C-Boy, on the other hand, is mute. Reader is uptight and criminal, reacting viciously, for example, when she learns of William, her rival for Boswell's affections; C-Boy is natural in everything he does, especially when it involves being in tune with his body, such as dancing or communicating by gesture. Henley describes Reader as a malevolent manipulator who *"twists like a viper"* trying to maneuver her clients as prey (87), whereas C-Boy, *"the utter perfectionist," "capable of all sorts of fantastic feats,"* is the personification of flexibility of mind and body who *"twists and turns like rubber"* (92). Henley explained to me, "I envisioned C-Boy as extremely intelligent, soulful, and very gifted, kind of like a genius artist-dancer."[14] Obviously, the irony of the play is that Boswell ignores C-Boy, who becomes a kind of alter ego for him, as a useless commodity, eventually throwing him out of the house into homelessness, but pays attention to the mentally deranged Reader as his mentor and spiritual leader. In effect, *Signature* demonstrates how modern society, which diminishes our libidinal desires for human happiness, produces misery. Boswell, himself neurotic, seeks advice from what he believes to be an icon of social consciousness, who turns out to be the epitome of human wretchedness—i.e., mentally ill. Henley, however, understands that the modern *angoisse* is universal and thus admires the hapless, and often confused and misguided, Boswell for his Sisyphuslike determination to fight against the existential despair, unlike his brother who succumbs to it.

In all of Henley's canon, *Control Freaks* perhaps best represents the Freudian notion of how an untamed id, reflected by the innate urge toward sex and aggression, is in contrast to the norms and values of the external world, channeled through society's roles and institutions. The libidinal urges of Betty Willard, Carl Willard, and Paul Casper conflict with their desire to mesh with the goal of civilization: to create a unity out of mankind. The triptych of Betty, Carl, and Paul demonstrates that humans are, as Freud suggested, violent and impersonal rather than loving or caring; as such, this death instinct opposes the socialization process of modern society, thus creating existential madness, or, as Camus phrased it, the absurd condition. The title of the play suggests the dichotomy of id (freaks— or individuals out of control in society) and ego/superego (control in the form of ethical and moral judgments society asks us to ascribe to). In short, "control freaks" is the ideal title for the dilemma of the modern neurosis, as Henley strips the illusions behind the masks. Moreover, Los Angeles becomes the perfect milieu for the absurd condition, a microcosm in which the id's selfishness rules in order to mesh with socially channeled dreams and aspirations; Henley noted, "In Los Angeles, everybody's out for themselves. But everybody's trying, everybody's got these *dreams*, some of them pathetic and unreachable — but at least they do have hopes and aspirations."[15] Sister's plight is markedly different from the neurotic condition of the other characters in the play, for Sister suffers from the guilt of incest with her older brother; whereas Carl, Paul, and Betty are guiltless, civilization places a heavy taboo on incest, exacerbating Sister's neurotic condition to the point of multiple personalities, an affliction associated with schizophrenia.

Writing about the Met Theatre's 1993 production of the play, Barbara Isenberg astutely remarked, "Everyone in *Control Freaks* lies to everyone else, and the play is awash in brutality, deceit and desperation."[16] Betty Willard and her husband Carl are brutes akin to animals, personified by the instinctive impulses of sex, violence, and aggression. Betty, who teaches cold reading classes, met her husband when he came in for acting lessons;

the two of them put their acting skills to good use as they wear the mask in order to act according to civilized sanctions but are actually vicious, ruthless, and deceitful beneath their artificial veneer.

Betty is a social misfit. She was evicted from her apartment on Christmas no less, apparently her landlord refusing to impart the good will of Noël toward someone with brute instincts no better than an animal. On the spur of the moment (Betty lacks the logic or bon sens to think about the repercussions of her plans), she married Carl in the Elvis Presley Chapel in Las Vegas. Although Betty and Carl have imposed on Sister by moving in temporarily with her, they have plans to throw her out of her own house, a brutal response to decency and a slap in the face to hospitality codes. Betty even considers killing Carl when Paul makes her a lucrative offer to murder Sister and take her fortune, nonchalantly admitting about her sister-in-law, "I wouldn't mind seeing her dead."[17] Betty seems to comfort her husband by serving him milkshakes, massaging his shoulders, and catering to his every whim; however, underneath the mask of graciousness is cold brutality. Out of sheer ruthlessness, she lies to Carl, telling him that Paul asked her to perform oral sex on him, when in reality, Betty initiated the offer. This act of deceit is for the sole purpose of ego gratification, as Carl vows to defend his wife's honor by killing the alleged sex offender. Betty, low-life creature of atavistic pleasures that she is, proudly assets to her husband that Paul's penis was not the worst that she ever swallowed. Betty is the one who helps Paul concoct the outrageous plot to have Sister, conveniently unmarried and looking for love, marry Paul and then bilk her of her inheritance. She even complies with her husband's scheme to poison Paul, going one step further by poisoning her spouse and Sister at the same time. As Paul, Betty, Sister, and Carl share the poisoned wine, Betty becomes fully immersed in her violent and ruthless machinations by giving her poisoned concoction to Sister's cats—another blow to the sister-in-law Betty despises.

Betty's natural aggressiveness coincides with her sexual appetites, making her an icon for instinctual needs and drives. Miriam M. Chirico has commented on the sadistic and masochistic sexual drives that permeate the relationships among Betty, Carl, and Paul: "Each character in this play strives to control another without losing control over him or herself, and the form of control is usually sexual: wiping one's vaginal fluids on the face of an ex-lover to seduce him or compelling someone to lick a vibrator to save his life."[18] Paul describes Betty as a sex monger, an animal without regard for the human sense of compassion: "...you were a whore and burnt apartment buildings for money and drowned your son in a bucket" (130). Although the latter part of Paul's statement may merely be hyperbolic and certainly cannot be corroborated by anything in the play, Betty does admit that in order to avoid ejection from her apartment, she prostituted herself like some sort of tramp in an effort to raise the rent money: "I jerked two guys off in the parking lot. Neither of them paid me" (130). When her apartment was padlocked, she moved in with Carl, using her sex to lead him to believe that their relationship was grounded in love when, in reality, it was nothing more than lust catered to her advantage. However, like an animal in heat, Betty is not satisfied with one sex partner and thus cheats on her husband at virtually every opportunity. When first alone with Paul, at least ten years her junior, Betty offers to perform fellatio on him. Upon Paul's exit after his first visit to the Willard household, he begs Betty for a taste of her raw sexual animality. The stage directions indicate, "*Betty sticks her hand up between her legs. She gasps, then holds her wet fingers out to Paul*" (131). Paul's next visit is marked with a violent romp in the bushes with Betty once Carl is out of sight. In short, Betty's only idea of sex is through lust in an animalistic way that pits one lover against another so she can gain an advantage in the pecking order.

Carl, the second part of this triptych that gravitates toward the death instinct, is hypocritical, cunning, and savage. He tells Sister, "There's no one I can love any more than you" (121) while plotting her death. When hearing the news that his wife performed fellatio on Paul, Carl resorts to his animal instincts, which, for him personify a sense of "dignity": "We are thinking wrong here and now I have to commit murder. Otherwise, I have no dignity. No human dignity. No right to walk upright. I'd have to regress to all fours" (123). Moreover, this animalistic machismo is the way to flatter his wife so that she will fix him his milkshake, his only palliate in an otherwise violent world. That violence is visibly demonstrated in several ways: in his fisticuffs with Paul, which has to be broken up by the two women (136); in his torture of Paul, forcing him to crawl on his knees to beg for the antidote to the poison (143); and in his cavalier attitude toward murder, eliminating the competition when necessary, especially with regard to Paul and even his own sister: "Sister better watch her step if she knows what's good for her. If she doesn't straighten up and fly right, she could be next. (*Taking a can of poison from the sack.*) I got plenty of pest control. For anyone who gets pesty" (131). His excuse for buying poison to murder his own sister after she signs release papers is ostensibly to eliminate the neighborhood dog, whom Carl blames for defecating in the bushes. In one of the most overt displays of raw animality in Henley's theater, Carl is seen defecating on his own lawn and then has the gall to blame the neighbor's dog for the infraction. Obviously, Carl's gross animality is not the way to keep a wife, which attests to the fact that his last three marriages have ended in divorce or desertion. However, the natural aggressiveness and malevolence of humanity is best depicted in the way Carl has treated his own sister. In his sister's youth, Carl sodomized and raped her, also admitting that his sister implausibly had oral sex with him numerous times without her conscious knowledge when she was drowsy from sleep. Sister frantically realizes that she has been touched by evil, but Carl dismisses the trauma, implying that he was merely trying to show her the ropes (145). Carl's statement to Sister, "There's no one I can love any more than you" (121), thus can be taken by his sibling to be an ironic display of Freud's notion that the death instinct can overwhelm Eros.

Paul Casper, the owner of the building that the Willards eye for their Furniture World venture, would be ideal as a silent partner because he fits perfectly into the Willards' world of ruthless violence and wanton sex. Paul's broken nose most likely attests to the violent world to which he belongs, and his silver necklace and dagger earring typify his penchant for daring behavior. Betty assesses Paul's personality type for Carl: "That guy's bad news. He's got problems. Severe problems" (122). During Paul's first appearance on stage, he reveals that he is selling Carl a building that is about to be exploded, making Carl look like a sucker, and then, to create a further rift between Betty and her husband, he states, "You're nothing but an ornament to Carl. He only wants the deodorized airbrushed version of you. I want all of you. Every sweet dirty part" (129). Paul's wily sexual innuendoes to Betty soon have her believing that she never should have married Carl. Paul's primitive, instinctual sexual and violent drives are oblivious to the norms and values of society's institutions, for he seduces Betty at every opportunity, in her home no less, regardless of the fact that she is married and the sexual orgies take place while Carl is on the premises. Once Paul hears about the deal that allows Sister to co-sign for the building, using her fortune as collateral, his violent instincts reign, and he suggests marrying Sister, a woman he has never laid eyes on, then killing her for the money. Paul then ruthlessly manipulates the innocent Sister into a love relationship strictly for his own advantage and certainly without regard for Sister's fragile emotional state. When Paul's best laid plans go awry as Carl poisons him, Paul's aptly violent response is to shoot Betty, whom he suspects is the double crosser. Finally, Paul, forced to confess that he has used Sister for his own selfish purposes, cannot even exit gracefully but instead resorts to vicious callousness meant to hurt Sister — the only type of comment a person of his caliber could offer: "I don't love you. You're pathetic. I just wanted your money. I was using you the whole time. You're nothing to me. Nothing to me but unfinished toast" (143).

On the surface, characters such as Carl, Betty, and Paul whose ids, reflected in sex and violence, seem to overwhelm any attempt at social-ization, are reduced to pure evil. Henley thus had reservations about such vicious and perhaps unredeemable personae, who appeared to be atypi-cal in her canon. Henley stated, "I didn't like those characters very much at first, [and] I really had to trust myself. They were scaring me."[19] In her interview with Cynthia Wimmer-Moul, Henley reiterated this same notion: "Also, writing about these evil people was challenging because they weren't people I loved. In all my other plays, even though people behave very badly, I love them. I didn't love these people, but they were real; so that was interesting."[20] However, beneath the surface, we discover that these ostensibly vicious characters are very much aware of the conscious socialization process affecting the ego and superego. Betty and Carl aspire to commercial success in modern society; their goal is to turn Furniture World into a decent living for both of them. The Willards actually seek to be integrated into community norms and values. Betty even has dreams of capping off her marriage with what appears to be a typical bourgeois honeymoon if their capitalistic venture is successful. Carl, meanwhile, attempts to play the role of the successful capitalist, albeit dressing in a suit that he does not realize is cheap and carrying a plastic briefcase that he probably believes makes him at least appear to be professional. Fur-thermore, despite Carl's predilection for defying the norms of society by defecating in the bushes, he obviously is concerned with maintaining a proper business image, indicated by his meticulous attention to his toupee. Even Paul must have some business acumen, for his highly sought-after building precipitates much of the violence in the play. Henley comments on the characters' vital need to conform to societal expectations:

> The play definitely says something about women's and men's roles in the world. About constantly trying to fill them and not being able to. Carl try-ing to be the man who comes in with the tie and has his breakfast and goes off with the briefcase. Betty, Carl's wife, trying to be the little woman with the apron [,] running around making breakfast and going shopping and having pretty underwear. The grotesquerie of trying to fill those roles.[21]

In short, the neuroticism of these characters is apparent because of the conflict between their overt libidinal desires and the socializing norms of civilization. We should recall Henley's previously cited comment about how, on the one hand, selfishness appears endemic to life in Los Angeles—obviously, a libidinal desire for happiness—while, concomitantly, social aspirations motivate individual behavior just as powerfully. Henley, at first hesitant about showing compassion for what she considered to be evil characters that she created, ultimately understood that *Control Freaks*, as the title indicates, does indeed present balanced personae. Henley eventually must have realized that these characters were nothing more than extreme versions of her typical neurotics, and in a very incisive statement, acknowledged, "But now I really *love* them. So much. Because this play really embraced a darkness and truth about the terror of life."[22]

Although we are tangentially aware of the neuroses of Betty, Carl, and Paul, the neurotic condition of Henley's protagonist, Sister, is the focal point of the play.[23] Henley told Mary Dellasega, "It's a play about incest, basically. That's one of the themes that is the darker side of the human spirit and passions. In that sense I think it's kind of the path I was on."[24] Dr. Susan Forward, who has treated more than fifteen hundred victims of childhood sexual abuse, notes that incest is a particularly devastating emotional and psychological traumatic experience because of the cultural taboo associated with the violating act, as well as the fact that the child is thrust into an adult role before he or she is prepared for it; even worse, the child loses trust, having been betrayed by a family member who is supposed to be a nurturer.[25] After years of counseling victims of incest, Laura Davis concluded, "Adult survivors believe the abuse was their fault, that they're not worth much, and that somehow they're different than other people."[26] Sam Kirschner, Diana Adile Kirschner, and Richard L. Rappaport, psychologists who have done extensive research on the post-traumatic effects of incest, concur with Davis in her assessment that incest victims share in the belief that they are unlovable: "The most pervasive difficulties with which survivors struggle are issues in self-esteem and self-concept."[27] Kirschner, Kirschner, and Rappaport also found that victims in which the incest involved the combination of older brother and younger sister were less likely to get married.[28] This fundamental guilt shared by incest victims results in their feeling of being unloved and lacking self-respect; Forward and Buck attribute the source of this guilt to the adult believing that she has been somehow robbed of her childhood by the violator while simultaneously understanding that nothing can compensate for the loss.[29]

Davis notes that the extreme childhood trauma of incest often causes the abused victim to develop multiple personalities.[30] When the former victim cannot endure the pain and guilt of the trauma, she may form a new personality as a means of coping. This dissociation process has been previously documented in films and books such as *Sybil*, *The Three Faces of Eve*, and *When Rabbit Howls*. Kirschner, Kirschner, and Rappaport write that multiple personality disorders in incest victims often take the form of "psychological splitting" in which the survivor develops two distinct aspects of self-representation: a "good me" and a "bad me."[31] The official diagnosis of this neurotic condition is schizophrenia, which occurs in various forms, but may still be reduced to certain generic characteristics. *The Diagnostic and Statistical Manual of Mental Disorders* describes schizophrenia as an affliction that is not due to a general medical condition or to a direct physiological effect of a substance but is instead a cognitive or emotional dysfunction characterized by delusions or hallucinations.[32] The most common form of hallucination among schizophrenics is experienced as auditory voices, such as two or more personae conversing with one another.[33] Schizophrenics share a sense of dysfunction with regard to work, education, or self-esteem; most are socially impaired and have relatively limited social contacts. The majority of schizophrenics (60–70%) thus never marry.[34] Interestingly enough, a 1989 study found that 85% of patients diagnosed with schizophrenia (multiple personality disorder) had a history of sexual abuse.[35]

Although Sister's multiple personality disorder is fully manifested only when she is alone, Betty intuitively seems to recognize that Sister shares some form of mental illness. In conversation with Carl, Betty acknowledges that his sister is "weird" (137), "some sorta kook" (119) and laments to Paul that Carl's mother left her inheritance to Carl's "screwed-up sister" (130). Sister's neuroticism is essentially derived from the guilt she has built up over the years from her rape that she only suspects her brother committed. Incest becomes a violation not only of Sister's body and spirit, but also of civilized society's cultural values and mores. Sister's natural and libidinal desires for sex have been tainted by an act that is heinous enough to violate the purpose of civilization, which is to create a unity of mankind; victims of incest, seen as participating in an act of taboo, instead begin to view themselves as nonparticipants in society. This dichotomy between Sister's libidinal desire for happiness and the cultural norms of society has produced her *angoisse*, which takes the form of schizophrenia.

As if Carl had not done enough damage by raping and sodomizing his sister when she was an adolescent, he exacerbates Sister's guilt by demeaning her at virtually every opportunity. When Sister boasts to Carl and Betty that she is capable of attracting a man and getting dolled up when she puts on makeup, Carl's encouragement to her is to suggest that she clean up the dog mess, which he created, in the yard. When Paul shows an interest in marrying Sister, Carl, never one to be discreet with his comments, blurts out within earshot of his sibling, "Someone's finally taking my little sister off my hands. After all these years, she's finally found a man. Me and Mother never thought it was possible" (136). Carl, of course, always seems to find ways to insult Sister, as when he tells his wife that Sister's grief over charring the gingerbread men must be based on "the

PMS disease" (138). When Sister complains about Betty not fitting into the household, Carl snaps at his sibling, again turning the conversation personal: "Jealous 'cause you can't get a man. You can't get a man" (127). During this particular episode, Sister is in the garden, pulling up carrots. She reacts violently to Carl's insult: "You wanna fuck her? Stick these carrots up every place in her; make her scream like a pig? Fine! (*She breaks carrots in two and throws them at him.*)" (127). While tossing the carrots at Carl, she calls him a "rotten fucking failure!!" (127). This episode has phallic overtones, with Sister subliminally trying to castrate the one who violated her. However, the episode ultimately only serves to reinforce the guilt from the incest, because when Carl picks up a carrot and jams it in Sister's mouth, the symbolic rape subliminally suggests to Sister that the incest also included fellatio.[36]

Sister is a prime example of how pent-up guilt and hostility causes the neurosis of schizophrenia. She has literally adorned herself with a tattoo of a face without eyes surrounded by a cracked heart — an eternal reminder of her own misery. Her body suffers the effects of the guilt as well, for Sister is described as *"nearly bald with horrible little bloody tufts sticking out all over her head"* (124), the blight being masked by an assortment of wigs. Sister has lost trust in her brother ever since her childhood betrayal, and his constant and continuous demeaning behavior remind her daily that she is a social misfit, unable to establish a relationship with a man. Sister, believing that she is unlovable and thus attempting to redeem herself in the eyes of her family, her most immediate social unit, therefore jumps at the opportunity to marry Paul, sight unseen. Her attitude is truly naive, intimating that being loved might assuage the neurosis: "Then we could have another wedding. We'd all be one big happy family. Running Furniture World, celebrating birthdays, borrowing cups of sugar, lending each other lawn mowers. It could be a very excellent setup. I'm gonna set my cap for him" (118–119). Sister acknowledges to Betty that this insatiable desire to be loved, to redeem her sense of lost self-esteem experienced by most incest victims, is why she has always acquiesced to any hint of male sexual advances (132), albeit unsuccessfully establishing a relationship with anyone. The perfect example of how Carl's presence serves to reinforce Sister's latent pent-up guilt occurs near the end of the play; Sister, after recently seeing Paul lustily embrace Betty and thus reduce her idyllic dreams of possible marriage, is reassured by Paul that he is indeed in love with her. Paul seems to have provided some of the psychotherapy that Sister needs, and she is temporarily healed: "Innocence is proclaimed! The verdict is not guilty! And someone could love me after all" (142). However, Carl intervenes, almost as if he were the voice of Sister's hidden past, reinforcing the subliminal notion that Sister is somehow going to be interminably unloved: "He doesn't love you. He's nothing more than an opportunist. He's just using you to get your money. Your inheritance" (142). This becomes the breaking point for Sister, whose years of pent-up hostility and guilt now result in her threatening Carl with a huge butcher knife.

Like most schizophrenics, Sister experiences hallucinations in the form of auditory voices through multiple personae. When Sister is alone, she splits into three personalities that include Sister, Spaghetti, and Pinkie. Spaghetti and Pinkie know each other; Spaghetti also knows about Sister but Pinkie does not, while Sister has no knowledge of either Pinkie or Spaghetti.[37] Spaghetti is the more vicious voice, abrasive at times, cynical, sexual, and wry. She challenges the conventions of teatime and the beauty of birds singing in the morning, admitting that she sometimes resembles the voice of evil (128). At odds with Pinkie, Spaghetti even goes so far as to slap her alter ego. Pinkie, on the other hand, is whimsical, sanguine, innocent, and flighty; she spends her time partially trying to reign in Spaghetti's rebellion and rage.

The denouement of *Control Freaks* is atypical of any of the plays in Henley' s canon. Typically, Henley's theater demonstrates that the eternal struggle against the modern *angoisse* cannot be overcome, yet her protagonists continue to try and maintain their dignity in an absurd universe. Her protagonists generally wind up enjoying brief interludes, usually of laughter and love, that temporarily break the cycle of despair. However, at the end of *Control Freaks*, Sister kills Carl, stabbing him over and over and demeaning him further as he falls into his own fecal matter (suggesting that the onus is on Carl, and certainly not on the neighborhood dog). In a gesture of liberation, Sister takes off her dress and shoes, and, in the guise of her new wardrobe, flies out into the audience. Pinkie now learns about Sister, and, in turn, Sister finds out about Pinkie and Spaghetti. This partially suggests that Sister is on the road to empowerment because her knowledge of the other two personae is at least a start in recognizing the neurosis. However, only naivete would lead us to conclude that Sister's deeply rooted neurosis in the form of schizophrenia can be resolved so abruptly. Henley admitted to me that she views this redemption as the first step in Sister's healing.[38] We can perhaps admit that she enjoys temporary relief from the modern *angoisse*, but there is no guarantee that the murder that she just committed will not increase her guilt over this act of aggression, and guilt, as Freud stated, is the purpose of the unifying effect of civilization.

8

Revelers, L-Play, and *Impossible Marriage*

Revelers occurs in northern Wisconsin, along the shore of Lake Michigan, once again discounting any notion that Henley is merely a regional playwright. Henley takes the familiar family crisis—the starting point of *Crimes of the Heart, The Wake of Jamey Foster*, and *The Debutante Ball*— and combines it with a highly charged ritualistic event[1]—the nexus for *The Miss Firecracker Contest* and *The Lucky Spot*—to accentuate the tension of the modern neurosis. The "family crisis" is the reunion of Dash Gray's former theater students, who have formed a family of sorts that has reunited at Victor Lloyd's lake cottage to commemorate a memorial to their theater teacher and mentor; this ritualistic ceremony includes performances and eulogies to honor Dash, followed by a sprinkling of the deceased's ashes.[2] The play is structured in two acts, with a total of five scenes and a prologue, and although half of the drama occurs outdoors at dawn and sunset, giving the play an ethereal aura similar to what Henley described as the atmosphere of *A Midsummer Night's Dream*,[3] the romantic elements are superseded by the taut reality of the repressive forces of modern civilization. The underlying focus of the play is the essence of ontological insecurity and spiritual bankruptcy as a result of the conflict between the id's libidinal desire for happiness and the unifying cultural norms and values of society. *Revelers* strips the illusion of wearing masks so as to conform to a proscribed notion of success, forcing us to confront the modern neurosis in all its despair.

Dash Gray is the acting teacher and spiritual mentor that his former students, who are now his disciples, have come to honor in memoriam.

His spirit is with the revelers, who have fashioned a life-size cutout replica of their former acting teacher, depicted in his glory as a dashing man in his forties with blazing eyes and sneering lips. Dash Gray — the name sounds like that of a Hollywood heart throb — is gesturing triumphantly in the cutout replica, with his red umbrella pointing accusingly at his syco-phants. Dash's real name was Daniel Frank Gray, but his students endear-ingly called him Dash, which suggests an icon of spiritual vitality and energy. Dash is remembered as an "innovative genius of the Chicago the-atre world,"[4] a flamboyant mentor who inspired his students to become one with great art. On the other hand, Dash is depicted as mean-spirited, capable of demeaning his students, and idiosyncratic in his affections for certain acolytes. Henley, who wrote the play based on a memorial service conducted by her former acting teacher's students at the University of Illi-nois, was ambivalent about Dash's portrayal:

> I had mixed feelings in that I had feared and hated the acting teacher. He had advised me to return to Mississippi, get married, and stay south. In a fit of rebellion I'd thrown his final assessment of me unread into the trash bin at Arby's Roast Beef. The unsettling thing was I had learned much from this tyrant: ways of looking into characters by asking vital questions. What is the character's greatest dream, greatest fear? What smell do they like best? Questions I still ask in my work today.[5]

In short, although Dash is considered to be the icon of cultural validation, imposing his own value judgment that the creation of great art guaran-tees one's signature in life, he is also despised as latently interfering with one's personal happiness. In Freudian terms, Dash is glorified by his syco-phants in their memorial to an icon, replete with his life-size replica sub-liminally reminding his acolytes of great art as the unifying purpose of civilization; he represents the push and pull of the constant socialization process affecting the ego and superego. On the other hand, the libidinal desire for happiness conflicts with the constraints that Dash has set for his former students; the id becomes deeply repressed, thus causing depression and feelings of insecurity. Although the neurosis produced in these for-mer acting students creates a terrible need for nurturing and love to assuage their broken dreams and unfulfilled lives, the result is typically unrequited love.

Jasper Dale, the anointed prodigal son, has seemingly followed into Dash Gray's footsteps as the purveyor of great art. He insists that even though he may be a failure, his striving for the purity of art that Dash sought gives him integrity. Jasper vainly states, "I'm not asking for awards or banquets. I only want it acknowledged that I'm a world-class actor"

(170). Jasper Dale even has a glamorous theatrical-sounding name, suggesting an extroverted heartthrob that could capture an audience with his charismatic appeal. Now in his forties, Jasper, the gay artistic director of the small theater venture, the Red Lantern Theater, no longer the starry-eyed optimist, is reduced to unsightly warts growing spiral hairs, long, greasy hair, and torn sweaters. By blindly following his mentor and former lover's lead to make wonderful art the rallying point of his raison d'être, Jasper has ruined his life. Jasper persisted in seeking his mentor's approval, even after Dash, in a fit of rage, shattered Jasper's grandmother's china, ostensibly because Jasper fed his dog a piece of linguine from the dinner table. Dash put the blame squarely on Jasper's shoulders, acknowledging that the outrage was the result of their relationship in "domestic hell" (169). Jasper laments, "I was never able to reinstate myself with Dash. He even stopped casting me — he claimed my extreme charisma unbalanced productions" (170). Jasper never had any talent, and his only claim to fame, *Earth!*, a musical version of *The Good Earth* in which he directed, starred in, and for which he wrote the libretto, lyrics, and music, was a financial and critical disaster. Jasper's complete lack of artistic talent is demonstrated by the song he has chosen to memorialize Dash with, a tune that came from his first musical, *Cookie's Cooked*, which Jasper readily admits may not be his most accomplished or sophisticated work:

> Oh, Cookie, my baking powder
> My sugar lump
> My little honey
> My little stump.
> I like to sift your flour
> Love t'shake ya by the hour
> When I twirl my spoon in your bowl... [182]!

Jasper is reduced to working at Chicken Bob's in order to earn a living. The truth is that he virtually bankrupted the Red Lantern Theater because *Earth!* was overpriced, Asians picketed the performances, and, in a drunken stupor, he desperately made poisonous telephone calls to the theater's VIP patrons; Dash despised Jasper for conning him into getting involved with the disastrous venture.

Nevertheless, Jasper has completely bought into Dash's notion that great art is the unifying force of civilized life. Jasper refuses to recognize that, as Freud intimated, art is merely a means of representing life delusionally, in contrast to the id, which seeks pleasure and happiness. Jasper is conflicted and confused, the victim of broken dreams and an unfulfilled life. Jasper is in love only with Dash, who obviously did not share the affection; this becomes an obsession for Jasper, a case of unrequited love that can never be resolved. Jasper thus adopts the persona of Dash, insulting his friends one by one, strictly because they do not conform to Dash's high artistic standards. Showing his disdain for film as an inferior art to the theater, Jasper says of Victor, "Believe me, Vickie looks far better in the movies than she does in real life. Out there they can make any dog shine" (156). When Caroleena insists that Victor has acting ability, Jasper demeans her even further: "Please, she's a half-baked affair. A facile technician who lacks… Hmm, how shall I say it kindly? Who lacks all divine soulfulness. Dash and I always had to beat it out of her" (156). Dash also has disdain for Timothy Harold, Victor's associate, a cartoonist whose art he considers to be mass produced, "homogenized with MSG" (170) so as to be more palatable for public consumption. Jasper, true to his mentor, also despises Kate Spoon for the simple reason that Dash threw apple cores at her during performances. Kate, now married and far removed from Dash's creative inspiration, is no longer considered an artist and therefore is persona non grata as far as Jasper is concerned; he even suggests editing her out of Dash's memorial video. Caroleena is also unworthy of Jasper's attention since she is merely a Jill-of-all-trades technical person at the Red Lantern Theater but does not have the experience or training to perform onstage; she is, in Jasper's eyes, merely an expendable young "wannabe" who feels empowered by associating with true artists such as Jasper and Dash. Jasper is so intent on valorizing Dash's artistic integrity that he even excludes from the memorial ceremony Earl Bell, Dash's younger lover and companion for the last five years (and thus Jasper's rival), in order to eliminate the competition and thereby validate his own connection to Dash as the only legitimate artist. The only character to escape Jasper's disdain is Eddy Canary, the one student Dash fêted as a potential genius in the artistic community; unfortunately, Jasper's refusal to recognize Eddy as an artistic failure is a testimony to the artificiality of Dash's values that he so cherishes. As a result of Jasper being conflicted between his own happiness and the socializing norms of civilization seen through Dash's desire for artistic integrity, Jasper reacts aggressively to anyone not conforming to his mentor's unifying vision of society. Jasper becomes deeply conflicted to the point where suicide notes become the norm. He rationalizes his neurosis, reflected through crumpled suicide missives, as mundane: "It's nothing. I write these all the time. I wrote several last night. It's how I deal with depression. Doesn't everyone do it? I thought everyone did it?" (179). Suffering as a deeply wounded victim of unfulfilled dreams and a dispirited life, Jasper feels so depressed and divorced, so wedded to his existential madness, that he considers suicide as a viable alternative so as to be reunited as sprinkled ash with Dash — the only person that Jasper believes can assuage the *angoisse*. However, in Henley's theater, suicide is never a viable alternative, so Jasper is forced to live with his misery.

Caroleena Lark is not part of Dash's original theater circle of flatterers, but she nevertheless desperately seeks to belong to a group that has fashioned their mentor as the icon of civilized values. We know very little about her family history except for Jasper's casual remark to Victor that Caroleena was an abused child (171) and the fact that her father committed suicide in Mexico (194). Perhaps her sordid background of neglect forced her into this situation in which, in a subliminal attempt to feel worthy of being wanted and loved, she accepts Dash as her father figure and the Red Lantern Theater as her family. Caroleena, in her twenties, is much younger than Dash's fortyish acolytes, and her technical and administrative roles in the Red Lantern Theater further separate her from the performance artists. Caroleena, however, is determined to see herself as part of Dash's minions, boasting to Victor, "I have a formidable acting gift and hope someday to work on the stage, but for now I'm a Jill of all trades. I build sets, hang lights, do maintenance, box office, props, concessions, lobby displays. I'm indispensable to the operation" (161–162). Caroleena even adopts the role of a psychic, believing that no theater company would ever part company with someone who can supply such a valuable commodity.

Caroleena's id is so dominated by the socializing forces of civilization in the form of Dash and his disciple Jasper that she completely loses her personal identity in their personae. Caroleena, in her pathetic attempt to merge herself with Dash's cry of collective unity through artistic integrity, is infatuated with Jasper. However, this is merely another example of Henley's females engaged in unrequited love, for Jasper sees Caroleena as nothing more than a nuisance. Caroleena understands that her obsession with Jasper is unrequited love that she feels unable to control: "I'm in love with someone who will never love me. Ssss. It's a hopeless, doomed situation" (194). For her memorial tribute to Dash, Caroleena, in her vision of what it means to be a performance artist, walks across a tightrope to impress Dash's former students. Exalted at being in the limelight of attention, Caroleena's spirit becomes one with Dash as she actually adopts his persona. When asked to relinquish her time because her turn is up, Caroleena, as Dash, points the red umbrella at Dash's minions, eliminating the competition for Dash's favor one by one. Having previously reiterated to Kate Spoon that she is no longer the young ingenue (173), Caroleena reminds her that Dash threw apple cores at her. She admonishes Jasper for not inviting Earl Bell to the memorial ceremony and then proceeds to castigate him for bankrupting the Red Lantern Theater through the financial disaster of his extravagant musical, *Earth!* Finally, Caroleena exposes Vickie as having moved away from classical theater into film and cartoons, thus subverting Dash's dream of artistic integrity for her own purposes. Caroleena then proceeds to hurt Eddy as Victor rejects the one Dash anointed as a creative genius in favor of Timothy Harold, branded by Caroleena/Dash as a Philistine (188).

Caroleena's attempt to become one with her ego and superego through the social norms and values provided by the Red Lantern Theater, Jasper, and Dash's goal to create a unity out of individual human beings conflicts with the id's natural desire for happiness. She is conflicted because her raison d'être represents the desires of others. Caroleena's deeply rooted neurotic condition, overtly manifested by the unrequited love she has for Jasper, allows for her own psychoanalytic self-assessment, as she tells Jasper, "It's just... I'm sick. I'm sick" (157). Caroleena has a terrible need for nurturing and love to assuage the effects of the neurosis. Instead, her *angoisse* only deepens through further rejection. Not part of Dash's original theater class, Caroleena, isolated and alienated from the others due to her age and her duties at the Red Lantern, has her name omitted from the cake made in memory of Dash. Moreover, her faux pas in which she waxed the theater lobby as guests arrived has initiated a lawsuit from a man who apparently slipped on the wet floor. Jasper is more than glad to fire her because of this mishap, which, in reality, is his chance to end a relationship with a woman he considers to be a leech. Caroleena, ontologically insecure and spiritually sterile because of the misery caused by her adherence to what she believes are the only acceptable social norms and values to live by, is devastated by the news: "But I can't live without it. I can't live without the Red Lantern Theatre [*sic*]. Please. I can't live without it" (174).

Kate Spoon Mulligan is a housewife in her forties living in St. Louis with her husband and their five children. On the one hand, Kate has fully accepted the social norms of marriage and family to achieve happiness. The result is instead misery, as Kate realizes that she married a man she never loved, and four out of five of her children no longer speak to her. On the other hand, she dreams of personal success by accepting Dash's call for artistic integrity despite the fact that she lacks acting talent. In other words, Kate's adherence to the artificial socializing goals of a community of theater artists creates cultural restrictions on her life, thus producing angst. Ever since Dash threw an apple core at her during her reading of Euripides's *Trojan Women*, Kate's raison d'être is to ingratiate herself as a member of Dash's elite circle. No longer active on the stage as a performer, Kate latently justifies her involvement in Dash's dream of a community of artists by donating money to support the Red Lantern Theater. At the reunion, Kate tries to reunite with Dash's spirit by endearing herself to his star players: she recalls Jasper's performance in *Cannibal Road* as sexy (158) and glorifies Eddy as Dash's chosen one. Her performance of Hecuba's lament is her subliminal attempt to justify her artistic integrity in front of Dash's sycophants, hoping that this time the result will not be hurled apple cores. After her recital, she seeks approval of her art without regard to the fact that her former classmates applaud her chiefly because of her financial contributions to the theater: "I'm not just at RLT because of my contribution. You saw today, in my speech, I have talent. Didn't you see it, Jasper? Didn't you see I have a gift?" (186). Jasper's response is to imitate Dash throwing an apple core at Kate.

Kate Spoon feels guilty about abandoning Dash's vision of a life of artistic integrity and realizes that her attempts to regain the dream are futile. She becomes conflicted, alienated, depressed; in short, the norms and values ascribed by Dash, the icon of modern culture and civilization, directly result in her loss of happiness and concomitant depression. Kate consistently demeans herself as unworthy of emulation and love in the eyes of what she considers to be more successful peers. At the mention of Eddy Canary, Dash's favorite son, Kate demurs: "He hardly knew me in the first place. I'm no one he should know" (154). When Eddy touts his epiphany, the only novel he had written but eventually destroyed, he does it to impress Kate, who responds, "But why? I'm no one; I'm nobody" (158). Kate is also defensive around Jasper, pleading for his acceptance: "I know you think I'm not artistic. I don't go around barefoot slurping my hair, and you assume I'm not artistic but I am. In my heart I know I am" (159). Kate frankly admits to feeling inferior around icons like Dash, who threw apple cores at her, and Jasper, who is determined to edit her out of the video memorial, both of whom have never recognized her as a viable artist: "No one has ever believed in me. I'm used to it by now" (160). Moreover, Kate, now in her forties and reminded by Caroleena that the world is no longer her oyster, realizes that these lost opportunities contribute to her neurosis. She laments to Jasper, "I'm so unphotogenic. I don't take a good picture. I always photograph like an older person. Like I'm not young anymore" (177). Kate admits that these negative feelings about herself exacerbate her depression and alienation: "My husband Otto was right! No one likes me unless I'm giving them his money. I'm just an ugly, stupid woman filled with vain, pathetic, pathetic dreams!" (188). As a result of her deeply rooted feelings of *angoisse*, Kate reacts with the primordial hostility of what Freud would call the death instinct. She becomes naturally aggressive toward herself and her peers. She vandalizes the life-size replica of Dash by writing "Fuck You" in lipstick across his face.[6] Then, in a Babe-like suicide attempt gone awry, Kate, trying to drown herself in the lake laden down with rocks in her pockets, ultimately realizes that she did not want to be nibbled on by fish. This destructive aggression is turned against the ego in the form of Kate's superego, which exacerbates her guilt. Thus, by the end of the play, Kate simply withdraws from aggression and turns inward, refusing to participate in the sprinkling of Dash's ashes because, in her own words, "Dash didn't think I had talent. He wouldn't approve" (197).

There is a strong contrast between Dash's two remaining members of his theater circle — Victor Lloyd and Eddy Canary. Dash believed that these two acting students, in particular, demonstrated great potential. Vickie winds up as a highly successful film actress, while Eddy virtually drops out of society to become a bum. Vickie, reflective of an ego pushed to extremes, is miserable, while Eddy, satisfying the libidinal appetites of an unchecked id, cannot function in society.

Victor, now in her forties, is a very busy Los Angeles film star who owns the cottage on the shore of Lake Michigan that is the setting for Dash's memorial service. Vickie was one of Dash's protégés who distinguished herself as Lady Macbeth and, in Dash's own words, was born to play Blanche Dubois — a role that many actresses dream of playing. She fully accepted Dash's ideology of defining the self through artistic expression and has carried the philosophy to the pinnacle of success. Although she is despised by her fellow thespians for rejecting the stage in favor of film, considered by Dash and his star pupils to be quite the inferior art form that, like television, merely caters to mass public consumption, much of the resentment is due to pure jealousy. Henley herself would probably admit that most theater performing artists would readily jump at the chance to act in films (as she tried to do in Los Angeles) — what Jasper considers to be merely a homogenized art form. The fact that Victor is artistically successful, even though she is now playing Herlagator the cartoon alligator, is not what causes her to be miserable; instead, her *angoisse* derives from the fact that her ego has been fully subjugated to the socialization process that she was indoctrinated with by Dash. She has, in effect, superseded all expectations that Dash had of her being accepted into a community of ascribed norms and values. Her id has been diminished, and thus her libidinal desires have vanished because of the cultural restrictions placed upon her due to Dash's tutelage. In short, Victor is terribly conflicted, which results in neurosis that is characterized by depression and a feeling of emptiness.

Victor, like Meg and Elain, suffers from narcissism, a neurotic condition in which the libido is withdrawn from the external world and directed to the ego. Like any narcissist, Vickie needs to be at the center of attention and is only interested in her own grandiose sense of self-importance. Rather than dirty her hands with the peons, Vickie's assistant Bert makes arrangements for the lake cottage accommodations, sends flowers to the Red Lantern Theater, and even writes and mails Vickie's greeting and condolence messages for her. Vickie, probably realizing that she was not going to be the center of attention at Dash's memorial service, prefers instead to do a video to be played during the ceremony. Vickie is not even sure of the date of the memorial service, and when she returns to her lake cottage, she stumbles onto the ceremony completely by mistake, thinking that the ritual was conducted the week before and that her former colleagues would be long gone. In other words, Vickie, the egotistical movie star, could have attended the ceremony but simply chose not to be bothered. Vickie has long since abandoned her former friends, simply because her haughty attitude as a narcissistic movie star precludes any empathy for others. She has promised over the years at least seven times to return to the Red Lantern Theater to play Blanche Dubois but is always too busy to lower herself to be with the peons who have yet to reach the pinnacle of success like she has; in short, she has nothing personally to gain from any altruistic gestures toward her peers but merely keeps their attention piqued by advertising her return in numerous fliers. She even refused to see Dash in his final hours of decent health, claiming that she was "distracted" at the time. Instead, she is more concerned with maintaining her image as the center of attention, worrying that, because her "legs are stoutish" (175), she will be replaced in the cartoon film by Christine Berry. Her narcissism also colors her love affairs because ego obviously overwhelms her suppressed libidinal desires. Although she is attracted to Eddy and formerly had an affair with him, she cannot force her ego to accept the reality that Dash's prodigal son, now withered and toothless, has aged. Even after sharing a sexual romp with Eddy under the stage, Vickie cannot divorce herself from ego to allow her libidinal desires to flourish; she warns Eddy, "Stay away. You frighten me. You're not young, you're not young, you're not young anymore" (179). A relationship with Eddy would act as Victor's crutch, for being seen with him would likely reduce her self-esteem in the eyes of others. Henley explained to me this love-hate dichotomy that Vickie has for Eddy: "I just think they have that great chemistry, that ability to make it work in the real world. I think it's always horrible to see somebody that you haven't seen in years, who you have an image of, and then, "Oh, my god, what happened to him?"[7] Vickie thus rejects her true love in favor of Timothy Harold, who is young and successful, having grossed millions of dollars at the box office by making cartoons that cater to public appeal. Timothy, with his laptop computer and cellular telephone, represents to Vickie the innovations of the future, while Eddy, with only blank pages of manuscripts, is the epitome of an art form that Vickie has long since subliminally abandoned. In short, Vickie believes that being in the company of someone with Timothy's status will enhance her self-esteem, thus providing the nurturance she needs to overcome the *angoisse.*

Vickie's neurotic condition has caused her to be ontologically insecure and spiritually bankrupt. She has suffered through two divorces, and although she is financially successful, she is psychologically disturbed and miserable about her life. She tells Jasper, "Oh, please, you wouldn't want my life. Look at my life. I have no family, no friends, no children, no mate. At present I'm performing opposite fire-breathing fiberglass.... It's all so endlessly empty" (171). Like Meg who felt guilty about her inability to care for others, Victor shares guilt over neglecting both her former friends in the theater and, in particular, Dash's spirit of artistic integrity. Confronted by Caroleena who accuses her of being "a shitty friend" (187), Vickie engages in an unusual moment of self-introspection:

> Oh, I'm such an empty, horrible person and I don't understand how it happened. I started out — I had this dream — I followed it, my dream, and now it's mine. But all the same I'm so unhappy. I don't know why I'm so unhappy. I don't think it should be this way. Oh, Jasper. I have to come back to you and the Red Lantern. I'll sell my estate in Pacific Palisades, invest the money in the theatre, move back to Chicago, find my center, do the classics [187]!

However, for a narcissist, the guilt merely exacerbates the modern neurosis. Vickie has no intention of giving up her successful film career in Los Angeles to move back to Chicago with her former colleagues; this would, in any narcissist's eyes, be a step backwards and a blow to self-esteem. After all, narcissists probably believe that no one leaves Los Angeles for Chicago, and certainly no successful film actress regresses to the austere world of the theater. Vickie cannot let guilt outweigh ego and thus tells Jasper, "Look, dearest. I know RLT means everything to you. But in the greater scheme of things, it's just not relevant. I mean, do you really think I'd be willing to give up everything and move back to Chicago just to be some grand guppy in a glob of spit?!" (192). Unlike Meg, who can temporarily assuage the neurosis through bonding with her siblings, Vickie cannot escape the absurd condition. Her ego gets the best of her at the expense of arrogant and haughty behavior toward others, much like Elain who is defined by her beautiful clocks and L-Tip whose need to be constantly in the limelight fuels her grandiose feelings of self-worth and importance.

Whereas Victor has allowed her ego and superego to follow Dash's dictum of artistic integrity, taking her to the heights of her profession, Eddy Canary, Dash's other star pupil, has spiraled downward to oblivion as a result of an id that seeks happiness despite social constraints imposed upon humanity. Eddy is described in the Cast of Characters as a "poet/ bum"; deemed by Dash to be a poetic genius with searing wit, blinding insight, and untamed passion, Eddy certainly had the type of artistic potential that Dash could easily recognize. After acting in the original production of *Cannibal Road*, which he wrote and performed while in Dash's class more than twenty years ago, Eddy gave up acting and writing and became a bum. Ostensibly working on a novel for several years that was to be his epiphany, Eddy actually wrote nothing for publication. His social life deteriorated as well. Although Eddy was married to Jenny Brown, he was actually in love with Victor. When Jenny learned of the secret liaison, she ran off to the Yucatan and died shortly thereafter. Eddy then seemed to give up writing altogether and dropped out of society. At one point, Eddy was shot by a stray bullet in Baltimore, but for months, no one could identify the body. More recently, he was institutionalized in an Oslo insane asylum for pulling out all his teeth with a pair of pliers. He has since become homeless, begging on the streets shoeless while holding a sign that reads "Shakespeare for Spare Change." In short, Eddy has rejected all cultural norms and values ascribed by society's institutions.

Instead, Eddy's id, his primitive, atavistic instincts that naturally seek pleasure, overwhelm any rational, ethical, or moral constraints on his ego and superego. He is more concerned with satisfying the bodily instincts than pleasing the soul or satisfying ego typically confined by social mores. He can do virtually nothing without a cigarette or a drink, an oral fixation that hearkens back to a childhood time of happiness when he was nurtured by his mother. His sexual appetite certainly has not abated, for Eddy spends much of the night before the memorial service under the stage with his former love, Victor. Eddy, who admits that his homelessness has developed his taste for "an acute sense of the rotten" (193), and comes out from under the stage bruised, bloodied, and covered in filth, exclaiming, "dirt is a masterpiece!" (178) while taking a slug of vodka. One might wonder why Eddy is even at the reunion because his having produced nothing of any artistic value would only exacerbate the guilt that weighs on him as failing to adhere to Dash's call for artistic integrity as a means of assigning value to life. However, Eddy admits that he went to the memorial service only to see his old flame Vickie, in other words, merely to satisfy his sexual appetite and nothing more.

Eddy is certainly an anomaly in Henley's canon, for most of her protagonists gravitate to the demands that society places on the ego and superego, diminishing their instinctual libidinal desires. Eddy, on the other hand, has dropped out of society to adhere to the demands of his id; nevertheless, he is just as conflicted and neurotic as any of Henley's characters. Dash's memorial service, a ritualistic social event, only serves to accentuate Eddy's neurosis further. There is evidence that Eddy feels guilty about his refusal to adhere to social norms and values, ostensibly doing so to free himself from cultural restrictions. In reality, he cannot escape the fact that he wasted his enormous potential by dropping out of society. When Kate Spoon asks him if has written anything, he shakes his head, then smiles with dread (158). Eddy admits to Victor that his stasis is caused by a fear of not being able to live up to Dash's standards: "I'm afraid if I write, it won't be any good" (176). Only a severely conflicted or neurotic person would pull out all of his own teeth. Moreover, the neurosis has affected Eddy physically as well. Only in his forties, he has aged well beyond his years. Victor calls him "a sad, sad case" (192) and "a decayed regret" (165), intimating that Eddy's plight is the result of guilt from a wasted life. Eddy even describes himself as having deteriorated to "a frail, teetering state" (169) whose "infrastructure's disintegrating" (184). Eddy's emotional and physical dysfunction is visibly demonstrated during the memorial service for Dash. Asked to write something poetic for the ceremony, Eddy can only come up with a blank page. During his presentation of the eulogy, Eddy is so physically wasted that he collapses on stage — quite a descent from his acting days in Dash's class. His highly anticipated speech is reduced to an extemporaneous one-liner that a layman without any artistic sensibility could deliver: "Dash. I'm sorry you are dead. (*Eddy pauses a moment, then walks off stage and takes a swig from his bottle.*)" (184). Thus, even a person such as Eddy, who has dropped out of society to cater to his id, cannot escape the modern neurosis. *Revelers* therefore becomes one of Henley's darker plays, with no chance of egress, no defining moment of consciousness to assuage the existential madness even temporarily.

In 1996, while *Revelers* was being produced at Center Theater in Chicago, Henley was stringing together bits of dialogue and evocative images that she had recorded in her notebooks. However, nothing seemed to jell or to hold these isolated fragments together as a play. Henley recalls that this fragmentation was the genesis for *L-Play:*

I finally got the idea for the play when I realized I had no idea. I felt frag-
mented, decentralized, clueless. I had become confused over who was more
truthful, more enlightened: Sophocles, the Three Stooges, Edgar Allan
Poe, Elvis, Nero? There are so many worldviews, endless realities, tones,
messages. I decided to go with it — the mosaic of life.[8]

L-Play developed into twelve vignettes of approximately ninety minutes
in duration (Henley's later plays have become recognizably shorter than
her earlier dramas), the title of each scene beginning with L. There are eight
distinct episodes, with "Learner" and "Lunatic" each depicted in three
vignettes that round out the twelve "scenes." The styles of each vignette
vary from realistic (e.g., "Loneliness," "Learner," "Lost") to expression-
istic ("Loser") to symbolist, echoing the dramas of John Millington Synge,
W.B. Yeats, or Maurice Maeterlinck ("Leaving"), and finally to allegori-
cal, reminiscent of Thornton Wilder's *The Skin of Our Teeth* ("Life"). The
vignettes are not arranged in chronological order but instead are juxta-
posed from prehistoric times ("Life") to the 1930s ("Loneliness") and then
to the present (ten scenes) or what Henley refers to as a time "later than
you think" ("Loser"). Nine of the settings are undesignated, providing the
play with the universality expected in absurdist dramas; however, three
of the vignettes are clearly designated as recognizable Henley locales: South
Louisiana ("Loneliness"), Los Angeles ("Linked"), and Urbana, Illinois
("Learner"). Although the structure of the play is nonlinear and the tone
sometimes approaches the tragicomedy associated with absurdist drama,[9]
the play's often-realistic dialogue, distinct settings, and specifically motivated characters do not resemble any similar corresponding elements
found in theater of the absurd.

The major motif that unites the vignettes in *L-Play* is E.M. Forster's
"only connect," which was the epigraph for *Howards End*, now repeated
here in scene 2, "Linked." The unifying element of the play is that each
scene's title begins with L, which is half a box — a letter that needs connection. Henley stated, "*L-Play* is really about trying to connect, trying to
make the box. It's about how we go about finding anything solid in this
world, where it can be the Marquis de Sade's world, Disney's world, Woody
Allen's world, Degas' world. So many different perspectives on this one
world that we live in."[10] Henley poses the question of whether we can connect with someone or find dignity amidst the existential despair. Leo Seligsohn astutely noted that "Love" is conspicuously absent as one of the L
words but does not seem to be a careless omission: "Rather, it's around
the void created by the absence of this particular L-word that Henley seems
to be building her half-hidden message: Absent love, human existence is

little more than this 12-ring circus— grim, chaotic and ridiculous."[11] Love has been replaced by the modern *angoisse*, the ubiquitous state of humanity conflicted by the social pressures exerted on the ego and superego opposing the id's instinctual desire for happiness; unfortunately, these short vignettes offer little chance for us to learn much about the past lives of these characters, thereby making it difficult to assess the actual cause of each person's neurosis. The play ends with Dean Martin's rendition of "That's Amoré," a sarcastic reverberation of the motif that, in Henley's plays, the only love prevalent is unrequited (thus aptly describing the point of the final episode, "Learner"). Henley, in short, agrees with Freud in acknowledging that love is a fleeting means of mitigating the neurotic condition.

Scene 10, "Life," is the only episode that occurs before the twentieth century (prehistoric times) and thus offers no clues about the effect of civilization on the human psyche. The scene has all the earmarks of a Brechtian parable in a *lehrstücke*, including a narrator who tells the tale of the Three Ones, similar to cave-dwelling Neanderthals, who are visited by a character named Shoe. The Ones are shoeless primitives, so Shoe, dressed in black with a red shoestring and a crisp, white tongue, conceivably would offer a good complement to their needs— an opportunity to connect. In Henley's dramas, connection is made through an isolated moment of consciousness that can temporarily negate the absurd condition. However, the Narrator tells us that the Ones "never celebrated occasions and failed to share or savor the moment."[12] The Shoe is essentially a gift to the Ones, who, as prehistoric humans living without civilization, do not know how to react to the Shoe's generosity. Confused by the Shoe's altruism, the Ones tie the Shoe up and put him in a cage with the intent of killing him. The Narrator notes, "Blood lust was in the air. Wild revelry ensued" (228). The Ones then do a primitive dance that builds to *"animalistic debauchery"* (228). Gradually, the Small One and the Middle One, largely due to curiosity, individually begin to form a bond with the Shoe. The Big One nearly beats the Small One to death, but the Middle One manages to depart briefly with his new friend before the Big One can intervene. Eventually, the Big One cuts the Shoe to shreds while the Small One laughs and the Middle One smiles sickly; then they engage in an act of cannibalism, eating the Shoe with the blood dripping from their mouths. Henley depicts a world without misery or *angoisse*, for there is no civilization here and thus no socializing force to rein in the ego and superego. The Ones merely exist to satisfy their ids— their violent and primitive instincts. Happiness for them is attainable before the dawn of civilization; the murder of the Shoe leads to their reunification, the happiness that results from the elimination of an interloper who threatened the tightly knit bond between the three Ones. This natural aggression, which Freud termed the death instinct, opposes the goals of civilization. The Shoe brings the Ones to "life," teaching them the joy and horror of feeling human, replete with myriad emotions and desires, including violent ones; the consequence is that he is murdered for his efforts. The Ones embrace what the Shoe has taught them and learn to be human. In short, the Ones do not suffer from neurosis because their ids are completely satiated; in the remaining eleven interludes of the play, which all occur in the twentieth century, civilization's socialization process interferes with subliminal desires for human happiness, thus producing alienation and *angoisse*.

Scene 1, "Loneliness," which is the next in chronological order, is reminiscent of *The Lucky Spot*, with its 1930s setting in Louisiana during Christmas Eve. Monica French, a waitress in her thirties, could be the personification of what Cassidy Smith might have evolved into once she settles down into a respectable job after the wildness of her youth wanes. Just as Cassidy had sanguine dreams of marrying Reed Hooker, Monica, now with a child, hopes to wed William Pitt, the owner of the diner where she works for low wages and measly tips. She makes the obligatory Christmas Eve telephone call to her mother, but we get the impression that her life is characterized by misery in the form of loneliness, especially since it is Christmas and Monica chooses to work rather than to be with her family. She is estranged from her own loved ones, forgetting to get her daughter Lou Ellen a Christmas present and explaining that she will not be reunited with them during the holiday "'Cause Mama doesn't want me. She doesn't want me" (203). Monica bonds with penniless fourteen-year-old Joan Wells who has come to the diner this Christmas to be with Mr. Pitt, her grandfather, the only relative she has. Joan is virtually Cassidy's age, so Monica perhaps intuitively sees this carefree drifter as a younger version of herself. When Price Summers enters, the atmosphere changes for the worse; the stage directions indicate, "*There is something unsettling and inappropriate about his genial exuberance*" (204). Whereas Joan is dressed in rags for the cold weather and has no money, Price is dressed in warm clothing and throws money around carelessly, tossing fifty cents to the destitute Joan, who has offered to pray for him for a fee. Price has come to the diner to settle a grudge that he has with Monica, blaming her for Senator Emiling's suicide at the time when the two of them were working on the senator's campaign. Price's murder of Monica reminds us about Carnelle's remark concerning eternal grace and what individuals can reasonably expect out of life. "Loneliness" pays homage to the millions of unloved, alienated, and isolated individuals who, like Sisyphus, toil through life seeking dignity in a meaningless universe. This sense of *angoisse* is particularly exacerbated on Christmas Eve, a terrible time for lonely people, such as Monica and Joan, who are estranged from their own family members. Even the brief bond between outcasts Monica and Joan is untenable, ending swiftly when Price fulfills his longtime vendetta. Henley seems to pose the question of whether happiness can ever be attained by the disenfranchised who wander through life aimlessly without connecting with anyone before death, which may come early and unexpectedly.

Scene 2, "Linked," concerns two fairly intelligent single professionals who sit in a sweltering, dilapidated Los Angeles apartment trying to connect, to link, with a compatible mate. Gertrude and Jay, both in their thirties, are drinking heavily late at night, attempting to brainstorm about how to break the terror of the modern *angoisse*. Gertrude is dictating a letter that Jay plans to send to his ex-lover, Kattrina; Gertrude sees Jay's friend as a suitable candidate for psychotherapy and has Jay make a reference to her mental instability in the letter: "In a few years, perhaps after some hours on the couch, you may possibly evolve into a semblance of a human being" (207). Jay, a supreme egotist, is only wondering who will make his car payments if he breaks off the relationship with Kattrina. Meanwhile, Gertrude, who claims she is "so lonely" (208), cannot maintain a relationship with anyone either. For example, she broke off her affair with Alan because he had the gall to oversalt her French fries. When asked to prepare a list of the men she can date, Jay can only come up with dead people. Gertrude remarks, "This is depressing. 'Only connect. Only connect.' Who said...?" (209). When interrupted by the continuous hacking cough of their next-door neighbor, Gertrude, as egotistical as is Jay, can only selfishly wonder, "God, she's still alive. Isn't it awful?!" (210). In contrast to the lonely indigents of the 1930s in South Louisiana depicted in Scene 1, Henley in this scene intimates that the modern *angoisse* extends beyond the working class to educated professionals in contemporary Los Angeles. Like their 1930s rural counterparts, the denizens of the modern-day urban metropolis are also linked by this ubiquitous malaise that condemns them to a life of searching for a meaningful relationship, but even worse, contemporary society has forced individuals to attend to ego at the expense of the needs of others.

Scene 3, "Loser," epitomizes how the dichotomy between individual happiness and the socializing norms of society produces the modern neurosis that leads to existential madness and despair. Malcolm, like so many of us in modern society, desperately seeks to belong or connect, to be successful within the confines of social institutions, which would necessarily establish his own self-esteem. Mr. Chatwick, Malcolm's boss, has invited him to what is described as "an intimate affair" at his home; moreover, Mr. Umpton, Malcolm's rival at work, has not been included as one of the party guests. Malcolm views the invitation as an opportunity to connect, to feel wanted and important: "Perhaps my clothes are somewhat shabby underneath this coat. And my shoes are vivid, ostentatious, even vulgar. Yet I am invited. I'm included in the gathering" (212). Malcolm is ushered into Chatwick's study and savors the moment as a time when he feels he will be rewarded for his contributions at work, thus making him feel vital and appreciated. Malcolm muses to himself: "I have arrived. The inner sanctum. I have arrived. A view. Look. A view. The water. The mountains. Sky. Standing here with my whiskey among comfortable furniture; admiring the view" (213). Chatwick tells Malcolm that not only is he being fired, but also Umpton is getting what Malcolm hoped would be his own promotion. Malcolm, a loyal employee for seventeen years, has been dismissed because of a shaved pimple on his neck. Chatwick has invited Malcolm to the party only to amuse the other guests due to his ability to make funny noises from his armpits. Malcolm, depressed at hearing the news of his dismissal, is forced to remove his coat, and then, virtually naked except for shabby rags covering his body, makes flatulent sounds from underneath his armpits while the audience roars with laughter. What was to be a defining moment in Malcolm's life turns out to be humiliation and embarrassment; Henley again takes an important ritualistic celebration, a stressful situation in which tensions are accentuated, and turns it into a traumatic experience. Malcolm's innate violent urges are repressed because he must conform to social expectations; the id is overwhelmed by the cultural restrictions placed on the ego. Having bought into the notion that self-esteem and self-worth, or belonging, means conforming to the expectations imposed on an individual by social institutions and thus being rewarded for doing so, Malcolm is conflicted when he has no other recourse than to restrain his unconscious libidinal desires. In short, "Loser" depicts how individuals who inevitably must be acculturated into community norms and values at the expense of innate happiness will eventually wind up neurotic.

"Learner" comprises scenes 5, 9, and 12 and is indeed a learning experience for Henley's unnamed protagonist. Learner, an emaciated young man with glasses who is conscious of his frail physicality and his lack of intellectual prowess, is attracted to a young woman named Lucheea in the Modern Poetry class that they are both enrolled in as undergraduates. Learner initially tries to interact with Lucheea, who is partially disabled with a back brace, by carrying her books. He becomes obsessed with

Lucheea as an ideal vision of beauty, hoping that if she can at least recognize him, he will be able to connect, to belong: "How I wanted to hold her pale face with my bony hands and stare into her eyes (brown her eyes!) until I would know her and she would see me too" (217). Learner follows the existential dictum that "To Be Is to Be Perceived"; however, Lucheea has no interest in him, and, once her back brace is removed, tells Learner that his services are no longer needed. Alone in his garret apartment, Learner decides to write an L-poem for his muse, hoping, as the letter L suggests, to connect, to close the box. He ponders possible motifs for the L-Poem: "Loneliness, linked, loser, lunatic, learner, leaving, lost, life, love, life, lost, love, life..." (227). The first eight words represent the titles of the eight vignettes in *L-Play*; only love is absent. Learner has inadvertently characterized his dilemma: the only love present is unrequited (and shortly Henley will conclude that the only marriage is impossible). Learner's L-Poem receives a D+ for a grade and, when read in class, is ignored by Lucheea, who was "lost in private reverie" (234). When Learner asks Lucheea what she thought of his poem, she nonchalantly brushes him off with the noncommittal "I didn't know where it was going" (234). Thus, the Freudian notion that love represents life delusionally and cannot function as a major source of happiness to assuage our inability to belong or connect in modern society becomes apparent, especially as Learner is sarcastically mocked by Dean Martin's rendition of "That's Amoré."

"Lost," which is scene 6, occurs at a bar in a raunchy pool hall when the older Ben is giving his friend Wes advice on how to seduce Shelly. Ben, who has dated Shelly, claims that she loves him because of his thoughtfulness and exhorts Wes to develop a similar attitude toward her by giving her a gift. Wes is a loser who is even rejected by his own mother for being unemployed and is so academically inept that he flunked band class. Shelly is beautiful but most likely as lost as Wes, for although we do not know much about her life, she does reveal that she visits the Women's Crisis Center for advice. Shelly wants to belong or connect just as much as Wes, and when Wes gives her a gift of a small bottle of cologne, she wonders what the occasion is and why she deserves such a present. Wes puts on the charm, flattering the humble Shelly in what she views as his attempt to be sweet. When Wes gets up to get Shelly a beer, the stage directions indicate that she is lost as well, but brief moments of happiness are possible in a world where the reality of pain and anguish are endemic to our lives: "(*She sits, lost and nervous for a moment, then looks down at the tiny bottle of cologne; her face glows.*)" (222). This gift from a virtual stranger may in reality be nothing more than a cheap trinket, but to Shelly, the gesture of grace momentarily assuages the pain of the modern *angoisse* by reminding her of her own dignity and self-worth.

Scene 8, "Leaving," is presented in a symbolist style that is atypical of Henley's gritty realism. The time and place are unidentified, as in many of the symbolist dramas written in the late nineteenth and early part of the twentieth century, and the two characters, the Grandmother and Granddaughter, both in half-masks indicating their ages, remind us of archetypes of a symbolist play such as Maeterlinck's *L'Intruse*. All of the movements are stylized (the masks place the emphasis on voice and body), while the dialogue's staccato rhythm, again unlike Henley's contemporary vernacular, recalls the symbolist playwrights in their use of stichomythia to explore the soul rather than the intellect. The grandmother, deteriorating physically and mentally, is preparing for her imminent death, alone with her daughter because no one else has come to give her solace. The daughter attempts to find out who her mother's lover was during a particularly meaningful summer interlude, but the Grandmother refuses to divulge any information. The Granddaughter pleads for some answers to the mystery of life: "If only you could tell me something, something. Please" (226). In short, the Granddaughter is trying to connect with her mother before the latter dies to find out about what type of passion would lead her to cut off her own hand and send it to her lover. During an interview that I conducted with Henley, she put this scene in perspective: "I thought that the mask would tell the story of how removed they both are, and they're trying to reach each other. The Granddaughter really wants to know something human, something real about her grandmother, and they can't get through the mask."[13] The Grandmother can provide no answers, trying to placate her daughter with the gift of a red balloon, as if placating a child with a trifle. The Grandmother, when asked what she believes in, responds, "Sophistry" (225), indicating that the nature of life is fallacious and its meaning is absurd. Henley seems to be posing the question of whether it is possible to die with dignity and the possibility of any memory of happiness amidst the deeply rooted existential despair manifested by otherwise ubiquitous alienation and isolation — or lack of connection — endemic to our lives.

The other distinct possibility is to surrender to the modern neurosis and therefore die as one of the millions of afflicted. This obviously will be the fate of "Lunatic," depicted in scenes 4, 7, and 11. When we first see her, the lunatic is living alone in suburbia, obviously suffering from severe neurotic disorder. She is incapable of living by herself and needs to be hospitalized. We get the impression that the tales she tells may be hallucinations, as in the incident in which she awoke one morning to find someone else in bed with her:

I was wearing roller skates and there was fruit all over the bed. Apple cores, oranges, pineapples, dates. I was shocked to see I had part of a banana up my "vagina," as they call it on the six o'clock news. Part of it seemed to have been eaten but this is, of course, conjecture. It was snowing outside, which was odd because the last thing I remembered was swatting flies in summer [226].

We do not know the cause of the neurosis since nothing is revealed about her personal history, but the importance of self-esteem comes up in her monologues. She seems to rely on the media as her means of socialization, wondering if the women bearing children on television became fat and thus lost their sense of self-worth. Committed to the mental asylum, the lunatic spends most of her day working on jigsaw puzzles that lack the requisite pieces, yet assuring herself, "As soon as I put everything together, all together, I'll be set free to leave" (223). Seemingly concerned about her image, the lunatic wonders where she will go first — either to the porno store or to the mall — once she leaves: "Which would be more degrading?" (223). During the last episode, the lunatic has deteriorated physically as well, having lost a leg when she tried to hack it off with garden clippers after believing it was filled with excrement. She is dressed in a tattered circus outfit, the result of the solo act she believes she is performing before a live audience. We get the impression that the lunatic has fully succumbed to the existential madness, the modern *angoisse*, and is helpless to do anything about it. As her long monologue digresses in stream of consciousness fashion, the torrent of words suggests her emptiness. Even specific stage directions coincide with the idea that the lunatic's gap between happiness and the socializing norms of civilization can never be bridged because of such deeply rooted anomie: "*(A long beat, filled with a horribly sweet need and loneliness.)*" (232). The lunatic admits, "And my life is completely empty. Wheat fields of emptiness" (232). Obviously, the lunatic has failed to connect, and the result is that she will die alienated and isolated, incapable of fitting into the norms and values of civilized society.

L-Play depicts the loss of happiness in modern society, reducing humanity to *angoisse* as a result of the failure to connect. This connection can be construed as meaningful contact — the need to belong; concomitantly, connection refers to the ability to unite id and ego. The only episode that conveys an unchecked ego-id relationship is "Life," since that vignette occurs in prehistoric times before civilization places burdens on our collective consciousness; happiness is thus possible when norms and values do not interfere or quash the id. However, in modern civilization where the id is subdued and where ego is channeled collectively, to use Henley's variation on the dreaded L-word, humanity is lost, lonely, and trying to link; the quest for dignity in modern society results in despair, alienation, anomie, or unrequited love. The only positive note in *L-Play* is the gift that Shelly receives in "Lost"—a momentary reprieve from the modern *angoisse*, a glowing moment, similar to Sisyphus's brief respite at the top of the mountain before he is again burdened. We can expect to be afflicted with the modern neurosis—horribly demonstrated by the fate of the lunatic—or, like the Grandmother in "Leaving," we can try to die with dignity, perhaps alone, with fleeting memories of the past.

In 1995, when Henley was pregnant, she was commissioned by the Roundabout Theatre to write a new play. Henley's mother urged her to write a drama that would lift her spirits during the pregnancy, assuming that brooding over another dark play might somehow put the baby under stress. Henley turned to Oscar Wilde's witty farces as her starting point for *Impossible Marriage*:

> For the first time I read all of Wilde's plays. What a good time that was. I started looking at drawings by Aubrey Beardsley: sensual, formal, and forbiddingly erotic. When the play started to come together, I realized the characters' insides were vastly different from their facades. I began staring at Chagall's circus figures, blue flying lovers, red horses with wings, green angels with horns ... I tried to imagine these feelings inhabiting the Beardsley figures.[14]

Set in the pastoral gardens of Kandall Kingsley's country estate during mid–May in Savannah, Georgia, where the flowers are in full bloom, *Impossible Marriage*, in three scenes without an intermission, has an ethereal air of a Wildean comedy and a magical, dream-haunted aura of Shakespeare's *A Midsummer Night's Dream*, with echoes of the latter particularly reinforced in scene 2 when Kandall admonishes Sidney for disturbing the fairies living under the toadstools. In the spirit of nineteenth-century Edwardian drawing room comedy and Wilde's witty repartee, Henley has created aristocratic characters who speak eloquently and lyrically; there are no Leon Darnells, Brocker Slades, Delmounts, Cassidy Smiths, or Sue Jack Tiller Hookers among this Southern gentry. Moreover, if the color of her earlier "Southern" plays was red with violence and mayhem, the color here, much more appropriate for Edwardian farce, is a subdued pink, with the only opportunity for violence being Sidney's inept shooting of himself in the foot while aiming the gun at his father; nineteenth-century ire substitutes for twentieth-century anger.

In scene 3 of the play, Edvard Lunt remarks about the importance of civility, and Floral Whitman responds, "Being civilized is a rot."[15] Edvard counters: "I disagree. Without the tormenting friction between the civilized and the primitive, life would be bereft of its most rapturous flavor" (263). *Impossible Marriage* is primarily concerned with this conflict between the civilized and the primitive; in Freudian terms, the play focuses on the dichotomy between the id's desire for happiness and the means by which the ego and superego are confined by the norms and values of contemporary society. This aristocratic society in Savannah is highly socialized and restricted by cultural norms rather than by their own sense of fulfillment; Henley suggests that this is the reason she returned to a Southern landscape:

> I wanted an environment where there were more boundaries, where marriage was an institution that was valued and would put Floral more on a pedestal than, say, Los Angeles. I wanted an environment where there's an organized society for the characters to bounce off of. A pregnancy from an out-of-wedlock affair would have more mileage in that environment.[16]

Henley discussed the paradox endemic to *Impossible Marriage*: "There are so many things that can work in this world if you follow your instincts and your heart instead of some predestined structure."[17] In essence, there is a curse on the House of Kingsley; through the family's legacy as a paragon of virtue and civilized behavior according to ascribed norms and values, the id has been suppressed; thus, the family members have become conflicted or neurotic. The Kingsley family has had a long history of repressing their guilt — keeping secrets — due to social influences, thus increasing the *angoisse*, forcing them into unfulfilled lives; the Kingsleys may be wealthy, but they are spiritually bankrupt. In the Edwardian tradition in which violence and suicide are repressed, *Impossible Marriage* instead focuses on the id's release of lust and sexuality to assuage the neuroticism temporarily; Floral, however, seems to personify the notion that innate aggressiveness conflicts with social norms and values, creating a struggle between Eros and Death that can never be resolved.

Henley sets the play during the wedding day and the day before the wedding of twenty-year-old Pandora Kingsley and her fiftyish husband-to-be Edvard Lunt, a highly charged celebration that will only exacerbate family tensions. There is a lot of anxiety in the Kingsley household, particularly because marriages typically do not seem to work for this clan, and certainly, as a result of the thirty-year difference in the ages of the bride and groom, a happy union seems to be impossible here as well. The wedding ceremony thus serves to intensify the already volatile family situation, unearthing skeletons kept in the closet and bringing latent secrets to the forefront.

Kandall Kingsley, now in her fifties, has been an icon for social responsibility and respectability in the community. She remained married to her husband, now deceased, for many years simply because she wanted to convey to her daughters the sanctimony of the institution of marriage. Although Kandall admits that she never loved her husband, she was confined by the parameters of conventional mores in a highly restricted Southern community, so she was forced to accept the hypocrisy of her marriage. Kandall, conflicted by her innate desires yet forced to live according to the standards of others, shares a jaded view of life as she gives advice to Floral: "Eventually, we'll all be dead. Your travails will have ended and you can rest in peace, knowing you have experienced the pain, confusion, and various contretemps that give life girth" (267). Kandall, like Boswell in *Signature*, is suffering from some terminal disease, a secret she has kept from the rest of her family. Now that she is dying, Kandall has a chance to reassess her life and thus realizes that she has sacrificed her desires for happiness for the sake of family and social convention. In short, Kandall is conflicted because her id has been subsumed by the demands that cultural restrictions have placed on her superego. She wonders aloud if it is too late to change her life (272), perhaps to allow the id to flourish despite public opinion. This dichotomy forms the essence of the play or what Henley referred to as shades of incompatibility: "How do we marry our dark and light sides? How do you marry lust with love? Being a mother with being a woman."[18]

Kandall's chance to break the curse by changing her life so as to dispense with public opinion in favor of innate happiness comes in the way of Sidney Lunt, Edvard's eldest son. Sidney shares with Kandall the need to disrupt the marriage of Edvard and Pandora because of the importance they place on cultural values. Kandall acknowledges that the difference in the ages of the bride and groom will preclude any chance that the marriage can be successful, while Sidney sees the wedlock as an insult to his mother and seven siblings. When Sidney tells Edvard that his wife will commit suicide if he marries Pandora, Kandall and Sidney are united in their attempt to avert scandal or any disruption to the social code. Sidney is so appalled by the wedding plans that he insists that he, along with his siblings, will also commit suicide if the ceremony takes place. Kandall, oblivious to her own daughter's happiness, insists, "We cannot have a scandal of this magnitude in my garden" (253) and then plans to call off the wedding. Sidney, opposed to the pastoral setting of the wedding, whacks the flowers with his cane (239), claiming to attend the ceremony "to disrupt and annihilate" (257); Kandall, a kindred spirit, assures Sidney that they share the same passion: "I too would like nothing better than to see this engagement broken" (257).

Sidney, considering himself a failure and a coward, has a moment of intense passion when he bonds with Kandall, who at the time was musing about her own abject loneliness and impending death. Sidney, never having bonded with a woman, shares Kandall's misery to the point where he spontaneously kisses her on the lips, admitting, "I love you" (259). However, Henley's focus is on Kandall, not Sidney, to see if the dying matriarch can change her life from the confines of public opinion that have forced her to live with a secret that has become a curse. Kandall, now near death, realizes that her life has been a miserable sham, sacrificing happiness for the sanctity of cultural norms and values. To assuage the abject loneliness, the existential madness from which she suffers, she asks Sidney to kiss her, despite the fact that he is thirty years her junior. In doing so, Kandall, in effect, gives approval to her daughter's marriage, supposedly ill-fated because public opinion would not approve of Pandora marrying a man thirty years her senior. Sidney, cognizant of the mask that he wears for society, cannot respond accordingly. Nevertheless, Henley apparently views Kandall as a tragic and pathetic person who tries to change her persona much too late in life. When Kandall learns that Floral was also keeping the father of her child a secret because of her mother's expected disapproval of a violation of established social conventions, she seems to realize that community norms and values have cursed the family. Henley discussed the change that Kandall attempts to make at the end of the play: "Basically, she's intuitive and intelligent. When Floral says, 'People can change.... I've seen it happen,' she means her mother. Her mother has changed from caring about public opinion to saying essentially, 'Oh, who gives a damn? We lived and touched real life and inevitably we had some scandal.'"[19] Henley infers that Kandall's intuition, her id, is essentially in conflict with her intelligence, which forced her to conform to the way public opinion would expect her to behave as a member of Southern gentility. Henley's homage to Kandall's willingness to change is to allow her to eat raspberries with her fingers while the juices drip; this abrupt lack of decorum, coupled with a long overdue submission to her latent erotic impulses in the form of enticing Sidney to seduce her, seems untenable for an audience to fathom, even after we have heard Floral state, "Table manners are important. So that when we eat berries with our fingers and let the juices drip down our lips, a statement is made" (263). In short, Kandall's debilitating illness may make her desperate to change so as to live life without boundaries and thus without neurosis, but we wonder how serious the commitment may be and whether it can be sustained.

Although Pandora's wedding is the focal point of the play, the protagonist is clearly Floral Whitman, Pandora's older sister, who is on stage more than any of the other characters. Floral is one of Henley's most complex, and therefore most intriguing, characters, a role challenging for actresses to portray because she is so multi-faceted; Holly Hunter, who played Floral during the Roundabout Theatre's 1998 production, explained the challenge of the role: "She is a radical, she is rebellious, a truth-teller, really manipulative. She is courageous, a protector and a fighter, an extremist. She has wickedness, she is a schemer, she has plans."[20] Floral is terribly conflicted by an id that is repressed by the constant socialization process and cultural restrictions in this small Southern community; the civilizing forces mold Floral's ego and superego into a unity of individuals at the expense of her libidinal desires. Pamela Renner discussed Floral's terribly divided self: "A wellspring of the play's mischievous vision on the pitfalls of conformity to social rules, Floral is also a casualty of sorts, leaking tears and bitter regrets, and pining for something she can't articulate."[21] The result of Floral's neurosis is that she feels intolerably alone, frustrated, and unfulfilled, as if her life is characterized by broken dreams. Her terrible need for nurturing results in promiscuous behavior. Suicide is not considered; instead, she takes out her frustrations against her sister.

Floral's supposedly wonderful marriage to Jonsey is an overt display of what is actually a hypocritical life of lies and illusions that form the core of their relationship. Jonsey, an embarrassingly handsome man in his thirties and wealthy enough to provide for his wife luxuriously, would presume to be the ideal husband. Pandora remarks, "Jonsey is the most wonderful dancer in the country. All the women seek his company. He's acclaimed" (251). Jonsey remembers their wedding as a day of perfection, recalling, "Everyone was transformed by our love. It was effortless" (241). Jonsey constantly reminds Floral that he loves her, waxing eloquent in the process: "Tonight I'll pour sweet oils for your bath and rub your belly and feet. My wife. My cherished mother-to-be" (244). Jonsey also caters to his wife's needs, treating her like a queen: "I run her bath, massage her feet with oils, dab her wrists and neck with fine perfumes. I powder every crevice of her body and feel only calm" (255). Although he flirts with other women to maintain his reputation as a cad, he never cheats on Floral, despite the fact that his flirtations cause rumors that he has been unfaithful to her. Jonsey loves Floral, but for some unknown reason, he cannot have sex with her. He is haunted by the traumatic experience of having watched his father drown in a boating accident twenty-seven years earlier, which may have adversely affected his sex life, extinguishing his libido. One might assume that he is gay, certainly not a closet homosexual but perhaps someone who refuses to recognize himself for what he really is; if the latter were true, then Jonsey is also conflicted because his innate sexual preferences are suppressed in favor of flirtations with women so as to portray a certain image of himself, as if wearing the mask, to a conformist Southern society. Henley, however, told me that instead she perceived of Jonsey as a man without a libido (certainly not too uncommon), someone for whom the world is too perfect and whose pristine life would only be tainted by sex.[22] Nevertheless, Jonsey hints to Floral that his flirtations are merely a mask to justify in the public domain the fact that he is actually capable of loving her: "I assumed you knew that my attention to others was merely a guise to make us appear normal" (270).

Floral, in desperate need of counseling to assuage her neurosis, sought spiritual guidance from Reverend Jonathan Larence. In modern American drama, the reverend continues a long line of inept clergymen who cannot offer adequate spiritual support, including Reverend Tooker in Tennessee Williams's *Cat on a Hot Tin Roof* and Father Dewis in Sam Shepard's *Buried Child.* Reverend Larence is the wrong person to offer spiritual advice, for he himself is conflicted between demands by his id and superego, thus causing him to be miserable. When Pandora compliments him on his benevolence, the reverend corrects her: "I'm afraid I'm not. I'm not. No, no. But I thank you for the thought" (241). When Pandora asks him for advice about marrying Edvard, pending the imminent suicide of his wife, which would obviously be scandalous for the Kingsley household, Reverend Larence cannot provide any wisdom, admitting, "I have so little" (253). His pitiful attempt at providing some response, a feeble call for a modicum of love, prompts Sidney to remark, "How grateful I am to have forsaken organized religion of any sort" (253). On the day of Pandora's wedding, when his services are needed, he has to be hauled out of a ditch in which he spent the night. After Sidney's miscalculated attempt to disrupt the wedding ceremony, Reverend Larence blames himself for his own lack of spiritual support:

> Don't ask me for help. I'm through giving help. Here, take this collar. Have it. It's more fit for a beast than a man. I'm sick from answering prayers and doing good deeds. It has turned me into a raving lunatic and left me with desperate, unquenchable desires. I want to spit on all altars for the remainder of my days. God, I am wretched [265–266].

The reverend is conflicted between the id's desire for sexual gratification and the demands placed on his superego by the public who regard him as an icon of righteousness and a pillar of the community. Thus, instead of providing Floral with spiritual guidance, he seduces her instead, allowing his id to lead him temporarily toward latent happiness and gratification;

however, he cannot marry Floral because she is another man's wife, advising her to stay with Jonsey "Because it is the right thing to say" (260). As a result of cultural restrictions that would never allow him to wed a woman believed to be carrying Jonsey's baby, Reverend Larence insists that his happiness must be sacrificed for the sake of maintaining his image in the community; in short, his love for Floral will always be an impossible marriage. Reverend Larence describes his neurosis as an "onerous affliction" (261), a dialectic so confusing to him that when asked whether he has ever been married, the question seemingly leads to a response that reveals his conflicted personality: "Yes, I mean no, no!" (241). Reverend Larence's conflicted desires cause him to regard himself as a hypocrite (259), understanding that the only solution to his dilemma is to abandon the church.

Floral is neurotic because she is torn between the id's animality and the socializing forces of civilization. Floral's id seems to seek the happiness that Kandall refused by remaining in a loveless marriage; Floral subliminally understands that by not adhering to her unconscious demands for lust, she may die unfulfilled. Floral is occasionally prone to fits of wild animality and rage, as witnessed, for example, by her impromptu romp in the dirt, grass, and leaves. When Floral's overwhelming cravings get the better of her and she lurches for a taste of wedding cake, Kandall wonders, "Forgive me, I thought we were civilized human beings, not animals" (262). Furthermore, Floral is the one who complains that marriage is too much a matter of tradition linked by ceremonial events ritualistically performed for the sake of public opinion and the need to create a unity out of individuals: "Once you are married you're stuck. Nothing ever changes. Every year there's a turkey at Thanksgiving and a goose at Christmas. Jonsey gives me one more letter opener for my collection and no one ever sends me any mail" (266). Although Jonsey truly loves Floral, the feeling is not mutual; instead, she turns to Reverend Larence, who cannot love her in return. We have the classical case of unrequited love, again the Racinian ladder where A loves B who loves C who cannot reciprocate. Floral's pregnancy is the visible reminder of this neuroticism — hypocrisy that she must live with; moreover, Henley makes every effort to indicate that Floral's tumescence is visibly exaggerated to the extent that the pregnancy cannot be hidden from the community. Floral simply has to live with this cumbersome, daily-visible reminder of her neurosis attributed to the fact that her id's primitive and animalistic desire for happiness that forced her into an out-of-wedlock sexual tryst conflicts with the fact that the baby is not her husband's child; the result is that the burden of bearing a child adversely weighs on an ego and superego channeled through social norms. She admits, "Being civilized is a rot" (263). When Alexis Greene asked

Henley if Floral was in tune with her pregnancy, Henley's response suggested the neurosis that forms Floral's raison d'être: "When she connects to it, she totally connects, as much as she might be denying it."[23] Floral, like any mother, is trying to connect with her baby, a normal reaction disrupted by the truth that the offspring is a product of only lust, not love, and moreover a relationship that could never be sanctioned by the conservative Savannah community. Floral essentially lives life as a lie, telling her friends and family that the child is the product of a happy marriage: "And Jonsey and I are very much in love. We're having a child together. Our first child" (254). Floral even reminds her family that she sought counseling because Jonsey, who actually worships her, was unfaithful — a sham that deemphasizes her conflicted persona while putting the onus on someone else. Floral's hypocrisy is further revealed when she tells Edvard, "In any case, I'd like you to know I'm extraordinarily particular about who I see privately. I'm not a virgin, but other than that, I am wholesome in the extreme" (262). However, the most telling moment of Floral's hypocrisy occurs when Reverend Larence admits that he cannot love her because social constraints prevent him from having an affair with a married woman; Floral, after urging the reverend to seduce her, now hypocritically rejects the id's desire for happiness as she insults the clergyman in an attempt to fall back on demands placed on her ego through the socialization process:

> I never cared for you at all. I am happily married. Happily, happily, happily. My child will come from a good home. Without any hint of scandal. (*To her child.*) And everything will be possible for you. My dear, my most secret dear. It will all be possible [261].

At this point, Jonsey enters, and the hypocrisy continues with him as well. Floral expresses her love for her husband, but the stage directions reveal how conflicted she really is: "(*Floral kisses Jonsey desperately on the lips. They slowly pull apart and regard each other with profound sadness.*)" (261).

Floral is living a hypocritical life because her child's father is Reverend Larence, not her husband Jonsey, yet she is forced to pretend that her child is legitimate, thus turning her very visible pregnancy into a facade. Floral understands that the cultural restrictions of this Southern community will inevitably lead to her divorce of Jonsey. She is further tormented by the fact that she must suffer in a loveless marriage because of the socializing norms of a community that would not accept an out-of-wedlock child; thus, she suffers from the same curse that plagued her mother, who was also trapped in a loveless marriage that was visibly represented as a union filled with eternal joy.

Floral, a deeply neurotic victim of broken dreams and an unfulfilled life, has a terrible need for nurturing and contact with the Other, forcing her to be promiscuous, like Meg and Carnelle. The other manifestation of the modern *angoisse* is an aggressive, jealous hostility toward Pandora's wedding and the concomitant need to make sure the event goes awry. Floral is jealous because her younger sister is truly in love with the man she plans to marry, whereas Floral is trapped in a loveless marriage. Pandora's youth (she is ten years younger than Floral) and her ability to commune with nature also adversely affect Floral, who is now concerned with her warts, which she blames on contact with frogs, almost as if nature were anathema to her. Pandora is in tune with the blooming May flowers while Floral spends her time crying in the garden. Floral explains to Pandora why she is jealous of her: "My marriage is a morbid predicament without passion or hope. You have such brave gaiety, romantic notions, youthful daring, and translucent beauty" (268). The sardonic Floral is two-faced and hypocritical about her jealousy, admitting to her sister that she loves her (241) while plotting to destroy her marriage plans. Floral casts doubt about Edvard's character, asking Pandora to consider the type of man who would divorce his wife of twenty-three years and leave his children for another woman. Floral also infers that Pandora's youth and innocence would be incompatible with Edvard's middle-aged discretions, thus making them the objects of ridicule in the community: "So you have no doubts about your future? No gnawing concerns? I mean, the fact that he is over twice your age, myopic, rumored to be a drunkard, decidedly a philanderer, and has been known to wear a ponytail, makes no matter to you?" (242). Unable to get Pandora to break off the marriage, Floral tries to develop a rift between the two lovers by telling Edvard that his future wife is having second thoughts about the wedding. Having failed to scare Edvard into believing that Pandora is tentative about the wedding, she tries to convince him that marriage means conforming to civilized standards, and therefore he should get on a train and never return to Savannah. Floral's neurosis has pushed her beyond a normal jealousy of her younger and more beautiful sister to a malevolent hatred of her as well. When Kandall mentions that Pandora threw herself out of a moving automobile when Edvard shouted her name, Floral responds, "Pity she didn't break her neck" (246). It is unusual for an individual to have such hatred toward a sibling, and thus Floral's love-hate relationship toward Pandora only serves to increase her anomie and *angoisse*. As Freud mentioned, the neurotic instinct toward destruction is countered by civilization, which increases our sense of guilt from the socially unacceptable stance of malevolence toward a loved one. Floral's jealousy toward Pandora may be a reaction to a loveless marriage but inevitably becomes nothing more than a hollow gesture producing guilt that merely intensifies her misery.

The focal point of the play revolves around whether Pandora and Edvard Lunt can break the curse on the House of Kingsley or whether their intended marriage will be impossible and thus will follow in the footsteps of Pandora's kin, Kandall and Floral. The dilemma concerns whether Pandora will open the box and let instincts reign or resign herself to a loveless fate because of cultural restrictions placed on the ego and superego. Pandora, described in the stage directions as *"the image of youthful exuberance"* (240) of a twenty-year-old, is marrying a recently divorced man who is twice her age and has seven children. Floral, addressing Pandora's concern that Edvard has age spots and gray hairs covering his body, speaks for the community sentiment by stating that Pandora is setting herself up to be a nursemaid to a doddering old relic. Moreover, Edvard's European ancestry marks him as an outsider in the community and thus someone who is suspect. Even worse, his abandonment of his children, whom he admits to having difficulty communicating with to the extent that he cannot recognize his own son Sidney, makes him further estranged from a tightly knit Southern infrastructure where strong family bonds, or at least its ostentatious display, are indigenous to the culture. Finally, the threat of Edvard's former wife committing suicide over his marriage to Pandora creates scandal for the Kingsley household, which forces Kandall to attempt to abort the wedding.

Pandora and Edvard seem to think that their libidinal desire for happiness can overwhelm the cultural restraints imposed on them, so they choose to wed in defiance of the socializing norms of the community. Edvard, who can articulate "the tormenting friction between the civilized and the primitive" (263), hopes that erotic abandonment will tip the balance between the repressed id and the ethical and moral judgments made on the superego. Edvard claims that his lust, dormant for years in a flaccid marriage, is rekindled by Pandora's youthful exuberance. Edvard tries to defy the modern neurosis, insisting, "I adamantly reject the notion of meaningless existence" (244). He is about to unleash his long-dormant id, explaining to Floral the reasons for marrying Pandora despite the objections of the community: "The man who is no longer capable of scaling the mountain is quite different from the boy who has yet to try. Ah, indeed, if it were never too late to do anything, life would hold no meaning whatsoever" (244). Pandora feels empowered by the passion of love with an artist, a cultured man of sophistication who can open new horizons to her. She intuitively understands that realizing her passion is much better than the traditional and loveless life that plagued her mother and now her sister. Pandora uses the wedding ceremony — which will occur outside the arms of the church and in an another county, away from community gossip — as a defining moment of recognition in which dignity can briefly be established in an absurd universe. Although Pandora wishes that her love for Edvard will last forever, she also acknowledges that there is no permanent escape from the *angoisse* that will eventually debilitate her physically and psychologically:

> I play the lovely, joyous child everyone adores and is drawn to, but sooner than later my face will be less round, my eyes will dull, worry lines will cross my hardened brow, and I will become something that once was and now is not. My charms will not age well. Now is my time. I must take it [268–269].

Pandora, in her youthful enthusiasm, mistakenly believes that she has this one opportunity to seize the day. The effort that she and Edvard make to gratify the id's desire for happiness is only a momentary break in the absurd condition. We have the feeling that the clash between the id and the demands placed on the ego will inevitably produce an "impossible marriage," which Henley insists is "the only kind."[24] However, Pandora, nervous about losing the opportunity, will, like Edvard, eventually realize that there will be other glowing moments of awareness to enable one to find dignity in an absurd universe.

9

Conclusion

In this book, the first full-length critical study of Henley's plays, I have argued that Henley's oeuvre needs to be reexamined. Much of the criticism on Henley's dramas was written in the 1980s and early 1990s, focusing primarily on the early plays. In addition, by merely labeling Henley through stereotypes, these early critics have taken her plays too lightly and need to reassess them in a new critical perspective. I have tried to dispel the stereotypical notion of viewing Henley as a Southern Gothic playwright. Only one play that Henley has written since 1990 occurs in the South; meanwhile, the Gothic label, which characterizes Henley's protagonists as dysfunctional, eccentric, grotesque, or demented, is anathema to Henley. Time and again in interviews, Henley has reiterated that she does not view her protagonists as aberrations, and when I confronted her with the neuroticism of her characters, she reacted by stating that she thought they were typical of what we see in the twentieth-century rather than distortions or exaggerations.

Although Henley has professed disinterest in political or social agendas during interviews conducted with her, this has not deterred the critics, who often insist on analyzing the plays based on feminist interpretations. Henley writes about abusive mothers as well as domineering husbands and grandfathers; however, the critics have chosen to focus on how the patriarchy precipitates family violence. As the stereotyped argument goes, the patriarchy defines roles for women, reducing them to sex objects. Henley's females, branded with ritualized codes of Southern gentility, abort their rage in the form of self-destructive aberrant suicide attempts and violence toward men, sometimes in the form of homicide. The unusual amount of family violence in the plays is typically attributed to a statement that Henley must be making about battered women. Henley's females thus engage in a quest for identity free from rigid cultural norms, created by the patriarchy, that define the roles by which they must live. The females assert themselves either by bonding with other females or by becoming unruly women who affront the notion of the genteel Southern lady, usually making a spectacle of themselves at an important social event, celebration, or family reunion. These women mar their bodies to rebel against cultural norms and revolt by spoiling the traditional celebration, thus upsetting the patriarchal conventions of Southern culture.

Such sociological interpretations are difficult to sustain because, as I have argued, the revolt of Henley's protagonists is essentially psychological, not politically motivated. Such political arguments do not take into account any of the plays written since 1990, which amounts to half of Henley's canon; the only play since 1990 that could possibly be interpreted as a feminist statement about the patriarchy would be *Control Freaks*, which ostensibly could be viewed, albeit limitedly, as a sociological treatise on the ill effects of incest. In *Abundance*, there is no cause-effect relationship between the husband-wife union and the fates of either Macon or Bess; in *Impossible Marriage*, even the most jaded feminist critic would agree that Jonsey tries to be the ideal husband to Floral, although his worn-out libido may be his Achilles' heel. Finally, Henley's affection for Boswell as her most admired character (the only male protagonist in the canon) refutes the notion that her agenda is primarily feminist. Thus, the feminist interpretations of Henley's dramas apply principally to the early plays and then only to select ones. Ashbe's seduction of fraternity boy John Polk can hardly be construed as a revolt against patriarchal convention. Moreover, Carnelle's desire to win the Miss Firecracker Contest dispels any notion that Henley is making a political statement about beauty contests. Although Katty and Wayne live in a violent patriarchal microcosm, most of the feminist interpretations of *The Wake* tend to focus on Wayne's paternalistic treatment of his wife and Collard, certainly not the focal point of the play. In *The Lucky Spot*, the patriarchy is largely absent, whereas in *The Debutante Ball*, the relationship between Jen and Teddy seems to be the raison d'être for the social event going awry, and any attempt to bring the lesbianism of Bliss and Frances into play as a statement against the patriarchy is a stretch. The feminist argument against the confining hold that the patriarchy has on Henley's females seems to work best in *Crimes of the Heart*, and since the vast majority of the critical literature (discounting theater reviews) has been written on that play, we can understand how the stereotypes prevail. Furthermore, the stereotyped notion that female bonding is the solution to the patriarchal discourse obviously comes from the denouement of *Crimes* but then disappears from the rest of the canon, which many of the critics seem to either ignore or have not bothered to explore.

Perhaps the reason that no critical book has yet been written about Henley's theater is that critics and scholars cannot make a sustained argument about the political or social value of each of the plays in the canon. Henley herself has stated that she is more interested in examining the world rather than changing it or adhering to a particular agenda. Certainly, Henley's theater is significant enough to warrant a book examining all of her plays. As a Pulitzer Prize winning dramatist who has written approximately thirteen plays (three of which have been turned into films), she is recognized as perhaps the most artistically successful female American dramatist in the latter half of the twentieth century. Moreover, with worldwide productions of many of her plays, Henley has begun to develop an international reputation. Scholars must now recognize that Henley's appeal goes beyond viewing her as a regional playwright making political or sociological statements about the role of women in the South. Perhaps the reason for the lack of critical success of many of Henley's late plays is that critics who have pigeonholed her as a Southern playwright find the imposition of regional identity difficult to abandon, even though it amounts to a failed means of explaining her oeuvre.

I hope that this book changes the focus of the way we can appreciate Henley's theater. I have argued that the scope of her plays is much more universal than most critics realize. Henley's protagonists are ostracized, spiritually bankrupt, ontologically insecure, and often physically maimed optimists haunted by the specter of unfulfilled dreams. Like Sisyphus, Henley's characters seek to maintain a sense of dignity in what amounts to be an absurd universe. Although these characters intuitively feel their own nothingness in an estranged world, they long to connect with the Other (perhaps bonding with husbands or siblings), to become spiritually enlightened or to endure with a sense of dignity. Perhaps the value of her theater is that we can relate to her characters on a visceral level as individuals with broken dreams and unfulfilled lives who have an intense desire to find love in an absurd universe that guarantees little else but pain and disappointment. What is consistent in her plays is the idea that no one is empowered, yet each person struggles for acceptance of their own self-worth and the belief that they must count in some small way. Like O'Neill's Yank Smith or Miller's Willy Loman, Henley's protagonists share the desire of needing to belong, to be paid attention to amidst the desperate futility of life. And when the very few of her protagonists do find love, it is usually unrequited or results in the pain and anguish of "an impossible marriage." Thus, there is no wonder why her protagonists suffer from neuroses of all sorts, many of which lead to violent, self-centered, or promiscuous behavior in an attempt by these individuals to gain attention for themselves. Yet, like Sisyphus, despite the overwhelming despair, the existential madness of the modern *angoisse*, Henley's characters endure and have faith in the human spirit that provides only momentary periods of happiness; audiences that watch Henley's plays seem to intuitively understand and accept this noble battle that we face daily.

Henley can best be understood through comparison with her mentor, Chekhov. Like the Russian dramatist, Henley writes about people of all ages and classes; although her favorite subjects are the disenfranchised walking wounded from the working class, she displays the modern neurosis affecting the middle and upper classes as well. Her plays occasionally veer into pathos and sentimentality, but they are, like Chekhov's dramas, consistently laced with tragicomedy; Henley understands that life is a bizarre, sardonic comedy and that we must be able to laugh in the face of the ubiquitous existential madness that engulfs us daily. Moreover, Henley's tragicomic vision, borrowed from her mentor, reminds us that the act of striving for love, self-esteem, or dignity typically goes unfulfilled, yet one must be able to laugh at life's absurdities or else succumb to its neuroses. In addition, like Chekhov's characters who seek to overcome the ghosts of the past, Henley's protagonists cannot flourish or become whole because they often hide behind veiled secrets. Henley's characters learn that the more secrets one has, the greater the facade that they must live with and the more difficult it is to remove the mask; Henley, like Chekhov, exposes human frailties and, in doing so, teaches us about life and human misery. Finally, just as Chekhov depicted his characters as part of a family that could be endearingly amusing but never mocked or despised, Henley also shares compassion for her deeply afflicted personae affected by the traumas of humanity. Chekhov, the physician, knew much about pain and suffering during the nineteenth century; Henley follows in this same tradition, observing the absurdity of twentieth-century life and teaching us to cope with the modern *angoisse*.

Notes

Introduction

1. John Simon, "Sisterhood Is Beautiful," *New York*, 12 January 1981, 42.

2. This was confirmed in a telephone conversation Henley had with Joanne B. Karpinski. See Karpinski, "The Ghosts of Chekhov's *Three Sisters* Haunt Beth Henley's *Crimes of the Heart*," in *Modern American Drama: The Female Canon*, ed. June Schlueter (Madison, N.J.: Fairleigh Dickinson University Press, 1990), 229.

3. William W. Demastes, *Beyond Naturalism: A New Realism in American Theatre*, Contributions in Drama and Theatre Studies, no. 27 (New York and Westport: Greenwood Press, 1988), 136.

4. Matthew C. Roudané, *American Drama Since 1960: A Critical History* (New York: Twayne, 1997), 139.

5. Tish Dace, "Henley, Beth," in *International Dictionary of Theatre — 2: Playwrights*, ed. Mark Hawkins-Dady (Detroit: St. James Press, 1994), 467.

6. Scott Haller, "Her First Play, Her First Pulitzer Prize," *Saturday Review*, November 1981, 40.

7. Frank Rich, "The Theater: Beth Henley's *Crimes of the Heart*," *New York Times*, 5 November 1981, C21.

8. Kay K. Cook, "Henley, Beth, "in *The Oxford Companion to Women's Writing in the United States*, eds. Cathy N. Davidson and Linda Wagner-Martin (New York: Oxford University Press, 1995), 386.

9. Gerald M. Berkowitz, *American Drama of the Twentieth Century* (London and New York: Longman, 1992), 200.

10. Lisa J. McDonnell, "Diverse Similitude: Beth Henley and Marsha Norman," *Southern Quarterly: A Journal of the Arts in the South* 25, no. 3 (1987): 100.

11. In *Dirt and Desire: Reconstructing Women's Writing, 1930–1990*, Patricia Yaeger tries to break down the stereotypical ways of reading Southern women's literature, "dominated by a huge Faulkner industry that both overshadows and tames the terms we use for reading southern women's fiction" (xv). Yaeger argues that the explosion of the grotesque or monstrosity in Southern women's literature should be read with a new paradigm that suggests how the open, bleeding, corpulent, maimed wound reflects, not merely (as in the case of Flannery O'Connor) a latent sadism, but more likely a growing need for social retribution from a society that straitjackets the oppressed; Southern women, Yaeger argues, thus display an incredible anger about being made into magnolias, for example. The Southern Gothic therefore takes on a social commentary about how the grotesque becomes a sign for an emergency within the body politic. Unfortunately, Yaeger does not discuss Henley in her book. See Yaeger, *Dirt and Desire: Reconstructing Women's Writing, 1930–1999* (Chicago and London: University of Chicago Press, 2000). Much more apropos is Miriam M. Chirico's essay on Henley and the grotesque, which argues that Henley's use of the grotesque in terms of deformity, disease, death, and decay, develops from implied or narrated images of the Southern Gothic in the early plays to dramatized human experience at its most violent and lascivious stages in the later dramas. Chirico focuses on Henley's penchant for the intermingling of

violence and horror with moments of beauty and kindness, thus producing a paradox that is inherent in the grotesque. See Chirico, "'Dancing on the Edge of a Cliff': Images of the Grotesque in the Early Plays of Beth Henley," in *Beth Henley: A Casebook*, ed. Julia A. Fesmire (New York and London: Routledge, 2002), 1–31.

12. Jonnie Guerra, "Beth Henley: Female Quest and the Family-Play Tradition," in *Making a Spectacle: Feminist Essays on Contemporary Women's Theatre*, ed. Lynda Hart (Ann Arbor: University of Michigan Press, 1989), 119.

13. *Ibid.*, 119–121.

14. Alan Clarke Shepard, "Aborted Rage in Beth Henley's Women," *Modern Drama* 36, no. 1 (1993): 96.

15. Sally Burke, *American Feminist Playwrights: A Critical History* (New York: Twayne, 1996), 194.

16. Helene Keyssar, *Feminist Theatre: An Introduction to Plays of Contemporary British and American Women* (Basingstoke and London: Macmillan, 1984), 157–159.

17. Karen L. Laughlin, "Criminality, Desire, and Community: A Feminist Approach to Beth Henley's *Crimes of the Heart*," *Women and Performance: A Journal of Feminist Theory* 3, no. 1 (1986): 35–51.

Chapter 1

1. Richard Corliss, "I Go with What I'm Feeling," *Time*, 8 February 1982, 80.

2. Kevin Sessums, "Beth Henley," *Interview*, 17 February 1987, 85.

3. *Ibid.*

4. Lee Alan Morrow and Frank Pike, eds., *Creating Theater: The Professionals' Approach to New Plays* (New York: Vintage, 1986), 13.

5. Margy Rochlin, "The Eccentric Genius of *Crimes of the Heart*," *Ms*, February 1987, 12.

6. Cynthia Wimmer-Moul, "Beth Henley," in *The Playwright's Art: Conversations with Contemporary American Dramatists*, ed. Jackson R. Bryer (New Brunswick: Rutgers University Press, 1995), 117.

7. Amy Peach was chosen partly out of defiance and partly because she feared flamboyance. Henley recalls that at age fourteen, she went unchaperoned to Mississippi State College for Women to attend the Miss Mississippi Contest. Out of what she calls "pubescent euphoria" at being on her own for the first time, she ran up to a college student and said, "One day I am going to be a writer and I will

call myself Amy Peach! Remember that name!" The young man callously responded, "Little girl, if you were just half as cute as you think you are, you'd still be ugly." See Beth Henley, *Collected Plays, Volume 1: 1980–1989* (Lyme, N.H.: Smith and Kraus, 2000), viii.

8. Richard Christiansen, "Pulitzer Prize Winner Beth Henley: Pressing on, Despite the Pressure," *Chicago Tribune*, 19 June 1983, sec. 12, 16.

9. See Sid Smith, "Playwright's Progress," *Chicago Tribune*, 20 September 1992, sec. 13, 12. Also see Mary Dellasega, "Beth Henley," in *Speaking on Stage: Interviews with Contemporary American Playwrights*, eds. Philip C. Kolin and Colby H. Kullman (Tuscaloosa and London: University of Alabama Press, 1996), 258. For detailed analyses of the comparisons between the two plays, see Jean Gagen, "'Most Resembling Unlikeness, and Most Unlike Resemblance': Beth Henley's *Crimes of the Heart* and Chekhov's *Three Sisters*," *Studies in American Drama, 1945–Present* 4 (1989): 119–128, and Joanne B. Karpinski, "The Ghosts of Chekhov's *Three Sisters* Haunt Beth Henley's *Crimes of the Heart*," in *Modern American Drama: The Female Canon*, ed. June Schlueter (Madison, N.J.: Fairleigh Dickinson University Press,1990), 229–245.

10. Many reviewers and critics have written that *Crimes of the Heart* was submitted to the Festival of New American Plays in Louisville without Henley's knowledge of it. Actually, this rumor got started after Jon Jory of the Actors Theater telephoned Henley and assumed that her nervous reaction was due to the fact that Bailey had not informed her of his submission. The truth is that Henley's shyness virtually prevented her from speaking to Jory when he called; Bailey, however, had actually told Henley earlier that he sent the script to Jory.

11. See Jack Kroll, "New Blood in Louisville," *Newsweek*, 19 March 1979, 92, 96; Julius Novick, "Too Much, Too Small," *Village Voice*, 12 March 1979, 87; and T.E. Kalem, "Third Running of the Derby," *Time*, 5 March 1979, 73.

12. For a review of this production, see Bernard Weiner, "A Rich Comedy-Drama on Three Odd Sisters," *San Francisco Chronicle*, 2 May 1979, 55.

13. Simon, "Sisterhood Is Beautiful," 42, 44.

14. Humm, "Off-Broadway Review," *Variety*, 31 December 1980, 60.

15. Edith Oliver, "The Theatre: Off Broadway," *New Yorker*, 12 January 1981, 81–82.

16. Marilyn Stasio, "Theater," *After Dark*, March 1981, 28–29.

17. See Terry Curtis Fox, "The Acting's Teething," *Village Voice*, 7 January 1981, 71; Frank Rich, "Stage: *Crimes of the Heart*, Comedy about 3 Sisters," *New York Times*, 22 December 1980, C16; and Glenne Currie, "Talent on Display in Various Plays," *Los Angeles Times*, 5 January 1981, sec. 6, 5.

18. For example, Eugene O'Neill was 32 years old when he won his first Pulitzer; Tennessee Williams and Arthur Miller won theirs at age 34.

19. The only cast deviations from the Off-Broadway production included Sharon Ullrich as Chick and Raymond Baker as Doc.

20. See Clive Barnes, "*Crime* Is a Prize Hit That's All Heart," *New York Post*, 5 November 1981, in *New York Theatre Critics' Reviews — 1981*, 137–138; Robert Brustein, "Broadway Inches Forward," *New Republic*, 23 December 1981, 25–27; Brendan Gill, "The Theatre: Backstage," *New Yorker*, 16 November 1981, 182–183; Hobe, "*Crimes of the Heart*," *Variety*, 11 November 1981, 84; T.E. Kalem, "Southern Sibs," *Time*, 16 November 1981, 122; Stanley Kauffmann, "Two Cheers for Two Plays," *Saturday Review*, January 1982, 54–55; Howard Kissel, "*Crimes of the Heart*," *Women's Wear Daily*, 6 November 1981, in *New York Theatre Critics' Reviews — 1981*, 140; Jack Kroll, "Theater," *Newsweek*, 16 November 1981, 123; Don Nelson, "*Crimes* Is Heartwarming," *Daily News*, 5 November 1981, in *New York Theatre Critics' Reviews — 1981*, 139; Frank Rich, "The Theater: Beth Henley's *Crimes of the Heart*," *New York Times*, 5 November 1981, C21; John Simon, "Living Beings, Cardboard Symbols," *New York*, 16 November 1981, 125–126; Marilyn Stasio, "Scenes: An Off-Season," *Penthouse*, June 1982, 44; and Edwin Wilson, "Beth Henley: Aiming for the Heart," *Wall Street Journal*, 6 November 1981, in *New York Theatre Critics' Reviews — 1981*, 138.

21. Rich, "The Theater: Beth Henley's *Crimes of the Heart*," C21.

22. Kauffmann, "Two Cheers for Two Plays," 55.

23. Kroll, "Theater," 123.

24. Simon, "Living Beings, Cardboard Symbols," 125.

25. Walter Kerr, "Offbeat — But a Beat Too Far," *New York Times*, 15 November 1981, D3, D31.

26. See John Heilpern, "Great Acting, Pity about the Play," *Times*, 5 December 1981, 11; Gerald Weales, "American Theater Watch, 1981–1982," *Georgia Review* 36 (Fall 1982): 526; and John Beaufort, "A Play That Proves There's No Explaining Awards," *Christian Science Monitor*, Eastern Edition, 9 November 1981, 20.

27. Leo Sauvage, "Reaching for Laughter," *New Leader*, 30 November 1981, 19–20.

28. Michael Feingold, "Dry Roll," *Village Voice*, 18 November 1981, 106.

29. For reviews of this production, see Anthony Masters, "*Crimes of the Heart*," *Times*, 19 May 1983, 15; Sheridan Morley, "Kids on the Skids," *Punch*, 8 June 1983, 52; and Benedict Nightingale, "Low-powered,' *New Statesman*, 27 May 1983, 25–26.

30. For reviews of the Blackstone performances, see Claudia Cassidy, "Our Stage and Stars, Lyric and Otherwise," *Chicago*, February 1984, 20–24, and Richard Christiansen, "*Crimes* Has a 'Heart'-warming Glow," *Chicago Tribune*, 15 December 1983, sec. 2, 24. For a review of the Immediate Theatre's production, see Christine Koyama, "*Crimes of the Heart* Acquits Itself Splendidly," *Chicago Tribune*, 24 May 1984, sec. 5, 13.

31. For a review of this production, see Bernard Weiner, "*Crimes* Captures the Heart of a Family," *San Francisco Chronicle*, 15 May 1984, 41.

32. For different opinions of this production, see Lloyd Grove, "Excess Kooks Foil *Crimes*," *Washington Post*, 8 June 1984, "Weekend," 11, and Megan Rosenfeld, "At Olney, the Best of *Crimes*," *Washington Post*, 8 June 1984, sec. B, 1, 6.

33. See Bernard Weiner, "Berkeley *Crimes of the Heart* Keeps Its Balance," *San Francisco Chronicle*, 16 November 1985, 37.

34. For a review of the production, see Richard Dodds, "Searching for the Guilty Party at *Crimes*," *Times-Picayune* (New Orleans), 19 May 1989, LAG 20.

35. See, for example, Jeremy Kingston, "*Crimes of the Heart*," *Times*, 18 August 1989, 14.

36. See Kevin Kelly, "*Crimes* Earnest but Without Insight," *Boston Globe*, 18 January 1990, "Arts," 74, and Kara Swisher, "*Crimes* Steals Heart of Va. Audiences," *Washington Post*, 25 January 1990, "Virginia Weekly," 2.

37. John Griffin Jones, ed., *Mississippi Writers Talking* (Jackson: University Press of Mississippi, 1982), 190.

38. For positive reviews, see Clive Barnes, "Circle Lives up to Its Rep," *New York Post*, 11 January 1982, in *New York Theatre Critics' Reviews — 1982*, 362–363; John Beaufort, "Sensitive One-act Plays at the Circle Rep," *Christian Science Monitor*, 19 January 1982, 19; Walter Kerr, "Two Parts Gimmickry, One Part Discretion," *New York Times*, 24 January 1982, sec. 2, 3, 10; Howard Kissel, "Confluence," *Women's Wear Daily*, 11 January 1982, in *New York Theatre Critics' Reviews — 1982*, 360–361; Jack Kroll, "The Best of Off-Broadway": *News-*

week, 25 January 1982, 71, 73; Frank Rich, "Stage: 'Confluence,' 3 One-Acters, at Circle Rep," *New York Times*, 11 January 1982, C14; and Douglas Watt, "Three Plays in Search of an Audience," *Daily News*, 11 January 1982, in *New York Theatre Critics' Reviews—1982*, 361.

Michael Feingold's review was neutral since he put the blame squarely on Henley's "mechanical skit-writing" and wordy prologue that needed editing yet found no fault with the production. See Feingold, "Israel in Greece," *Village Voice*, 13–19 January 1982, 101, 103. Humm was also neutral in his assessment, claiming, in his one-paragraph review, that the play is amusing at times, but the bizarre humor was more theatrically sound in *Crimes of the Heart*. See Humm, "Confluence," *Variety*, 27 January 1982, 88. Perhaps the sharpest critic of the play was John Simon, who defended Henley earlier in his two reviews of *Crimes of the Heart* (at the Manhattan Theatre Club and on Broadway at the John Golden Theater). Simon complained mostly about the production, especially Stein's portrayal of Ashbe (he insisted that a Southern girl should have been cast, particularly one with the right accent and some charm), and found fault with the set, costumes, and lighting, which he stated were not up to Circle Rep's usual standards. See Simon, "Slow Flow," *New York*, 25 January 1982, 56–57.

39. For example, the play was successfully staged by the Haight Ashbury Repertory Theater in San Francisco for its Lunchtime Theater program in January 1985. For a review of this production, see Bernard Weiner, "S.E.W. Theater Switch—Lightweight Sit-Com," *San Francisco Chronicle*, 22 January 1985, 58.

40. Markland Taylor, "*The Wake of Jamey Foster*," *Variety*, 27 January 1982, 90.

41. See Robert Brustein, "Good and Plenty," *New Republic*, 29 November 1982, 24–26; Curt Davis, "On Stage," *After Dark*, December 1982–January 1983, 10; Brendan Gill, "The Theatre: Steps Going Down," *New Yorker*, 25 October 1982, 160–161; Humm, "*The Wake of Jamey Foster*," *Variety*, 20 October 1982, 331; Howard Kissel, "*The Wake of Jamey Foster*," *Women's Wear Daily*, 15 October 1982, in *New York Theatre Critics' Reviews—1982*, 181–182; Julius Novick, "Affirmative Actions," *Village Voice*, 26 October 1982, 103; Frank Rich, "Theater: Beth Henley, *Wake of Jamey Foster*," *New York Times*, 15 October 1982, C3; Leo Sauvage, "Dark and Shallow Visions," *New Leader*, 15 November 1982, 19–20; John Simon, "All's Well That Ends 'Good,'" *New York*, 25 October 1982, 77–79; Douglas Watt, "*Jamey*'s' Wake Is Gravely Shallow," *Daily News*, 15 October 1982, in *New York Theatre Critics' Re-*

views—1982, 181; and Edmund Wilson, "Beth Henley's New Play," *Wall Street Journal*, 20 October 1982, 32.

42. See Gill, "The Theatre: Steps Going Down," 161; Rich, "Theater: Beth Henley, *Wake of Jamey Foster*," C3; Simon, "All's Well That Ends 'Good,'" 78; Watt, "*Jamey*'s' Wake Is Gravely Shallow," 181.

43. Kissel, "*The Wake of Jamey Foster*," 181–182.

44. Sauvage, "Dark and Shallow Visions," 20.

45. Gill, "The Theatre: Steps Going Down," 161.

46. Brustein, "Good and Plenty," 26.

47. Humm, "*The Wake of Jamey Foster*," 331.

48. Frank Rich, "The Varied Use of History in *Good* and *Plenty*," *New York Times*, 11 November 1982, C21.

49. Sylvie Drake, "Henley's Heart Is in the Theater," *Los Angeles Times*, 16 April 1983, sec. 5, 1.

50. For reviews of the Washington, D.C., production, see Lloyd Grove, "The Fitfully Funny *Wake of Jamey Foster*," *Washington Post*, 1 June 1984, "Weekend," 11, and David Richards, "Southern Eccentric," *Washington Post*, 2 June 1984, 65. For a review of the Chicago production, see Sid Smith, "*Wake* Warmed-over Dixie Melodrama,'" *Chicago Tribune*, 10 April 1985, sec. 5, 4.

51. Jones, ed., *Mississippi Writers Talking*, 181.

52. Sessums, "Beth Henley," 85.

53. Several critics and scholars, who should be nameless, have incorrectly reported the premiere as having occurred in Illinois. Often, the production history of the play in regional theaters before its appearance on Broadway has been confusing. The correct chronological order for the regional productions is Burbank, Jackson, Dallas, University of Illinois, Buffalo, London, and Chicago.

54. For a review of the Burbank production, see Sylvie Drake, "*Miss Firecracker* Launches Theater," *Los Angeles Times*, 15 March 1980, sec. 2, 8–9.

55. For a review of the University of Illinois production, see Joel Colodner, "*The Miss Firecracker Contest*," *Theatre Journal* 34, no. 2 (1982): 260–261.

56. The only noteworthy review of the Buffalo production was Douglas Smith, "*The Miss Firecracker Contest*," *Variety*, 4 November 1981, 84.

57. For reviews of the London production, see Ned Chaillet, "*The Miss Firecracker Contest*," *Times*, 28 April 1982, 10; James Fenton, "Pillow Talk and Power," *Sunday Times*, 2 May 1982, 39; Sheridan Morley, "Steamboat

Singalong," *Punch*, 5 May 1982, 742; and Benedict Nightingale, "Asking for Trouble," *New Statesman*, 14 May 1982, 30–31.

58. The Chicago production was criticized for the unevenness with which the performers handled the Southern accents; however, the cast was quite adept, including Glenne Headley's Popeye and Joan Allen's Elain. See Richard Christiansen, "*Miss Firecracker* a Bizarre Blast," *Chicago Tribune*, 1 July 1983, sec. 3, 10.

59. Frank Rich, "Theater: *Firecracker*, a Beth Henley Comedy," *New York Times*, 28 May 1984, 11.

60. See Edith Oliver, "The Theatre: Off Broadway," *New Yorker*, 11 June 1984, 112–113, and Richard Schickel, "Jagged Flashes of Inspiration," *Time*, 11 June 1984, 80.

61. Benedict Nightingale, "A Landscape That Is Unmistakably by Henley," *New York Times*, 3 June 1984, sec. 2, 3, 7.

62. See Clive Barnes, "*Firecracker* Is Happy Adjustment," *New York Post*, 29 May 1984, in *New York Theatre Critics' Reviews — 1984*, 251–252; John Beaufort, "*Miss Firecracker Contest*: Beth Henley's Latest Is Lush, Wacky Drama," *Christian Science Monitor*, 6 June 1984, 22; and David Richards, "Where's the Drama?" *Washington Post*, 8 July 1984, sec. H, 1, 5.

63. See Sylviane Gold, "A Fondness for Freaks," *Wall Street Journal*, 20 June 1984, 28, and Ron Cohen, "*The Miss Firecracker Contest*," *Women's Wear Daily*, 30 May 1984, in *New York Theatre Critics' Reviews — 1984*, 253.

64. See Douglas Watt, "*Miss Firecracker Contest* Just Doesn't Have the Spark," *Daily News*, 21 May 1984, in *New York Theatre Critics' Reviews — 1984*, 251, and John Simon, "Repeaters," *New York*, 4 June 1984, 79–80.

65. For reviews of these regional productions, in chronological order of their staging, see Joe Brown, "*Firecracker* Lots of Sparkle but Little Bang," *Washington Post*, 16 August 1985, "Weekend," 7; David Richards, "Olney's Crazy Contest," *Washington Post*, 8 August 1985, sec. B, 1, 10; Steven Winn, "Southern Playwright Gets Bay Exposure," *San Francisco Chronicle*, 7 May 1986, 66; Nicholas de Jongh, "*Miss Firecracker*," *Guardian*, 16 July 1986, 11; Alvin Klein, "*Miss Firecracker* Is Staged in Fairfield," *New York Times*, 20 March 1988, sec. 22, 18–19; Alvin Klein, "Poignant, Daft *Miss Firecracker*," *New York Times*, 24 July 1988, sec. 12, 19; and Jan Breslauer, "*Firecracker Contest* Can't Find Its Spark," *Los Angeles Times*, 10 September 1993, F16.

66. Critics thought Roberts played the macho role to the hilt while Arquette came across as being too cute. Several complained that Purcell never established any charm in

the relationship between Cassie and Riley, yet they praised the subordinate members of the cast, such as Fletcher and Tobolowsky. For critical response to the film, see, for example, Vincent Canby, "Screen: *Nobody's Fool*, Comedy," *New York Times*, 7 November 1986, C18, and Stanley Kauffmann, "Dark Sides," *New Republic*, 15 December 1986, 22–23.

67. Samuel G. Freedman, "Beth Henley Writes a 'Real, Real Personal' Movie," *New York Times*, 2 November 1986, sec. 2, 1, 26.

68. Terrence Rafferty, "Nobody's Fool," *Savvy*, January 1987, 67.

69. For a sample of reviews of the film, see David Ansen, "When Ditsyness Was in Flower," *Newsweek*, 22 December 1986, 75; Paul Attanasio, "*Crimes* Doesn't Pay," *Washington Post*, 12 December 1986, C11; Vincent Canby, "Film: Henley's *Crimes of the Heart*," *New York Times*, 12 December 1986, C19; Richard Corliss, "Once a Comedy, Now an Elegy," *Time*, 22 December 1986, 70; Simon Cunliffe, "A Confederacy of Dunces," *New Statesman*, 24 April 1987, 23; Pauline Kael, "The Current Cinema," *New Yorker*, 15 December 1986, 81–82, 85–87; Stanley Kauffmann, "The Three Sisters," *New Republic*, 2 February 1987, 26–27; and Peter Travers, "*Crimes of the Heart*," *People Weekly*, 15 December 1986, 12. For an in-depth comparison of the film to the play, see Linda Rohrer Paige, "Southern Firecrackers and 'Real Bad Days': Film Adaptations of Beth Henley's *Crimes of the Heart* and *The Miss Firecracker Contest*," in *Beth Henley: A Casebook*, ed. Julia A. Fesmire (New York and London: Routledge, 2002), 128–153. Paige writes that the film is much less interesting and less complex than the play, largely because the absent characters now appear on screen, and character development is sacrificed in favor of entertainment value.

70. Kathleen Betsko and Rachel Koenig, eds., *Interviews with Contemporary Women Playwrights* (New York: William Morrow, 1987), 222.

71. There has been some confusion about the date of the premiere. In the Preface to the published version of the play in 1991, Henley herself cites Spring 1986 as the premiere. See Beth Henley, *The Debutante Ball* (Jackson and London: University Press of Mississippi, 1991), xii. Accepting Henley at her word thus makes for shoddy scholarship, as several critics reported the premiere to be in 1986. See, for example, Hilary Holladay, "Beth Henley," in *Contemporary Poets, Dramatists, Essayists, and Novelists of the South*, eds. Robert Bain and Joseph M. Flora (Westport, Conn: Greenwood Press, 1994), 242.

72. See Bask, "*The Debutante Ball*," *Variety*, 17 April 1985, 228, and Dan Sullivan, "All Odds, No Evens at the *Ball*," *Los Angeles Times*, 11 April 1985, sec. 6, 1, 4. For a dissenting opinion, see Welton Jones, "Henley's Southern Voice Is Shrill in *Debutante Ball*," *San Diego Union*, 13 April 1985, D10.

73. See John James, "Family Horrors Revealed," *Times Educational Supplement*, 16 June 1989, B31; Rachel Koenig, "Amusing, Not Amazing," *Punch*, 9 June 1989, 44; Michael Billington, "A Cracked Belle," *Guardian*, 1 June 1989, 24; John Peter, "The Shaming Shylock of Dustin Hoffman," *Sunday Times*, 4 June 1989, C9; Irving Wardle, "More Drawl Than Ball," *Times*, 31 May 1989, 21; and Matt Wolf, "*The Debutante Ball*," *Plays and Players*, No. 429 (July 1989): 31.

74. John Simon, "Bad Quirks, Good Quirks," *New York*, 11 May 1987, 82–84.

75. See John Beaufort, "*Lucky Spot*: Offbeat Comedy by Beth Henley," *Christian Science Monitor*, 30 April 1987, 30; Edith Oliver, "The Theatre," *New Yorker*, 11 May 1987, 80–81, and Henry Popkin, "On Broadway," *Plays and Players*, No. 406 (July 1987): 32–33.

76. See Humm, "Off-Broadway Review: *The Lucky Spot*," *Variety*, 6 May 1987, 615, and Julius Novick, "Not in the Cards," *Variety*, 12 May 1987, 99, 102.

77. Frank Rich, "Stage: *Lucky Spot* by Beth Henley," *New York Times*, 29 April 1987, C22.

78. For reviews of these productions, respectively, see Richard Christiansen, "Zany and Touching, *The Lucky Spot* Is a Fortunate Find," *Chicago Tribune*, 22 November 1990, sec. 1, 24, and Skip Ascheim, "Spotty Production of Henley's *Lucky Spot*," *Boston Globe*, 9 December 1998, D18.

79. With regard to differences between the film version and the play, see Paige, "Southern Firecrackers and 'Real Bad Days': Film Adaptations of Beth Henley's *Crimes of the Heart* and *The Miss Firecracker Contest*," 128–153.

80. For sample reviews of the film, see Richard Corliss, "Dreams to Avoid," *Time*, 1 May 1989, 68; David Denby, "The Day the Earth Stood Still for You," *New York*, 15 May 1989, 101–102; Hal Hinson, "*Firecracker*: Ignited by Hunter, Robbins," *Washington Post*, 12 May 1989, D7; Pauline Kael, "The Current Cinema," *New Yorker*, 29 May 1989, 103–109; Jack Kroll, "Southern Discomfort," *Newsweek*, 1 May 1989, 75; Eleanor Ringel, "*Miss Firecracker* Doesn't Have Spark Despite Stellar Cast," *Atlanta Constitution*, 12 May 1989, C1, C6; David Sterritt, "*Miss Firecracker* Fizzles— Despite Its Potential," *Christian Science Monitor*, 16 May 1989, 11; and Michael Wilmington, "*Miss Firecracker*: Beauty in Bursts of Affection," *Los Angeles Times*, 28 April 1989, sec. 6, 16–17.

81. See Sylvie Drake, "Henley's *Abundance* Goes West with a New-Found Maturity," *Los Angeles Times*, 24 April 1989, sec. 6, 1, 4; William A. Henry III, "Once Outposts, Now Landmarks," *Time*, 12 June 1989, 72; Welton Jones, "Two Mail-Order Brides Are 'Abundance,'" *San Diego Union*, 26 April 1989, E4; and David Patrick Stearns, "Two Powerful Tales of Greed Gone Wild," *USA Today*, 25 May 1989, D5.

82. See, respectively, James S. Torrens, "Trying Them Out Off Broadway," *America*, 8 December 1990, 453–454, and Mimi Kramer, "Picturing Abundance," *New Yorker*, 12 November 1990, 105–106.

83. Frank Rich, "*Abundance*, Beth Henley's Revisionist Western," *New York Times*, 31 October 1990, C15, C19.

84. See Clive Barnes, "Beth Henley Goes West," *New York Post*, 31 October 1990, in *New York Theatre Critics' Reviews— 1990*, 167–168; Robert Brustein, "She-Plays, American Style," *New Republic*, 17 December 1990, 27–29; Melanie Kirkpatrick, "Theater: Asians in America," *Wall Street Journal*, 9 November 1990, A8; Howard Kissel, "Plenty Is Lacking in *Abundance*," *Daily News*, 31 October 1990, in *New York Theatre Critics' Reviews— 1990*, 167; David Richards, "The Gershwins' *Oh, Kay!* Dances to Harlem," *New York Times*, 11 November 1990, sec. 2, 5, 33; John Simon, "Yo, Kay!," *New York*, 12 November 1990, 92–93; and Linda Winer, "Beth Henley's *Abundance* in a Bizarre Old West," *New York Newsday*, 31 October 1990, in *New York Theatre Critics' Reviews— 1990*, 168–169.

85. See, respectively, Richards, "The Gershwin's *Oh, Kay!* Dances to Harlem," 33; Simon, "Yo, Kay!," 93; and Kissel, "Plenty Is Lacking in *Abundance*," 167.

86. See Barnes, "Beth Henley Goes West," 168, and Winer, "Beth Henley's *Abundance* in a Bizarre Old West," 169.

87. Simon, "Yo, Kay!," 92. Simon does not explain what significance 1968 has in Henley's life nor does he discuss this "ex-husband" or female friend.

88. For reviews of these respective productions, see Gerald Nachman, "Beth Henley's Pioneer Women," *San Francisco Chronicle*, 23 September 1992, E2; Lloyd Rose, "*Abundance*: Wild & Wacky West," *Washington Post*, 22 March 1994, C7; Benedict Nightingale, "Way Out West Leads Nowhere Fast," *Times*, 3 November 1995, 37; and Alvin Klein, "The Schoolhouse Stages *Abundance*," *New York Times*, 28 May 2000, sec. 14, "Westchester," 12.

89. Beth Henley, "Introduction," in Beth Henley, *Collected Plays, Volume II: 1990–1999* (Lyme, N.H.: Smith and Kraus, 2000), viii.

90. For a review of this production, see Alvin Klein, "Hooray for Hollywood? More Like Horrors!," *New York Times*, 12 May 1996, sec. 13, "New Jersey," 12.

91. See Richard Christiansen, "*Control Freaks* Deviates from Taste, Subtlety," *Chicago Tribune*, 22 September 1992, sec. 1, 22, and Hedy Weiss, "Henley's *Control Freaks* Doesn't Deserve a Stage," *Chicago Sun-Times*, 22 September 1992, sec. 2, 32.

92. Dellasega, "Beth Henley," 259.

93. Tom Jacobs, "*Control Freaks*," *Variety*, 9 August 1993, 35.

94. Don Shirley, "*Freaks* Slips at End but It's a Fun Ride," *Los Angeles Times*, 19 July 1993, F1, F9.

95. The Chicago production of *Revelers* was reviewed in the *Chicago Sun-Times* by Hedy Weiss who astutely noted that the play was "a satire of the neurotic types who populate the world of theater and Hollywood" but deemed the writing to be flat, the characters nothing more than types, the pace monotonous, and LaMorte's direction shapeless and humorless. See Weiss, "Henley's *Revelers* No Fun at All," *Chicago Sun-Times*, 10 September 1996, 34.

96. Robin Pogrebin, "Sharing a History as Well as a Play," *New York Times*, 11 October 1998, sec. 2, 5.

97. In the definitive edition of her collected plays, 1995, an incorrect date, is provided for this production of *L-Play*. See Henley, *Collected Plays, Volume II: 1990–1999*, 201.

98. For reviews of this production, see Leo Seligsohn, "The 'L' in Confusion: Beth Henley Veers Into the Theater of the Absurd," *Newsday*, 27 August 1996, B7, and Ed Siegel, "*L-Play* Is a Lifeless Lemon, Largely Lackluster, Leaden," *Boston Globe*, 28 August 1996, C5.

99. This marked the seventh time Hunter appeared in Henley's stage productions. Henley explained why the Hollywood actress, a native Southerner, is well suited to act in her plays: "Holly has a strange ability to be passionate and vulnerable, but extremely tough and rageful. Also, she knows how to walk the edge between truth and humor. Holly hears the music of what I write." See Pamela Renner, "The Mellowing of Miss Firecracker,' *American Theatre* 15, no. 9 (1998): 19.

100. See Clive Barnes, "*Marriage* Reunites Holly with Her Beth Friend," *New York Post*, 16 October 1998, 41, and Fintan O'Toole, "New Georgia Play Is Just Peachy; Hunter's a Hoot in Henley's Latest," *Daily News*, 16 October 1998, "New York Now," 59.

101. Charles Isherwood, "*Impossible Marriage*," *Variety*, 19–25 October 1998, 84.

102. Donald Lyons, "No Faith in Love and Charity," *Wall Street Journal*, 21 October 1998, A20.

103. See John Simon, "The Boys in the Sand," *New York*, 26 October 1998, 82–83, and David Patrick Stearns, "Star Power Can't Save Henley's *Impossible Marriage*," *USA Today*, 20 October 1998, D4.

104. Edward Karam, "Verdict Misadventure," *Times*, 4 November 1998, 40.

105. Ben Brantley, "Fairies Adrift in Love's Garden," *New York Times*, 16 October 1998, E1, E4.

106. For a review of this production, see Graydon Royce, "Flat Script and Cast Hinder *Marriage*," *Minneapolis Star Tribune*, 13 July 2000, 4B.

107. Although the play was hardly noticed by the New York press, the few reviews that exist were negative. For example, see Bruce Weber, "Plan Your Family Reunion in Rehab," *New York Times*, 11 April 2000, E1, E3, and Charles Isherwood, "*Family Week*," *Variety*, 17–23 April 2000, 34.

108. Wimmer-Moul, "Beth Henley," 111.

109. Corliss, "I Go with What I'm Feeling," 80.

110. V. Cullum Rogers, "Beth Henley: Signature of a Non-stop Playwright," *Back Stage* 36, no. 12 (1995): 23.

Chapter 2

1. Sigmund Freud, *Civilization and Its Discontents*, in *The Standard Edition of the Complete Psychological Works of Sigmund Freud*, vol. 21, ed. and trans. James Strachey (London: Hogarth Press, 1961), 87.

2. *Ibid.*, 143.

3. *Ibid.*, 144.

4. Paul Ricoeur, *Freud and Philosophy: An Essay on Interpretation*, trans. Denis Savage (New Haven and London: Yale University Press, 1979), 309.

5. Gerald Levin, *Sigmund Freud* (Boston: G.K. Hall, 1975), 142–143.

6. Samuel I. Greenberg, *Neurosis Is a Painful Style of Living* (New York: New American Library, 1971), 53.

7. Albert Camus, *The Myth of Sisyphus and Other Essays*, trans. Justin O'Brien (New York: Alfred A. Knopf, 1969), 30.

8. *Ibid.*, 6.

9. *Ibid.*, 121.

10. *Ibid.*, 123.

11. Martin Esslin, *The Theatre of the Absurd* (Garden City, N.Y.: Doubleday, 1969), 350.

12. *Ibid.*, 364.

13. *Ibid.*, 375.

14. Scott Haller, "Her First Play, Her First Pulitzer," *Saturday Review*, November 1981, 44.

15. Evelyn Renold, "Baring Her 'Heart' on B'way," *Daily News*, 3 November 1981, 43.

16. Samuel G. Freedman, "Beth Henley Writes a 'Real, Real Personal' Movie," *New York Times*, 2 November 1986, sec. 2, 26.

17. Robert Berkvist, "Act I: The Pulitzer, Act II: Broadway," *New York Times*, 25 October 1981, D4.

18. Beverly Walker, "Beth Henley," *American Film*, December 1986, 30.

19. Terrence Rafferty, "Nobody's Fool," *Savvy*, January 1987, 67.

20. Jonnie Guerra, "Beth Henley: Female Quest and the Family-Play Tradition," in *Making a Spectacle: Feminist Essays on Contemporary Women's Theatre*, ed. Lynda Hart (Ann Arbor: University of Michigan Press, 1989), 120–121. To be fair to Guerra, she does mention that Henley makes fully visible women's experience of nothingness, but the statement refers sociologically to the negative effects the institution of marriage has in the plays. She does pay homage to a more universal sense of absurdism, or "nothingness" as she refers to it, in a footnote that supports Carol P. Christ's comment in her book, *Diving Deep and Surfacing: Women Writers on Spiritual Quest*, that "women's intense perception of their own nothingness sometimes gives them acute perceptions of the larger forces of nothingness, domination, death, and destruction that operate in men's world" (129).

21. William W. Demastes, *Beyond Naturalism: A New Realism in American Theatre*, Contributions in Drama and Theatre Studies, no. 27 (New York and Westport: Greenwood Press, 1988), 138–139.

22. Ayne C. Durham, "Beth Henley," in *Critical Survey of Drama: Supplement*, ed. Frank N. Magill (Pasadena: Salem Press, 1987), 192.

23. Gary Richards, "Moving Beyond Mississippi: Beth Henley and the Anxieties of Postsouthernness," in *Beth Henley: A Casebook*, ed. Julia A. Fesmire (New York and London: Routledge, 2002), 44.

24. Benedict Nightingale, "A Landscape That Is Unmistakably by Henley," *New York Times*, 3 June 1984, sec. 2, 3.

25. Freedman, "Beth Henley Writes a 'Real, Real Personal' Movie," 26.

26. Ted Bent, "Playwright Beth Henley's Only Crime Is Stealing the Hearts of Broadway Critics," *People*, 21 December 1981, 125.

27. Mary Dellasega, "Beth Henley," in *Speaking on Stage: Interviews with Contemporary American Playwrights*, eds. Philip C. Kolin and Colby H. Kullman (Tuscaloosa and London: University of Alabama Press, 1996), 254. This comment is similar to what Henley said to Barbara Isenberg in an interview for the *Los Angeles Times*: "If you just watch the evening news, odd things are happening all the time. And if you ever sit down and talk very seriously to people about their lives or their families' lives, it's always incredibly, unbelievably odd, scary and bizarre." See Isenberg, "She'd Rather Do It Herself," *Los Angeles Times*, 11 July 1993, "Calendar," 80. Also see Henley's remark to Cynthia Wimmer-Moul: "If you get things that are just Disneyland, it doesn't seem real to me. The six o'clock news is real, and that's got a lot more grotesque things in it than my plays." See Wimmer-Moul, "Beth Henley," in *The Playwright's Art: Conversations with Contemporary American Dramatists*, ed. Jackson R. Bryer (New Brunswick: Rutgers University Press, 1995), 116. Henley understands that these bizarre and eccentric feelings are simply part of human needs and struggles in modern society.

28. Kathleen Betsko and Rachel Koenig, eds., "Beth Henley," in *Interviews with Contemporary Women Playwrights* (New York: William Morrow, 1987), 215.

29. Alan Clarke Shepard, "Aborted Rage in Beth Henley's Women," *Modern Drama* 36, no. 1 (1993): 96–97.

30. Dellasega, "Beth Henley," 257.

31. *Ibid.*

32. Betsko and Koenig, eds., "Beth Henley," 221.

33. Laurin Porter, "Contemporary Playwrights/Traditional Forms," in *The Cambridge Companion to American Women Playwrights*, ed. Brenda Murphy (Cambridge: Cambridge University Press, 1999), 196.

34. Betsko and Koenig, eds., "Beth Henley," 221.

35. Dellasega, "Beth Henley," 257.

36. Carol Lawson, "Beth Henley's New Offbeat Play Is in Rehearsal," *New York Times*, 14 September 1982, C9.

37. Betsko and Koenig, eds., "Beth Henley," 215–216.

38. Barbara Kachur, "Women Playwrights on Broadway: Henley, Howe, Norman and Wasserstein," in *Contemporary American Theatre*, ed. Bruce King (Basingstoke and London: Macmillan, 1991), 19.

39. *Ibid.*

40. Spiritual bankruptcy, existential de-

spair, and unfulfilled lives are perhaps best exemplified in Henley's screenplay for the film *Nobody's Fool*, in which Cassie Stoolie, Henley's protagonist, lives unfulfilled in the small town of Buckeye Basin. Cassie is a sensitive girl who must contend with the mundane, parochial life of a small-town community, an aloof mother, a close cousin who "had a spell" and is now virtually catatonic, and a nerdy, obese younger brother who chastises his sister for her homely appearance. Cassie works as waitress in the Elk Lounge, where she sneaks Jack Daniels to avoid the pain of daily drudgery. Cassie's boyfriend abandoned her for another woman once Cassie became pregnant, and Cassie took revenge on him by stabbing him with a fork. Afterwards, Cassie attempted suicide, which was aborted when she fell harmlessly in a dumpster, much like Babe's fruitless suicidal machinations in *Crimes of the Heart*. Cassie joins an acting class (as Henley did earlier in her life) to assuage the neurosis and, in her own words, to "be different from me" so she can fantasize about performing on stage in front of a captive audience. When her acting teacher asks her for an emotion to display during the class, Cassie lets out a loud scream that obviously comes from her troubled soul.

Attending an outdoor production of *The Tempest*, Cassie meets Riley, who is working with the touring company as the set designer and lighting director. Riley, who is from Los Angeles, provides Cassie with the opportunity to fantasize about life outside of her parochial environment. As Cassie begins to establish contact with Riley, she becomes more distant from her former boyfriend, who has now married a wealthy woman; meanwhile, Cassie is forced to abandon the baby to her sister and her family. Cassie, frustrated because her former boyfriend is lost and probably viewing her relationship with a Hollywood type such as Riley as nothing more than unrequited love (Chekhov's favorite motif), begins to focus on suicide by shooting, drowning, and poisoning herself. As is the case in Henley's black comedies, the suicidal attempts go awry — Cassie reaches for rat poison but winds up with candy instead. Cassie, frustrated both by a father who abandoned her when she was fourteen to go to Mexico to drink and gamble, eventually dying from gangrene, and with a mother who tells her that to succeed in life she should become a stenographer, decides to date Riley. As Cassie and Riley establish a relationship, Cassie's fortunes seem to change. She is chosen from the acting class to present a speech from *Romeo and Juliet* at the annual courthouse gala and carnival. Meanwhile, Cassie

fears that Riley will eventually abandon her, which has become the typical experience in her life. During the carnival, Cassie is jeered at by the youngsters in Buckeye Basin who know her well (reminiscent of Carnelle's experience during the Miss Firecracker Contest), but after retreating from the stage, she returns to finish her speech triumphantly. Cassie's former boyfriend apologizes for his past transgressions and wants to get back together with her. However, after fantasizing about the future in Los Angeles, Cassie decides that Riley is her only chance to leave the misery of Buckeye Basin behind. She quits her job, throwing the drinks that she serves at the cafe in the air, exclaiming, "I don't care." Cassie informs her mother that she is leaving for Los Angeles, but her parent, semi-conscious in bed, shows no emotion. Cassie thus flees to Los Angeles with Riley — an attempt to assuage the modern neurosis albeit temporarily.

41. Nancy D. Hargrove, "The Tragicomic Vision of Beth Henley's Dramas," *Southern Quarterly: A Journal of the Arts in the South* 22, no. 4 (1984): 54.

42. Kevin Sessums, "Beth Henley," *Interview*, 17 February 1987, 85.

43. The idea of the neurotic sharing a moment of happiness amidst the existential despair is the subject of Henley's brief one-act play, *Hymn in the Attic*, in which Georgia Ray (Stevie's friend) and Miss Maybelle (Stevie's aunt) try to coax Stevie, a mentally retarded man, out of an attic in which he has barricaded himself in Canton, Mississippi. Stevie's very parochial life in Canton, replete with annoying children who smashed his pet frog against a pine tree and then left laughing about it, leaves little to assuage his neurosis. Only a brief interlude, such as Georgia Ray and Miss Maybelle's reproduction of the soothing Communion service, can provide momentary respite for those suffering from the modern *angoisse*.

44. Colby H. Kullman, "Beth Henley's Marginalized Heroines," *Studies in American Drama, 1945–Present* 8, no. 1 (1993): 27–28.

45. Scott Haller, "Her First Play, Her First Pulitzer," *Saturday Review*, November 1981, 42.

46. Beth Henley, introduction to *Monologues for Women* (Toluca Lake, Ca: Dramaline Publications, 1992), n.p.

47. Margy Rochlin, "The Eccentric Genius of *Crimes of the Heart*," *Ms*, February 1987, 14.

48. Henley has stated that her favorite playwrights also include Shakespeare and Sam Shepard. However, without a doubt, Chekhov influenced her more than any other dramatist, particularly his ability to orchestrate

characters on stage and his nonjudgmental attitude toward his protagonists that enables him to see the tragic and comic in each person. See John Griffin Jones, ed., "Beth Henley," in *Mississippi Writers Talking* (Jackson: University Press of Mississippi, 1982), 182.

49. Jay Sharbutt, "Beth Henley: Mississippi's Own Neil Simon?" *Times-Picayune* (New Orleans), 3 October 1982, sec. 8, 2.

50. V. Cullum Rogers, "Beth Henley: Signature of a Non-stop Playwright," *Back Stage* 36, no. 12 (1995): 23.

51. Betsko and Koenig, eds., "Beth Henley," 216.

Chapter 3

1. Beth Henley, *Am I Blue*, in *Collected Plays, Volume 1: 1980–1989* (Lyme, N.H.: Smith and Kraus, 2000), 83. All subsequent citations are from this edition and are included within parentheses in the text.

2. *Diagnostic and Statistical Manual of Mental Disorders*, 4th ed. (Washington, D.C.: American Psychiatric Association, 1994), 328.

3. *Ibid.*, 329.

4. *Ibid.*, 328.

5. Cynthia Wimmer-Moul, "Beth Henley," in *The Playwright's Art: Conversations with Contemporary American Dramatists*, ed. Jackson R. Bryer (New Brunswick: Rutgers University Press, 1995), 107.

6. Alan Clarke Shepard, "Aborted Rage in Beth Henley's Women," *Modern Drama* 36, no. 1 (1993): 98.

7. *Ibid.*, 99.

8. Colby H. Kullman, "Beth Henley's Marginalized Heroines," *Studies in American Drama, 1945–Present* 8, no.1 (1993): 22.

9. *The Wake of Jamey Foster*, based on the experience of her father's funeral, is Henley's most autobiographical play. She stated that the tensions of the crisis gave the family an excuse to drink, scream, and act out to the fullest. See John Griffith Jones, ed., "Beth Henley," in *Mississippi Writers Talking* (Jackson: University Press of Mississippi, 1982), 179.

10. Beth Henley, *The Wake of Jamey Foster*, in *Collected Plays, Volume 1: 1980–1989* (Lyme, N.H.: Smith and Kraus, 2000), 90. All subsequent citations are from this edition and are included within parentheses in the text.

11. *Diagnostic and Statistical Manual of Mental Disorders*, 654.

12. The catharses and tale telling of those attending the wake attenuates the drama's sense of physical action, making *The Wake of Jamey Foster* appear to be static, much like a classical Greek play in which a large part of the action occurs offstage and is related to us by the actors; certainly, the relationships that cause so much tension in the play have occurred in the past, so modern audiences attuned more to the visual than to the aural might have trouble with the play. This could explain the adverse critical reaction to the 1982 Broadway production.

13. Esmerelda is spelled two different ways in the text of the play: Esmerelda and Esmeralda. However, the former is used more often, so I use that as the spelling.

14. Miriam M. Chirico, "'Dancing on the Edge of a Cliff': Images of the Grotesque in the Plays of Beth Henley," in *Beth Henley: A Casebook*, ed. Julia A. Fesmire (New York and London: Routledge, 2002), 12.

15. Nancy D. Hargrove, "The Tragicomic Vision of Beth Henley's Drama," *Southern Quarterly: A Journal of the Arts in the South* 22, no. 4 (1984): 61.

16. Jonnie Guerra, "Beth Henley: Female Quest and the Family-Play Tradition," in *Making a Spectacle: Feminist Essays on Contemporary Women's Theatre*, ed. Lynda Hart (Ann Arbor: University of Michigan Press, 1989), 122.

17. Don Shewey, "A Director with an Eye for the Telling Detail," *New York Times*, 10 October 1982, sec. 2, 28.

18. Kathleen Betsko and Rachel Koenig, eds., "Beth Henley," in *Interviews with Contemporary Women Playwrights*, ed. Kathleen Betsko and Rachel Koenig (New York: William Morrow, 1987), 216.

19. A couple of critics disagree with my reading of Collard's role in the play. Without offering any explanation for his assessment, Charles S. Watson writes, "As the family assembles at the wake, Marshael gains support from her sister Collard, demonstrating once again the value of female bonding." See Watson, *The History of Southern Drama* (Lexington, Ky: University Press of Kentucky, 1997), 204. If anything, Watson's comment represents the ubiquitous stereotype that critics have of insisting that female solidarity is the unifying force behind Henley's plays. More interesting is Alan Clarke Shepard's depiction of Collard as a victim of patriarchal power. He focuses on the scene in which Wayne sexually harasses Collard by lifting her chin, thus making her feel like his sexual property. He links this scene with Collard's rejection of Brocker's sexual advances toward her. Collard then throws a nest of bird's eggs at Brocker when he serenades Marshael outside her bedroom. Shepard concludes, "Collard is distinguished

by openly resisting the imposition of patriarchal conventions." Collard's actions toward men are further embellished by her comment to Wayne, "Look, just because you'll always have the taste of leather in your mouth, doesn't mean the rest of us have to." This remark may refer to Wayne's cow leather briefcase, which would indicate his rise in the corporate world; however, the comment could also justifiably relate to the bit in his mouth. Shepard interprets the bit as Collard refusing to accept "the patriarchal bridle." Moreover, Shepard notes that Collard's abortion, which left her guilty, reflected by her unabashed desire for fried chicken consumption that she compared to eating her baby, makes Collard a survivor who challenges the conventions of gender while preserving her "nascent claim to self-determination." See Shepard, "Aborted Rage in Beth Henley's Women," 101–102.

20. See Betsko and Koenig, eds., "Beth Henley," 217, and Wimmer-Moul, "Beth Henley," 119.

21. Hargrove, "The Tragicomic Vision of Beth Henley's Drama," 61.

22. Wimmer-Moul, "Beth Henley," 120.

23. Susanne Auflitsch argues that Katty displays a mothering influence toward her nephew and nieces and becomes "the nurturing agent for the whole family, as is exemplified by her concern about health and food." Auflitsch believes that Katty is a counter image to women such as Babe and Carnelle, who have been inhibited by "dysfunctional mothers." See Auflitsch, "Beth Henley's Early Family Plays: Dysfunctional Parenting, the South, and Feminism," *Amerikastudien/American Studies* 46, no. 2 (2001): 275.

24. Henley has stated that in the play, she tried to project images of women in their various states of fertility: the virgin who dreams (Pixrose), the woman who wants to have a child but cannot (Katty), the woman who has children (Marshael), and the woman who aborts them (Collard). See Betsko and Koenig, eds., "Beth Henley," 220.

25. Billy J. Harbin, "Familial Bonds in the Plays of Beth Henley," *Southern Quarterly: A Journal of the Arts in the South* 25, no. 3 (1987): 93.

26. Shepard, "Aborted Rage in Beth Henley's Women," 98. Shepard laments that Marshael's action does not signal her escape from heterosexist oppression. Instead, he focuses most of his discussion of the play on Katty's reaction to her husband's sexual harassment of Collard, which elicits the aborted rage that these two women display toward the patriarchy. However, interpreting the play from the points of view of Katty or Marshael is like try-ing to critically analyze *Hamlet* by psychoanalyzing Horatio. In short, Shepard merely dismisses Marshael's *angoisse* so he can pursue his own agenda.

27. Hargrove, "The Tragicomic Vision of Beth Henley's Dramas," 68. Susanne Auflitsch also reinforces Hargrove's views concerning the symblic implications of setting the play during Easter, which suggests Marshael's resurrection, especially in the latter part of the play: "Thus, by wanting her friend Brocker to buy new Easter candy in the final scene, Marshael wants a rebirth for herself, her children, and maybe even for Brocker, who seems to sincerely love her." See Auflitsch, "Beth Henley's Early Family Plays: Dysfunctional Parenting, the South, and Feminism," 279.

28. Again, the denouement has been misread as a feminist or sociological statement against the patriarchy. Jonnie Guerra views the final scene as "signs both of Marshael's greater security with herself and of her liberation from the expectations of others," and her refusal to attend the funeral "seems to suggest her decision to detach her life from Jamey's and from the forces which ravaged their marriage." See Guerra, "Beth Henley: Female Quest and the Family-Play Tradition," 127. Laurin Porter, like Guerra who admitted that Brocker's serenade left Marshael more exhausted than rejuvenated (as Hargrove suggests), claims that Marshael drifts off to sleep, thus positioning herself in the role of a child. However, she does differ with Shepard and Guerra, concluding, "Gender roles remain unchallenged in this play, with a romantic comic structure, again heterosexual, pairing Brocker and Marshael and reestablishing the *status quo*." See Porter, "Contemporary Playwrights/Traditional Forms," in *The Cambridge Companion to American Women Playwrights*, ed. Brenda Murphy (Cambridge: Cambridge University Press, 1999), 200.

Chapter 4

1. See Karen L. Laughlin, "Criminality, Desire, and Community: A Feminist Approach to Beth Henley's *Crimes of the Heart*," *Women and Performance: A Journal of Feminist Theory* 3, no. 1 (1986): 35–51.

2. Jonnie Guerra, "Beth Henley: Female Quest and the Family-Play Tradition," in *Making a Spectacle: Feminist Essays on Contemporary Women's Theatre*, ed. Lynda Hart (Ann Arbor: University of Michigan Press, 1989), 120–121.

3. Helene Keyssar, *Feminist Theatre: An Introduction to Plays of Contemporary British and American Women* (Basingstoke and London: Macmillan, 1984), 158–159.

4. Janet L. Gupton, "'Un-ruling' the Woman: Comedy and the Plays of Beth Henley and Rebecca Gilman," in *Southern Women Playwrights: New Essays in Literary History and Criticism*, ed. Robert L. McDonald and Linda Rohrer Paige (Tuscaloosa and London: University of Alabama Press, 2002), 128.

5. Susanne Auflitsch, "Beth Henley's Early Family Plays: Dysfunctional Parenting, the South, and Feminism," *Amerikastiden/American Studies* 46, no. 2 (2001): 267–280.

6. Janet V. Haedicke, "'A Population (and Theater) at Risk': Battered Women in Henley's *Crimes of the Heart* and Shepard's *A Lie of the Mind*," *Modern Drama* 36, no. 1 (1993): 83–95.

7. Alan Clarke Shepard, "Aborted Rage in Beth Henley's Women," *Modern Drama* 36, no. 1 (1993): 102–103.

8. Alan Woods, "Consuming the Past: American Theatre in the Reagan Era," in *The American Stage*, ed. Ron Engle and Tice L. Miller (New York and Cambridge: Cambridge University Press, 1993), 261.

9. Laurin Porter, "Contemporary Playwrights/Traditional Forms," in *The Cambridge Companion to American Women Playwrights*, ed. Brenda Murphy (Cambridge: Cambridge University Press, 1999), 198.

10. Mary Dellasega, "Beth Henley," in *Speaking on Stage: Interviews with Contemporary American Playwrights*, ed. Philip C. Kolin and Colby H. Kullman (Tuscaloosa and London: University of Alabama Press, 1996), 257.

11. Barbara Kachur, "Women Playwrights on Broadway: Henley, Howe, Norman and Wasserstein," in *Contemporary American Theatre*, ed. Bruce King (Basingstoke and London: Macmillan, 1991), 19–20.

12. *Ibid.*, 19.

13. Kathleen Betsko and Rachel Koenig, eds., *Interviews with Contemporary Women Playwrights* (New York: William Morrow, 1987), 221.

14. William W. Demastes, *Beyond Naturalism: A New Realism in American Theatre*, Contributions in Drama and Theatre Studies, no. 27 (New York and Westport: Greenwood Press, 1988), 138–139.

15. John Griffin Jones, ed., *Mississippi Writers Talking* (Jackson: University Press of Mississippi, 1982), 182.

16. Sid Smith, "Playwright's Progress," *Chicago Tribune*, 20 September 1992, sec. 13, 12.

17. See Jean Gagen, "'Most Resembling Unlikeness, and Most Unlike Resemblance': Beth Henley's *Crimes of the Heart* and Chekhov's *Three Sisters*," *Studies in American Drama, 1945–Present* 4 (1989): 119–128, and Joanne B. Karpinski, "The Ghosts of Chekhov's *Three Sisters* Haunt Beth Henley's *Crimes of the Heart*," in *Modern American Drama: The Female Canon*, ed. June Schlueter (Madison, N.J.: Fairleigh Dickinson University Press, 1990), 229–245.

18. Karpinski, "The Ghosts of Chekhov's *Three Sisters* Haunt Beth Henley's *Crimes of the Heart*," 236.

19. Gagen, "'Most Resembling Unlikeness, and Most Unlike Resemblance': Beth Henley's *Crimes of the Heart* and Chekhov's *Three Sisters*," 124.

20. Matthew C. Roudané, *American Drama Since 1960: A Critical History* (New York: Twayne, 1997), 140.

21. Leo Sauvage, "Reaching for Laughter," *New Leader*, 30 November 1981, 19–20.

22. Anthony Masters, "*Crimes of the Heart*," *Times*, 19 May 1983, 15.

23. Jones, ed., *Mississippi Writers Talking*, 176.

24. Beth Henley, *Crimes of the Heart*, in *Collected Plays*, vol. 1, 1980–1989 (Lyme, N.H.: Smith and Kraus, 2000), 50. All subsequent citations are from this edition and are included within parentheses in the text.

25. Shepard, "Aborted Rage in Beth Henley's Women," 103.

26. Lana A. Whited, "Suicide in Beth Henley's *Crimes of the Heart* and Marsha Norman's *'night, Mother*," *Southern Quarterly: A Journal of the Arts in the South* 36, no. 1 (1997): 72.

27. Billy J. Harbin, "Familial Bonds in the Plays of Beth Henley," *Southern Quarterly: A Journal of the Arts in the South* 25, no. 3 (1987): 84.

28. Auflitsch, "Beth Henley's Early Family Plays: Dysfunctional Parenting, the South, and Feminism," 270.

29. Harbin, "Familial Bonds in the Plays of Beth Henley," 83.

30. Cynthia Wimmer-Moul, "Beth Henley," in *The Playwright's Art: Conversations with Contemporary American Dramatists*, ed. Jackson R. Bryer (New Brunswick: Rutgers University Press, 1995), 118.

31. Harbin, "Familial Bonds in the Plays of Beth Henley," 85.

32. Minrose C. Gwin, "Sweeping the Kitchen: Revelation and Revolution in Contemporary Southern Women's Writing," *Southern Quarterly: A Journal of the Arts in the South* 30, nos. 2–3 (1992): 58.

33. Harbin, "Familial Bonds in the Plays of Beth Henley," 89.

34. Sigmund Freud, "On Narcissism: An Introduction," in *The Standard Edition of the Complete Psychological Works of Sigmund Freud*, vol. 14, ed. and trans. James Strachey (London: Hogarth Press, 1957), 75.

35. *Ibid.*, 98.

36. Christopher Lasch, *The Culture of Narcissism: American Life in an Age of Diminishing Expectations* (New York: W.W. Norton, 1979), 8, 32–33.

37. *Ibid.*, 33.

38. *Diagnostic and Statistical Manual of Mental Disorders*, 4th ed. (Washington, D.C.: American Psychiatric Association, 1994), 661.

39. *Ibid.*, 659.

40. Laughlin, "Criminality, Desire, and Community: A Feminist Approach to Beth Henley's *Crimes of the Heart*," 42.

41. Thomas P. Adler, *Mirror on the Stage: The Pulitzer Plays as an Approach to American Drama* (West Lafayette: Purdue University Press, 1987), 45.

42. Wimmer-Moul, "Beth Henley," 118.

43. Nancy D. Hargrove, "The Tragicomic Vision of Beth Henley's Drama," *Southern Quarterly: A Journal of the Arts in the South* 22, no. 4 (1984): 59, 61.

44. Lisa J. McDonnell, "Diverse Similitude: Beth Henley and Marsha Norman," *Southern Quarterly: A Journal of the Arts in the South* 25, no. 3 (1987): 97.

45. Ganga Viswanath and Christine Gomez, "Woman's Quest for Identity in Beth Henley's *Crimes of the Heart*," *Indian Scholar* 8, nos. 1–2 (1986): 5.

46. Lasch, *The Culture of Narcissism: American Life in an Age of Diminishing Expectations*, 37.

47. For details about orality in the play, see Laura Morrow, "Orality and Identity in *'night, Mother* and *Crimes of the Heart*," *Studies in American Drama, 1945–Present* 3 (1988): 23–39, and Lou Thompson, "Feeding the Hungry Heart: Food in Beth Henley's *Crimes of the Heart*," *Southern Quarterly: A Journal of the Arts in the South* 30, nos. 2–3 (1992): 99–102.

48. Morrow, "Orality and Identity in *'night, Mother* and *Crimes of the Heart*," 23.

49. *Ibid.*, 32.

50. *Diagnostic and Statistical Manual of Mental Disorders*, 733.

51. Lenny, the wallflower who lacks self-esteem, can be compared to perhaps her precursor, the shy, reclusive Laura, in Tennessee Williams's *The Glass Menagerie*. Both women have disabilities (Lenny a shrunken ovary, Laura a limp), both await "gentleman callers," both are pathetically tied to home. Critics have readily made the comparison. See, for example, Megan Rosenfeld, "Beth Henley's World of Southern Discomfort," *Washington Post*, 12 December 1986, sec. C, 10.

52. Morrow, "Orality and Identity in *'night, Mother* and *Crimes of the Heart*," 35.

53. Harbin, "Familial Bonds in the Plays of Beth Henley," 85.

54. Thompson, "Feeding the Hungry Heart: Food in Beth Henley's *Crimes of the Heart*," 100.

55. C.W. E. Bigsby makes the point that two key male figures (Zackery and Old Granddaddy) never appear in the play. See Bigsby, *Modern American Drama, 1945–1990* (New York and Cambridge: Cambridge University Press, 1992), 320.

56. Morrow, "Orality and Identity in *'night, Mother* and *Crimes of the Heart*," 33.

57. Thompson, "Feeding the Hungry Heart: Food in Beth Henley's *Crimes of the Heart*," 99.

58. Betsko and Koenig, eds., *Interviews with Contemporary Women Playwrights*, 217.

59. *Ibid.*, 215.

60. Alexis Greene, ed., "Beth Henley,'" in *Women Who Write Plays: Interviews with American Dramatists* (Hanover, N.H.: Smith and Kraus, 2001), 220.

Chapter 5

1. Sally Burke, *American Feminist Playwrights: A Critical History* (New York: Twayne, 1996), 196.

2. Jonnie Guerra, "Beth Henley: Female Quest and the Family-Play Tradition," in *Making a Spectacle: Feminist Essays on Contemporary Women's Theatre*, ed. Lynda Hart (Ann Arbor: University of Michigan Press, 1989), 124.

3. Robert L. McDonald, "'A Blaze of Glory': Image and Self-Promotion in Henley's *The Miss Firecracker Contest*," *Southern Quarterly: A Journal of the Arts in the South* 37, no. 2 (1999): 154–155.

4. Lisa Merrill, "*The Miss Firecracker Contest*," *Women & Performance* 2, no. 2 (1985): 76.

5. Laurin Porter, "Contemporary Playwrights/Traditional Forms," in *The Cambridge Companion to American Women Playwrights*, ed. Brenda Murphy (Cambridge, U.K.: Cambridge University Press, 1999), 200.

6. Kathleen Betsko and Rachel Koenig, eds., "Beth Henley," in *Interviews with Contemporary Women Playwrights* (New York: William Morrow, 1987), 220.

7. Karen Jaehne, "Beth's Beauties," *Film Comment* 25 (May-June 1989), 11.

8. For example, Susanne Auflitsch views the female characters in the play as haunted by the memories of their mothers, who were victims of a male-dominated society. However, the argument is too much of a stretch, for there is no evidence that Carnelle's surrogate mother, Aunt Ronelle, is dysfunctional because of the patriarchy. Auflitsch, who gets the title of the play wrong, even contributes to the argument that the dysfunction is physiological, not sociological: "Another epitome of maternal dysfunctionality occurs in *The Wake of Jamey Foster*. After Aunt Ronelle's pituitary gland, which was affected by cancer, was replaced by that of a monkey, she started to grow long black hair everywhere on her body just like an ape. These severe side effects alienate Ronelle. Her transformation into an animal combined with an association of brain damage draws a vivid picture of maternal dysfunctionality." See Auflitsch, "Beth Henley's Early Family Plays: Dysfunctional Parenting, the South, and Feminism," *Amerikastudien/American Studies* 46, no. 2 (2001): 271.

9. *Diagnostic and Statistical Manual of Mental Disorders*, 4th ed. (Washington, D.C.: American Psychiatric Association, 1994), 654.

10. Beth Henley, *The Miss Firecracker Contest*, in *Collected Plays, Volume I: 1980–1989* (Lyme, N.H.: Smith and Kraus, 2000), 152. All subsequent citations are from this edition and are included within parentheses in the text.

11. Janet V. Haedicke notes that Carnelle's precursor as a desperate southern sexpot is Blanche DuBois in Tennessee Williams's *A Streetcar Named Desire*. Billy J. Harbin, however, views Elain differently, insisting that "Elain's dialogue frequently echoes that of the lyrical Blanche DuBois." See Haedicke, "Margins in the Mainstream: Contemporary Women Playwrights," in *Realism and the American Dramatic Tradition*, ed. William W. Demastes (Tuscaloosa: University of Alabama Press, 1996), 208, and Harbin, "Familial Bonds in the Plays of Beth Henley," *Southern Quarterly: A Journal of the Arts in the South* 25, no. 3 (1987): 91.

12. Laurilyn J. Harris, "Delving Beneath the Stereotypes: Beth Henley's *The Miss Firecracker Contest*," *Theatre Southwest* 14 (May 1987): 5.

13. Richard Christiansen, "Pulitzer Prize Winner Beth Henley: Pressing on, Despite the Pressure," *Chicago Tribune*, 19 June 1983, sec. 12, 16.

14. Harris, "Delving Beneath the Stereotypes: Beth Henley's *The Miss Firecracker Contest*," 5.

15. One might wonder if Henley's point is to offer a sociological critique of beauty pageants and the confining notion that a woman's sense of self-worth is determined by the male gaze and what has been considered to be patriarchal assumptions of a definition of female attractiveness. Laurilyn J. Harris notes that *The Miss Firecracker Contest*, like *Crimes of the Heart*, explores the notion of female identity, which, she states, "is hampered by the rigid, shallow, stereotypical roles that define and confine them, roles imposed by a society that threatens to suppress all traces of nonconformity." See Harris, "Delving Beneath the Stereotypes: Beth Henley's *The Miss Firecracker Contest*," 4. Certainly, as Lisa Merrill suggests, women such as Elain and Carnelle who enter the contest to be judged by the male gaze are inevitably the losers because they become merely objects to be evaluated. See Merrill, "*The Miss Firecracker Contest*," 75. Henley, however, when interviewed for a feature in *Film Comment* that reduced the play to the question of how beauty came to be enshrined and debased in the South, defended the idea that the yearn for beauty was more universal. See Jaehne, "Beth's Beauties," 9. The idea that a beauty pageant is inherently sexist and that beauty can be determined by traditional patriarchal assumptions is never an issue in the play because Carnelle confirms the notion that winning the contest is a means of saving grace and acquiring beauty rather than being forced to accept an ideology that she refuses to condone.

16. *Diagnostic and Statistical Manual of Mental Disorders*, 661.

17. Cynthia Wimmer-Moul, "Beth Henley," in *The Playwright's Art: Conversations with Contemporary American Dramatists*, ed. Jackson R. Bryer (New Brunswick: Rutgers University Press, 1995), 115.

18. Jaehne, "Beth's Beauties," 12.

19. Laurilyn J. Harris argues that Elain breaks down because she attempts to challenge the stereotype as a beauty queen with which she is forced to live. See Harris, "Delving Beneath the Stereotypes: Beth Henley's *The Miss Firecracker Contest*," 4. My argument is that Elain's neuroticism stems from the contrast between her id and the cultural expectations of the superego, defined by her mother's nurturance; the neurosis cannot be quashed, no matter what Elain tries to do.

20. This is essentially the argument that Alan Clarke Shepard makes in his essay on aborted rage in Henley's plays. Admitting that Elain is a peripheral character in the play, Shepard still views Elain's conflicted personality as a brief rebellion that "illuminates a paradigm of female surrender" that runs through-

out Henley's oeuvre. See Shepard, "Aborted Rage in Beth Henley's Women," *Modern Drama* 36, no. 1 (1993): 96.

21. Jaehne, "Beth's Beauties," 12.

22. Critics who view the play from a sociological perspective cite Delmount as the personification of the male gaze governing the contest and anatomizing women's body parts. See, for example, Burke, *American Feminist Playwrights: A Critical History*, 197.

23. Larry G. Mapp, "Lessons from the Past: Loss and Redemption in the Early Plays of Beth Henley," in *Beth Henley: A Casebook*, ed. Julia A. Fesmire (New York and London: Routledge, 2002), 36.

24. Miriam M. Chirico, "'Dancing on the Edge of a Cliff': Images of the Grotesque in the Plays of Beth Henley," in *Beth Henley: A Casebook*, ed. Julia A. Fesmire (New York and London: Routledge, 2002), 9.

25. On a personal level, Henley finds Popeye endearing. With regard to the outfits for bullfrogs that Popeye sews, Henley recalls that her mother told her that her aunt made those costumes when she was a little girl. See Jaehne, "Beth's Beauties," 12.

26. Harris, "Delving Beneath the Stereotypes: Beth Henley's *The Miss Firecracker Contest*," 7.

27. Linda Rohrer Paige, "Southern Firecrackers and 'Real Bad Days': Film Adaptations of Beth Henley's *Crimes of the Heart* and *The Miss Firecracker Contest*," in *Beth Henley: A Casebook*, ed. Julia A. Fesmire (New York and London: Routledge, 2002), 150.

28. Lily is spelled two different ways in the play. The owner of the shop is "Miss Celia Lilly" (191), but the store's name is "Miss Lily's Dress Shop" (181).

29. Joel Colodner, "*The Miss Firecracker Contest*," *Theatre Journal* 34, no. 2 (1982): 260.

30. Gene A. Plunka, tape-recorded interview with Beth Henley, 29 June 2002, Los Angeles, California.

31. Robert J. Andreach, *Creating the Self in the Contemporary American Theater* (Carbondale and Edwardsville: Southern Illinois University Press, 1998), 130.

32. Harbin, "Familial Bonds in the Plays of Beth Henley," 92.

33. Janet L. Gupton, "'Un-ruling' the Woman: Comedy and the Plays of Beth Henley and Rebecca Gilman," in *Southern Women Playwrights: New Essays in Literary History and Criticism*, eds., Robert L. McDonald and Linda Rohrer Paige (Tuscaloosa and London: University of Alabama Press, 2002), 135.

34. Chirico, "'Dancing on the Edge of a Cliff': Images of the Grotesque in the Plays of Beth Henley," 15.

35. Alexis Greene, ed., "Beth Henley," in *Women Who Write Plays: Interviews with American Dramatists* (Hanover, N.H.: Smith and Kraus, 2001), 217.

36. *Diagnostic and Statistical Manual of Mental Disorders*, 659.

37. Stephen Holden, Diane Solway, and Laurie Winer, "1988: Previews from 36 Artists," *New York Times*, 3 January 1988, sec. 2, 31. Also, compare Henley's comment on the play in an interview with Kathleen Betsko and Rachel Koenig: "It's about the debutante and her mother, about mother-daughter love. About the fragility of love, how people need love so badly that the need literally cripples them in their struggle to attain it." See Betsko and Koenig. eds., "Beth Henley," 218.

38. Beth Henley, *The Debutante Ball*, in *Collected Plays, Volume I: 1980–1989* (Lyme, N.H.: Smith and Kraus, 2000), 279. All subsequent citations are from this edition and are included within parentheses in the text.

39. Laura Ross, "Henley's Late Date," *American Theatre* 2 (April 1985): 19.

40. Greene, ed., "Beth Henley," 205.

41. *Ibid.*, 206.

42. Beth Henley, "Preface," in *The Debutante Ball* (Jackson and London: University Press of Mississippi, 1991), xii.

43. Henley wrote the role of Frances for Phyllis Frelich, whom Henley had seen in *Children of a Lesser God*; Frelich eventually played Frances in the South Coast Repertory production in April 1985. Although several politically correct activists insisted that Frances was an insult to the deaf community, Henley defended her inclusion in the play:

> I also wanted to write a part for a deaf person that didn't have to be sweet and perfect. I wanted to write a real person. And there are so many images in that play of isolation, of people having the need for love and not being able to express it. Frances' mother is dying, she's out of place, she doesn't fit in, and she's fallen in love with a woman and didn't even know she was interested in women. Having Frances in the play sort of embodies people trying to communicate. How do we connect? How do we love? See Greene, ed., "Beth Henley," 207.

44. When Henley was asked about the brief episode of lesbianism in the play, she focused on the desperate need to be loved shared by both Bliss and Frances. Henley stated, "I think one of the things that the play is really about is love and self-love and also seeing through facades. I wanted it to express that these women really connect on some essential level that doesn't have to do with the fact that one's

from the country and one's from the city. It's just a need they both have, a desperate need to be loved and to be seen, and this need and acceptance of each other overcome other elements, such as that they're both women, or that one speaks French and one doesn't, or that one has probably never had a lover at all and the other one has had many." See Mary Dellasega, "Beth Henley," in *Speaking on Stage: Interviews with Contemporary American Playwrights*, eds. Philip C. Kolin and Colby H. Kullman (Tuscaloosa and London: University of Alabama Press, 1996), 255. Feminists argue that the only relationship in the play that is viable is the lesbian affair that Bliss has with Frances. However, when Alexis Greene pressed this point with Henley, she disagreed, stating, "Well it [the relationship between Frances and Bliss] probably won't work out eventually, but it will be good for a while. They both need each other so desperately and they've both been cruel to other people. But I don't know how it will end." See Greene, ed., "Beth Henley," 207.

45. *Diagnostic and Statistical Manual of Mental Disorders*, 654.

46. Holden, Solway, and Winer, "1988: Previews from 36 Artists," 31.

47. Tish Dace, "Henley, Beth (Elizabeth Becker Henley)," in *Contemporary American Dramatists*, ed. K.A. Berney (London and Detroit: St. James Press, 1994), 261.

48. Greene, ed., "Beth Henley," 206.

Chapter 6

1. Rebecca King states that Henley's choice of setting is not arbitrary, for Reed Hooker, whose own name suggests procurement, owes his fortune to the "pigeons" he has duped in gambling and speculation. Her analysis of the play is sociological, arguing that the play demonstrates the selfish forms of capitalism and liberal meritocracy that result in the social and economic plights of homelessness and unemployment that run throughout the Great Depression. King reveals that the Lucky Spot's name and history remind us of the risks involved in any capitalistic venture. She also acknowledges that setting the play in the South readily reveals the disparity between commercial capitalistic culture and the feudal aristocratic system it replaced. See King, "*The Lucky Spot* as Immanent Critique," in *Beth Henley: A Casebook*, ed. Julia A. Fesmire (New York and London: Routledge, 2002), 64–87.

2. Beth Henley, "Introduction," in *Collected Plays, Volume 1: 1980–1989* (Lyme, N.H.: Smith and Kraus, 2000), xv–xvi.

3. *Ibid.*, xv.

4. *Ibid.*

5. Beth Henley, *The Lucky Spot*, in *Collected Plays, Volume 1: 1980–1989* (Lyme, N.H.: Smith and Kraus, 2000). All subsequent citations are from this edition and are included within parentheses in the text.

6. King, "*The Lucky Spot* as Immanent Critique," 76.

7. *Diagnostic and Statistical Manual of Mental Disorders*, 4th ed. (Washington, D.C.: American Psychiatric Association, 1994), 646.

8. *Ibid.*

9. *Ibid.*, 650.

10. Henley, "Introduction," xv.

11. Esther B. Fein, "Role Call: Waif, Wife, Drummer Girl," *New York Times*, 26 April 1987, sec. 2, 5.

12. Charles S. Watson, *The History of Southern Drama* (Lexington, Ky: University Press of Kentucky, 1997), 204.

13. Tice Dace, "Henley, Beth," in *Contemporary American Dramatists*, ed. K.A. Berney (London and Detroit: St. James Press, 1994), 259.

14. Mary Dellasega, "Beth Henley," in *Speaking on Stage: Interviews with Contemporary American Playwrights*, eds. Philip C. Kolin and Colby H. Kullman (Tuscaloosa and London: University of Alabama Press, 1996), 256.

15. *Ibid.*

16. In his review of the Manhattan Theatre Club's 1990 production of *Abundance*, Frank Rich was the first to characterize the play as a revisionist western.. See Frank Rich, "*Abundance*, Beth Henley's Revisionist Western," *New York Times*, 31 October 1990, C15, C19. For more details about the play as historical revisionism, see Richard Wattenberg, "Challenging the Frontier Myth: Contemporary Women's Plays about Women Pioneers," *Journal of American Drama and Theatre* 4, no. 3 (1992): 42–61.

17. Roy Hoffman, "Brash New South Is Still a Stranger to Its Dramatists," *New York Times*, 2 July 1989, sec. 2, 5.

18. Beth Henley, "*Abundance*," in *Collected Plays, Volume 2: 1990–1999* (Lyme, N.H.: Smith and Kraus, 2000), 7. All subsequent citations are from this edition and are included within parentheses in the text.

19. Alexis Greene, "Beth Henley," in *Women Who Write Plays: Interviews with American Dramatists*, ed. Alexis Greene (Hanover, N.H.: Smith and Kraus, 2001), 218.

20. Cynthia Wimmer-Moul, "Beth Hen-

ley," in *The Playwright's Art: Conversations with Contemporary American Dramatists*, ed. Jackson R. Bryer (New Brunswick, N.J.: Rutgers University Press, 1995), 109. The situation that Henley depicts in the play also is autobiographical, for Henley initially went west to California with the hope of acting in films and writing screenplays for Hollywood, only to find herself wasting her time while getting offered only modeling jobs. She believed that her experience was universal rather than atypical and tried to express that in the play: "But I think I was dealing with what happens with people's dreams in *Abundance* — how people come out to California so full of hope to be an actress or to be in the movies and slowly they find themselves working at Chicken Bob's, or they want to be great novelists and they're trying to write bad TV scripts." See Dellasega, "Beth Henley," 256.

21. Greene, "Beth Henley," 218.

22. Dellasega, "Beth Henley," 256.

23. Wattenberg, "Challenging the Frontier Myth," 53.

24. Robert J. Andreach, "The Missing Five Years and Subjectivity in Beth Henley's *Abundance*," *Southern Quarterly: A Journal of the Arts in the South* 39, no. 3 (2001): 147. Andreach notes that the key to the play is understanding the difference in the growth and development of Bess and Macon. He takes a feminist approach to the play, arguing that Bess prospers because her five years spent with the Indians was an inner journey to develop imagination, her potential, thus allowing the formerly domesticated woman to channel her rage, not against the Oglalas, but against her husband and Macon, who betrayed her. Macon, however, in her search for the imagination, betrayed the women's movement by remaining on the frontier and being "conditioned by the collective history and psychology of submissiveness" (149).

25. Greene, "Beth Henley," 219.

26. Karen L. Laughlin, "Abundance or Excess?: Beth Henley's Postmodern Romance of the True West," in *Beth Henley: A Casebook*, ed. Julia A. Fesmire (New York and London: Routledge, 2002), 99.

27. James S. Torrens, "Trying Them Out Off Broadway," *America*, 8 December 1990, 454.

28. Rich, "*Abundance*, Beth Henley's Revisionist Western," C15.

29. For example, see *The World Encyclopedia of Contemporary Theatre*, Vol. 2: Americas, ed. Don Rubin (London and New York: Routledge, 1996), 433.

30. Laughlin, "Abundance or Excess?: Beth Henley's Postmodern Romance of the West," 89.

31. Greene, "Beth Henley," 218.

32. At the end of the play, Bess, now facing the end of her financial success, shares a brief moment of consciousness with the dying and ravaged Macon. Wattenberg states that Bess and Macon finally embrace "that which is and must be," which seems to imply that they share a recognition of the absurd condition. He writes, "While these women have aged considerably and Macon speaks of her imminent death, the play ends with Bess and Macon joining each other in a deeply felt laugh — a laugh that expresses their shared consciousness of life's limitations and the human will to endure these limitations." See Wattenberg, "Challenging the Frontier Myth," 53. I contend that although this may be a moment of shared consciousness, it is more of a bitter irony of how they have destroyed their lives because of the fact that they have ignored their friendship for each other; indeed, they do not share a moment of joy but rather a moment of regret. Henley accentuates the specter of lost dreams as Macon acknowledges that she can no longer whistle and then does so only upon Bess's urging.

Chapter 7

1. Alexis Greene, ed., "Beth Henley," in *Women Who Write Plays: Interviews with American Dramatists* (Hanover, N.H.: Smith and Kraus, 2001), 211.

2. "Introduction," in Beth Henley, *Collected Plays, Volume II: 1990–1999* (Hanover, N.H.: Smith and Kraus, 2000), viii–ix.

3. Beth Henley, *Signature*, in *Collected Plays, Volume II: 1990–1999* (Hanover, N.H.: Smith and Kraus, 2000), 58. All subsequent citations are from this edition and are included within parentheses in the text.

4. Alvin Klein, "Hooray for Hollywood? More Like 'Horrors!,'" *New York Times*, 12 May 1996, sec. 13, "New Jersey," 12.

5. Miriam M. Chirico, "'Dancing on the Edge of a Cliff': Images of the Grotesque in the Plays of Beth Henley," in *Beth Henley: A Casebook*, ed. Julia A. Fesmire (New York and London: Routledge, 2002), 21.

6. Cynthia Wimmer-Moul, "Beth Henley," in *The Playwright's Art: Conversations with Contemporary American Dramatists*, ed. Jackson R. Bryer (New Brunswick, N.J.: Rutgers University Press, 1995), 108–109.

7. Greene, ed., *Women Who Write Plays: Interviews with American Dramatists*, 211. One should keep in mind that the impetus for

writing the play occurred in Los Angeles when Henley, already feeling depressed on one particular day, grew more upset by the odious reading of her future by a graphologist on Melrose Avenue.

8. Providing a female with an obviously male name seems to create a Brechtian-type alienation effect that serves no apparent purpose. However, we must remind ourselves that the play is set in futuristic Hollywood, the trend-setting capital of the world, so the gender blending would seem to coincide with Henley's prefatory comment that the production company should be "racially mixed, giving a cosmopolitan, universal feel to the play" (58).

9. Greene, ed., *Women Who Write Plays: Interviews with American Dramatists*, 219.

10. Wimmer-Moul, "Beth Henley," 115.

11. Greene, ed., *Women Who Write Plays: Interviews with American Dramatists*, 212.

12. *Ibid.*

13. Gene A. Plunka, tape-recorded interview with Beth Henley, 29 June 2002, Los Angeles, California.

14. *Ibid.*

15. Kathleen Betsko and Rachel Koenig, eds., *Interviews with Contemporary Women Playwrights* (New York: William Morrow, 1987), 211.

16. Barbara Isenberg, "She'd Rather Do It Herself," *Los Angeles Times*, 11 July 1993, "Calendar," 80.

17. Beth Henley, *Control Freaks*, in *Collected Plays, Volume II: 1990–1999* (Hanover, N.H.: Smith and Kraus, 2000), 131. All subsequent citations are from this edition and are included within parentheses in the text.

18. Chirico, "'Dancing on the Edge of a Cliff': Images of the Grotesque in the Plays of Beth Henley," 26.

19. Isenberg, "She'd Rather Do It Herself," 80.

20. Wimmer-Moul, "Beth Henley," 114.

21. Greene, ed., *Women Who Write Plays: Interviews with American Dramatists*, 215.

22. Isenberg, "She'd Rather Do It Herself," 80.

23. Sister may be modeled on Laura Wingfield in Tennessee Williams's *The Glass Menagerie*. The notion of family members riddled by pettiness and physical deformities manipulating the intentions of a "gentleman caller" (Paul) parallels the plot of Williams's play. Sister has various similarities to Laura, both of whom draw upon the sympathies of audiences through their wallflower images and physical inadequacies. In particular, when Sister drops the gingerbread men from the oven tray and tries to piece the charred crumbs to-

gether, we are reminded of Laura's remorse over the shattered unicorn. For an in-depth comparison between the two characters, see Gary Richards, "Moving Beyond Mississippi: Beth Henley and the Anxieties of Postsouthernness," in *Beth Henley: A Casebook*, ed. Julia A. Fesmire (New York and London: Routledge, 2002), 52–56. Richards actually argues that Henley's play is a strategic parody of *The Glass Menagerie*, with Sister's aggressive and erotic behavior a marked contrast to Laura's passivity. Richards believes that *Control Freaks* allows Henley to efface Williams and the Southern tradition, repaying "the older playwright for whatever intentional or unintentional acts of violence his work has enacted on subsequent regional writers and their abilities to escape his control" (34).

24. Mary Dellasega, "Beth Henley," in *Speaking on Stage: Interviews with Contemporary American Playwrights*, eds. Philip C. Kolin and Colby H. Kullman (Tuscaloosa and London: University of Alabama Press, 1996), 258.

25. Susan Forward and Craig Buck, *Betrayal of Innocence: Incest and Its Devastation* (New York and London: Penguin, 1988), 19.

26. Laura Davis, *Allies in Healing: When the Person You Love Was Sexually Abused as a Child* (New York: HarperCollins, 1991), 18.

27. Sam Kirschner, Diana Adile Kirschner, and Richard L. Rappaport, *Working with Adult Incest Survivors: The Healing Journey*, Frontiers in Couples and Family Therapy Series, no. 6 (New York: Brunner/Mazel, 1993), 6.

28. *Ibid.*, 47.

29. Forward and Buck, *Betrayal of Innocence: Incest and Its Devastation*, 23.

30. Davis, *Allies in Healing: When the Person You Love Was Sexually Abused as a Child*, 136.

31. Kirschner, Kirschner, and Rappaport, *Working with Adult Incest Survivors: The Healing Journey*, 7.

32. *Diagnostic and Statistical Manual of Mental Disorders*, 4th ed. (Washington, D.C.: American Psychiatric Association, 1994), 274.

33. *Ibid.*, 275.

34. *Ibid.*, 278.

35. Kirschner, Kirschner, and Rappaport, *Working with Adult Incest Survivors: The Healing Journey*, 7.

36. This scene is reminiscent of the confrontation that Shelly has with Dodge in act 2 of Sam Shepard's *Buried Child*. With Vince trying to get Dodge to recognize him, Shelly instead becomes the focus of Dodge's attention; the aging patriarch then proceeds to insult her. Ostensibly, Shelly assumes a domestic role in peeling carrots, trying to fit into this

new environment with which she feels uncomfortable. However, on the subliminal level, Shelly is countering Dodge's insulting barrage by slowing castrating him. Interesting enough, one could also make parallels between Bradley's symbolic rape of Shelly at the end of act 2 by sticking his fingers in her mouth and Carl doing the same thing to Sister. One wonders whether Henley had Shepard in mind when she wrote this segment of the play.

37. Obviously, an actress would have to be quite accomplished to pull off this achievement, in essence, moving delicately from one persona to another without pausing for breath. Holly Hunter was superb at making the Sister/Pinkie/Spaghetti transformation during the original 1993 production at the Met Theatre in Los Angeles.

38. Gene A. Plunka, tape-recorded interview with Beth Henley, 29 June 2002, Los Angeles, California.

Chapter 8

1. Henley herself refers to the play as a ritual. See Mary Dellasega, "Beth Henley," in *Speaking on Stage: Interviews with Contemporary American Playwrights*, eds. Philip C. Kolin and Colby H. Kullman (Tuscaloosa and London: University of Alabama Press, 1996), 259.

2. Dash's last name is alternately spelled "Gray" and "Grey" in the text. His brother's name is listed in the Cast of Characters as Bob Gray.

3. Dellasega, "Beth Henley," 259.

4. Beth Henley, *Revelers*, in *Collected Plays, Volume II: 1990–1999* (Hanover, N.H.: Smith and Kraus, 2000), 165. All subsequent citations are from this edition and are included within parentheses in the text.

5. Beth Henley, "Introduction," in *Collected Plays, Volume II: 1990–1999* (Hanover, N.H.: Smith and Kraus, 2000), xii.

6. This love-hate relationship that Kate has for Dash is reminiscent of Henley's comment about her ambivalence toward her former acting teacher at the University of Illinois. Thus, Henley must identify with Kate to some degree.

7. Gene A. Plunka, tape-recorded inter-

view with Beth Henley, 29 June 2002, Los Angeles, California.

8. Henley, "Introduction," xii.

9. Leo Seligsohn unconvincingly suggests that *L-Play* borrows from the distorted lens of Eugène Ionesco and the contrivances of Samuel Beckett. See Seligsohn, "The 'L' in Confusion: Beth Henley Veers into the Theater of the Absurd," *Newsday*, 27 August 1996, B7.

10. Alexis Greene, ed., "Beth Henley," in *Women Who Write Plays: Interviews with American Dramatists* (Hanover, N.H.: Smith and Kraus, 2001), 221.

11. Seligsohn, "The 'L' in Confusion: Beth Henley Veers into the Theater of the Absurd," B7.

12. Beth Henley, *L-Play*, in *Collected Plays, Volume II: 1990–1999* (Hanover, N.H.: Smith and Kraus, 2000), 228. All subsequent citations are from this edition and are included within parentheses in the text.

13. Gene A. Plunka, tape-recorded interview with Beth Henley, 29 June 2002, Los Angeles, California. During this interview, Henley also told me that the inspiration for "Leaving" was the recent death of her own grandmother before the elderly woman could reveal more intimate details about her life to her granddaughter.

14. Henley, "Introduction," xiv.

15. Beth Henley, *Impossible Marriage*, in *Collected Plays, Volume II: 1990–1999* (Hanover, N.H.: Smith and Kraus, 2000), 263. All subsequent citations are from this edition and are included within parentheses in the text.

16. Greene, ed., *Women Who Write Plays: Interviews with American Dramatists*, 204.

17. Pamela Renner, "The Mellowing of Miss Firecracker," *American Theatre* 15 (November 1998): 61.

18. Robin Pogrebin, "Sharing a History as Well as a Play," *New York Times*, 11 October 1998, sec. 2, 25.

19. Greene, ed., *Women Who Write Plays: Interviews with American Dramatists*, 204–205.

20. Pogrebin, "Sharing a History as Well as a Play," 25.

21. Renner, "The Mellowing of Miss Firecracker," 19.

22. Gene A. Plunka, tape-recorded interview with Beth Henley, 29 June 2002, Los Angeles, California.

23. Greene, ed., *Women Who Write Plays: Interviews with American Dramatists*, 202.

24. *Ibid.*

Bibliography

Works by Beth Henley

Abundance. In *Collected Plays. Volume II: 1990–1999.* Lyme, N.H.: Smith and Kraus, 2000. 1–53.

Abundance. New York: Dramatists Play Service, 1991.

Am I Blue. In *Antaeus* 66 (Spring 1991): 208–224.

Am I Blue. In *The Best Short Plays — 1983*, edited by Ramon Delgado, 131–150. Radnor, Pa.: Chilton, 1983.

Am I Blue. In *Collected Plays. Volume I: 1980–1989.* Lyme, N.H.: Smith and Kraus, 2000. 65–85.

Am I Blue. New York: Dramatists Play Service, 1982.

Control Freaks. In *Collected Plays: Volume II: 1990–1999.* Lyme, N.H.: Smith and Kraus, 2000. 109–146.

Crimes of the Heart. In *Collected Plays. Volume I: 1980–1989.* Lyme, N.H.: Smith and Kraus, 2000. 1–63.

Crimes of the Heart. New York: Viking/Penguin, 1982.

Crimes of the Heart. In *Plays from the Contemporary American Theater*, edited by Brooks McNamara, 227–291. New York: New American Library, 1988.

The Debutante Ball. In *Collected Plays. Volume I: 1980–1989.* Lyme, N.H.: Smith and Kraus, 2000. 265–315.

The Debutante Ball. Jackson and London: University Press of Mississippi, 1991.

The Debutante Ball. New York: Dramatists Play Service, 1997.

Four Plays. Portsmouth, N.H.: Heinemann, 1992.

Hymn in the Attic. In *West Coast Plays.* Nos. 17/18, edited by Robert Hurwitt, 313–316. Los Angeles: California Theatre Council, 1985.

Impossible Marriage. In *Collected Plays. Volume II: 1990–1999.* Lyme, N.H.: Smith and Kraus, 2000. 235–273.

Impossible Marriage. New York: Dramatists Play Service, 1999.

"Introduction." In Beth Henley, *Monologues for Women.* Toluca, Ca.: Dramaline Publications, 1992. Unpaginated.

"Introduction." In *Collected Plays. Volume I: 1980–1989.* Lyme, N.H.: Smith and Kraus, 2000. vii–xvi.

"Introduction." In *Collected Plays. Volume II: 1990–1999.* Lyme, N.H.: Smith and Kraus, 2000. vi–xiv.

L-Play. In *Collected Plays. Volume II: 1990–1999.* Lyme, N.H.: Smith and Kraus, 2000. 199–234.

The Lucky Spot. In *Collected Plays. Volume I: 1980–1989.* Lyme, N.H.: Smith and Kraus, 2000. 205–263.

The Lucky Spot. New York: Dramatists Play Service, 1987.

The Miss Firecracker Contest. In *Collected Plays. Volume I: 1980–1989.* Lyme, N.H.: Smith and Kraus, 2000. 143–204.

The Miss Firecracker Contest. New York: Doubleday, 1985.

The Miss Firecracker Contest. New York: Dramatists Play Service, 1985.

The Miss Firecracker Contest. New York: Theater Communications Group, 1979.

Monologues for Women. Toluca Lake, Ca.: Dramaline Publications, 1992.

"Preface." In Beth Henley, *The Debutante Ball.*

213

Jackson and London: University Press of Mississippi, 1991. xi–xiv.

Revelers. In *Collected Plays. Volume II: 1990–1999.* Lyme, N.H.: Smith and Kraus, 2000. 147–198.

Signature. In *Collected Plays. Volume II: 1990–1999.* Lyme, N.H.: Smith and Kraus, 2000. 55–108.

The Wake of Jamey Foster. In *Collected Plays. Volume I: 1980–1989.* Lyme, N.H.: Smith and Kraus, 2000. 87–141.

The Wake of Jamey Foster. New York: Dramatists Play Service, 1983.

Secondary Sources

Adler, Thomas P. *Mirror on the Stage: The Pulitzer Plays as an Approach to Drama.* West Lafayette, In.: Purdue University Press, 1987.

Andreach, Robert. *Creating the Self in the Contemporary American Theatre.* Carbondale and Edwardsville: Southern Illinois University Press, 1998.

_____. "The Missing Five Years and Subjectivity in Beth Henley's *Abundance.*" *Southern Quarterly: A Journal of the Arts in the South* 39, no. 3 (2001): 141–150.

Ansen, David. "When Ditsyness Was in Flower." *Newsweek,* 22 December 1986, 75.

Ascheim, Skip. "Spotty Production of Henley's *Lucky Spot.*" *Boston Globe,* 9 December 1998, D18.

Attanasio, Paul. "*Crimes* Doesn't Pay." *Washington Post,* 12 December 1986, C11.

Auflitsch, Susanne. "Beth Henley's Early Family Plays: Dysfunctional Parenting, the South, and Feminism." *Amerikastudien/American Studies* 46, no. 2 (2001): 267–280.

Barnes, Clive. "Beth Henley Goes West." *New York Post,* 31 October 1990. In *New York Theatre Critics' Reviews — 1990.* Week of 19 November 1990, 167–168.

_____. "Circle Lives Up to Its Rep." *New York Post,* 11 January 1982. In *New York Theatre Critics' Reviews — 1982.* Week of 1 February 1982, 362–363.

_____. "*Crime* Is a Prize Hit That's All Heart." *New York Post,* 5 November 1981. In *New York Theatre Critics' Reviews — 1981.* Week of 2 November 1981, 137–138.

_____. "*Firecracker* Is Happy Maladjustment." *New York Post,* 29 May 1984. In *New York Theatre Critics' Reviews — 1984.* Week of 21 May 1984, 251–252.

_____. "*Marriage* Reunites Holly with Her Beth Friend." *New York Post,* 16 October 1998, 41.

_____. "*Wake of Jamey Foster*: Awake with Lively Folk & Humor." *New York Post,* 15 October 1982. In *New York Theatre Critics' Reviews — 1982.* Week of 1 November 1982, 182.

Bask, "*The Debutante Ball.*" *Variety,* 17 April 1985, 228.

Beaufort, John. "*Lucky Spot*: Offbeat Comedy by Beth Henley." *Christian Science Monitor,* 30 April 1987, 30.

_____. "*Miss Firecracker Contest*: Beth Henley's Latest Is Lush, Wacky Drama." *Christian Science Monitor,* 6 June 1984, 22.

_____. "A Play That Proves There's No Explaining Awards." *Christian Science Monitor.* Eastern Edition. 9 November 1981, 20.

_____. "Sensitive One-act Plays at the Circle Rep." *Christian Science Monitor,* 19 January 1982, 19.

Bent, Ted. "Playwright Beth Henley's Only Crime Is Stealing the Hearts of Broadway Critics." *People,* 21 December 1981, 124–125.

Berkowitz, Gerald M. *American Drama of the Twentieth Century.* London and New York: Longman, 1992.

Berkvist, Robert. "Act I: The Pulitzer, Act II: Broadway." *New York Times,* 25 October 1981, D4, D22.

"Beth Henley." In *Interviews with Contemporary Women Playwrights,* edited by Kathleen Betsko and Rachel Koenig, 211–222. New York: William Morrow, 1987.

"Beth Henley." In *Mississippi Writers Talking,* edited by John Griffin Jones, 168–190. Jackson: University Press of Mississippi, 1982.

"Beth Henley." In *Women Who Write Plays: Interviews with American Dramatists,* edited by Alexis Greene, 200–224. Hanover, N.H.: Smith and Kraus, 2001.

"Beth Henley." *People Weekly,* 22–29 December 1986, 91.

Bigsby, C.W.E. *Modern American Drama, 1945–1990.* New York and Cambridge: Cambridge University Press, 1992.

Billington, Michael. " A Cracked Belle." *Guardian,* 1 June 1989, 24.

Blau, Eleanor. "Of Jamey Foster, Who Isn't in New Beth Henley Play." *New York Times,* 13 August 1982, C2.

Bradley, Jeff. "Love Soothes Disasters in Sensitive Staging of *Crimes of the Heart.*" *Denver Post,* 17 September 1991, E8.

Brantley, Ben. "Fairies Adrift in Love's Garden." *New York Times,* 16 October 1998, E1, E4.

_____. "Granddaddy Is in a Coma, and That's the Good News." *New York Times,* 17 April 2001, E1, E5.

Breslauer, Jan. "*Firecracker Contest* Can't Find Its Spark." *Los Angeles Times*, 10 September 1993, F16.

Brown, Joe. "*Firecracker* Lots of Sparkle but Little Bang." *Washington Post*, 16 August 1985, "Weekend," 7.

Brustein, Robert. "Broadway Inches Forward." *New Republic*, 23 December 1981, 25–27.

_____. "Good and Plenty." *New Republic*, 29 November 1982, 24–26.

_____. "She-Plays, American Style." *New Republic*, 17 December 1990, 27–29.

Buckley, Peter. "Beating the Odds." *Horizon*, December 1982, 49–55.

Burke, Sally. *American Feminist Playwrights: A Critical History*. New York: Twayne, 1996.

Camus, Albert. *The Myth of Sisyphus and Other Essays*. Trans. Justin O'Brien. New York: Alfred A. Knopf, 1969.

Canby, Vincent. "Film: Henley's *Crimes of the Heart*." *New York Times*, 12 December 1986, C19.

_____. "Screen: *Nobody's Fool*, Comedy." *New York Times*, 7 November 1986, C18.

Carr, Camilla. "Introduction: Beth Henley: Straight from the Heart." In Beth Henley, *Four Plays*. Portsmouth, N.H.: Heinemann. vii–ix.

Cassidy, Claudia. "Our Stage and Stars, Lyric and Otherwise." *Chicago*, February 1984, 20–24.

Chaillet, Ned. "*The Miss Firecracker Contest*." *Times*, 28 April 1982, 10.

Chirico, Miriam M. "'Dancing on the Edge of a Cliff': Images of the Grotesque in the Plays of Beth Henley." In *Beth Henley: A Casebook*, edited by Julia A. Fesmire, 1–31. New York and London: Routledge, 2002.

Christiansen, Richard. "*Control Freaks* Deviates from Taste, Subtlety." *Chicago Tribune*, 22 September 1992, sec. 1, 22.

_____. "*Crimes* Has a 'Heart'-warming Glow." *Chicago Tribune*, 15 December 1983, sec. 2, 24.

_____. "*Miss Firecracker* a Bizarre Blast." *Chicago Tribune*, 1 July 1983, sec. 3, 10.

_____. "Pulitzer Prize Winner Beth Henley: Pressing on, Despite the Pressure." *Chicago Tribune*, 19 June 1983, sec. 12, 16–17.

_____. "Zany and Touching, *The Lucky Spot* Is a Fortunate Find." *Chicago Tribune*, 22 November 1990, sec. 1, 24.

Cohen, Robert. "The Year in Drama." In *Contemporary Literary Criticism Yearbook 1989*. Vol. 59, edited by Roger Matuz, 15–23. Detroit: Gale Research, Inc., 1990.

Cohen, Ron. "*The Miss Firecracker Contest*." *Women's Wear Daily*. In *New York Theatre Critics' Reviews — 1984*. Week of 21 May 1984, 253.

Colodner, Joel. "*The Miss Firecracker Contest*." *Theatre Journal* 34, no. 2 (1982): 260–261.

Cook, Kay K. "Henley, Beth." In *The Oxford Companion to Women's Writing in the United States*, edited by Cathy N. Davidson and Linda Wagner-Martin, 386–387. New York: Oxford University Press, 1995.

Corliss, Richard. "Dreams to Avoid." *Time*, 1 May 1989, 68.

_____. "'I Go with What I'm Feeling.'" *Time*, 8 February 1982, 80.

_____. "Once a Comedy, Now an Elegy." *Time*, 22 December 1986, 70.

Cunliffe, Simon. "A Confederacy of Dunces." *New Statesman*, 24 April 1987, 23.

Currie, Glenne. "Talent on Display in Various Plays." *Los Angeles Times*, 5 January 1981, sec. 6, 5.

Dace, Tish. "Henley, Beth (Elizabeth Becker Henley)." In *Contemporary American Dramatists*, edited by K.A. Berney, 258–261. London and Detroit: St. James Press, 1994.

Davis, Curt. "On Stage." *After Dark* 15 (December 1982–January 1983): 10.

Davis, Laura. *Allies in Healing: When the Person You Love Was Sexually Abused as a Child*. New York: HarperCollins, 1991.

de Jongh, Nicholas. "*Miss Firecracker*." *Guardian*, 16 July 1986, 11.

Dellasega, Mary. "Beth Henley." In *Speaking on Stage: Interviews with Contemporary American Playwrights*, edited by Philip C. Kolin and Colby H. Kullman, 250–259. Tuscaloosa and London: University of Alabama Press, 1996.

Demastes, William W. *Beyond Naturalism: A New Realism in American Theatre*. Contributions in Drama and Theatre Studies, no. 27. New York and Westport, Conn.: Greenwood Press, 1988.

Denby, David. "The Day the Earth Stood Still for You." *New York*, 15 May 1989, 101–102.

DeVries, Hilary. "Beth Henley Talks About Her Way of Writing Plays." *Christian Science Monitor*, 26 October 1983, 23, 26.

Diagnostic and Statistical Manual of Mental Disorders. 4th ed. Washington, D.C.: American Psychiatric Association, 1994.

Dodds, Richard. "Searching for the Guilty Party at *Crimes*." *Times-Picayune* (New Orleans), 19 May 1989, LAG 20.

Dolan, Jill. "Personal, Political, Polemical: Feminist Approaches to Politics and Theatre." In *The Politics of Theatre and Drama*, edited by Graham Holderness, 44–65. New York: St. Martin's Press, 1992.

Drake, Sylvie. "Chat with a Pulitzer Dramatist." *Los Angeles Times*, 15 April 1981, sec. 6, 1, 7.

_____. "Henley's *Abundance* Goes West with

a New-Found Maturity." *Los Angeles Times*, 24 April 1989, sec. 6, 1, 4.

_____. "Henley's Heart Is in the Theater." *Los Angeles Times*, 16 April 1983, sec. V, 1, 8.

_____. "*Miss Firecracker* Launches Theater." *Los Angeles Times*, 15 March 1980, sec. 2, 8–9.

Durham, Ayne C. "Beth Henley." In *Critical Survey of Drama: Supplement*, edited by Frank N. Magill, 192–197. Pasadena: Salem Press, 1987.

Esslin, Martin. *The Theatre of the Absurd*. Garden City, N.Y.: Doubleday, 1969.

Farber, Stephen. "Playwrights See New Promise on the Small Screen." *New York Times*, 14 December 1986, sec. 2, 33.

Fein, Esther B. "Role Call: Waif, Wife, Drummer Girl." *New York Times*, 26 April 1987, sec. 2, 5.

Feingold, Michael. "Dry Roll." *Village Voice*, 18 November 1981, 104, 106.

_____. "Israel in Greece." *Village Voice*, 13–19 January 1982, 101, 103.

Fenton, James. "Pillow Talk and Power." *Sunday Times*, 2 May 1982, 39.

Fesmire, Julia A., ed. *Beth Henley: A Casebook*. New York and London: Routledge, 2002.

Forward, Susan and Craig Buck. *Betrayal of Innocence: Incest and Its Devastation*. New York and London: Penguin, 1988.

Fox, Terry Curtis. "The Acting's the Thing." *Village Voice*, 7 January 1981, 71.

Freedman, Samuel G. "Beth Henley Writes a 'Real, Real Personal' Movie." *New York Times*, 2 November 1986, sec. 2, 1, 26.

Freud, Sigmund. *Civilization and Its Discontents*. In *The Standard Edition of the Complete Psychological Works of Sigmund Freud*. Vol. 21, edited and translated by James Strachey, 64–145. London: Hogarth Press, 1961.

_____. "On Narcissism: An Introduction." In *The Standard Edition of the Complete Psychological Works of Sigmund Freud*. Vol. 14, edited and translated by James Strachey, 73–102. London: Hogarth Press, 1957.

Gagen, Jean. "'Most Resembling Unlikeness, and Most Unlike Resemblance': Beth Henley's *Crimes of the Heart* and Chekhov's *Three Sisters*." *Studies in American Drama, 1945–Present* 4 (1989): 119–128.

Gardner, Elysa. "*Crimes* Is an Apt Title for Revival." *USA Today*, 17 April 2001, D4.

Gill, Brendan. "The Theatre: Backstage." *New Yorker*, 16 November 1981, 182–183.

_____. "The Theatre: Steps Going Down." *New Yorker*, 25 October 1982, 160–161.

Gold, Sylviane. "A Fondness for Freaks." *Wall Street Journal*, 20 June 1984, 28.

Goldberg, Robert, "A Mutant Sitcom on PBS." *Wall Street Journal*, 26 October 1987, 25.

Greenberg, Samuel I. *Neurosis Is a Painful Style of Living*. New York: New American Library, 1971.

Grove, Lloyd. "Excess Kooks Foil *Crimes*." *Washington Post*, 8 June 1984, "Weekend," 11.

_____. "The Fitfully Funny *Wake of Jamey Foster*." *Washington Post*, 1 June 1984, "Weekend," 11.

Guerra, Jonnie. "Beth Henley: Female Quest and the Family-Play Tradition." In *Making a Spectacle: Feminist Essays on Contemporary Women's Theatre*, edited by Lynda Hart, 118–130. Ann Arbor: University of Michigan Press, 1989.

Gupton, Janet L. "'Un-ruling' the Woman: Comedy and the Plays of Beth Henley and Rebecca Gilman." In *Southern Women Playwrights: New Essays in Literary History and Criticism*, edited by Robert L. McDonald and Linda Rohrer Paige, 124–138. Tuscaloosa and London: University of Alabama Press, 2002.

Gussow, Mel. "Critics' Awards to *Aloes* and *Crimes of the Heart*." *New York Times*, 11 June 1981, C17.

_____. "Louisville Again Mines Rich Ore of Stage Talent." *New York Times*, 20 February 1979, C7.

_____. "Women Playwrights Show New Strength." *New York Times*, 15 February 1981, sec. 2, 4, 24.

Gwin, Minrose C. "Sweeping the Kitchen: Revelation and Revolution in Contemporary Southern Women's Writing." *Southern Quarterly: A Journal of the Arts in the South* 30, nos. 2–3 (1992): 54–62.

Haedicke, Janet V. "Margins in the Mainstream: Contemporary Women Playwrights." In *Realism and the American Dramatic Tradition*, edited by William W. Demastes, 203–217. Tuscaloosa: University of Alabama Press, 1996.

_____. "'A Population [and Theater] at Risk': Battered Women in Henley's *Crimes of the Heart* and Shepard's *A Lie of the Mind*." *Modern Drama* 36, no. 1 (1993): 83–95.

Haller, Scott. "Her First Play, Her First Pulitzer." *Saturday Review*, November 1981, 40, 42, 44.

Harbin, Billy J. "Familial Bonds in the Plays of Beth Henley." *Southern Quarterly: A Journal of the Arts in the South* 25, no. 3 (1987): 80–94.

Hargrove, Nancy D. "The Tragicomic Vision of Beth Henley's Drama." *Southern Quarterly: A Journal of the Arts in the South* 22, no. 4 (1984): 54–70.

Harris, Laurilyn J. "Delving Beneath the Stereotypes: Beth Henley's *The Miss Firecracker Contest." *Theatre Southwest* 14 (May 1987): 4–7.

Heilpern, John. "Great Acting, Pity About the Play." *Times*, 5 December 1981, 11.

"Henley, Beth." In *Contemporary Theatre, Film and Television*. Vol. 21, edited by Kathleen J. Edgar, 150–151. Detroit: The Gale Group, 1999.

"Henley, Beth." In *Current Biography Yearbook — 1983*, edited by Charles Moritz, 185–188. New York: H.W. Wilson, 1983.

"Henley, Beth." In *Encyclopedia of Southern Literature*, edited by Mary Ellen Snodgrass, 150–153. Santa Barbara: ABC-CLIO, 1997.

"Henley, Elizabeth Becker." In *Contemporary Authors — New Revision Series*. Vol. 73, edited by Daniel Jones and John D. Jorgenson, 222–225. Detroit: The Gale Group, 1999.

"Henley, Elizabeth Becker." In *Major 20th-Century Writers*. Vol. 2, edited by Bryan Ryan, 1379–1381. Detroit: Gale Research, 1991.

Henry, William A. "Once Outposts, Now Landmarks." *Time*, 12 June 1989, 72.

Hinson, Hal. "*Firecracker*: Ignited by Hunter, Robbins." *Washington Post*, 12 May 1989, D7.

Hobe. "*Crimes of the Heart*." *Variety*, 11 November 1981, 84.

Hoffman, Roy. "Brash New South Is Still a Stranger to Its Dramatists." *New York Times*, 2 July 1989, sec. 2, 5, 24.

Holden, Stephen, Diane Solway, and Laurie Winer. "1988: Previews from 36 Artists." *New York Times*, 3 January 1988, sec. 2, 1, 30–31.

Holladay, Hilary. "Beth Henley." In *Contemporary Poets, Dramatists, Essayists, and Novelists of the South*, edited by Robert Bain and Joseph M. Flora, 238–248. Westport, Conn.: Greenwood Press, 1994.

Hughes, Leonard. "A Smart and Enjoyable *Crimes of the Heart*." *Washington Post*, 11 February 1993, "Prince Georges Weekly," 3.

Humm. "Confluence." *Variety*, 27 January 1982, 88.

_____. "Off-Broadway Review." *Variety*, 31 December 1980, 60.

_____. "Off-Broadway Review: *The Lucky Spot*." *Variety*, 6 May 1987, 615.

_____. "*The Wake of Jamey Foster*." *Variety*, 20 October 1982, 331.

Isenberg, Barbara. "She'd Rather Do It Herself." *Los Angeles Times*, 11 July 1993, "Calendar," 5, 80.

Isherwood, Charles. "*Family Week*." *Variety*, 17–23 April 2000, 34.

_____. "*Impossible Marriage*." *Variety*, 19–25 October 1998, 84.

Jacobs, Tom. "*Control Freaks*." *Variety*, 9 August 1993, 35.

Jaehne, Karen. "Beth's Beauties." *Film Comment* 25 (May-June 1989): 9–12, 14–15.

James, John. "Family Horrors Revealed." *Times Educational Supplement*, 16 June 1989, B31.

Jones, Welton. "Henley's Southern Voice Is Shrill in *Debutante Ball*." *San Diego Union*, 13 April 1985, D10.

_____. "Two Mail-Order Brides Are 'Abundance.'" *San Diego Union*, 26 April 1989, E4.

Kachur, Barbara. "Women Playwrights on Broadway: Henley, Howe, Norman and Wasserstein." In *Contemporary American Theatre*, edited by Bruce King, 15–39. Basingstoke and London: Macmillan, 1991.

Kael, Pauline. "The Current Cinema." *New Yorker*, 15 December 1986, 81–82, 85–87.

_____. "The Current Cinema." *New Yorker*, 29 May 1989, 103–104.

Kalem, T.E. "Southern Sibs." *Time*, 16 November 1981, 122.

_____. "Third Running of the Derby." *Time*, 5 March 1979, 73.

Karam, Edward. "Verdict Misadventure." *Times*, 4 November 1998, 40.

Karpinski, Joanne B. "The Ghosts of Chekhov's *Three Sisters* Haunt Beth Henley's *Crimes of the Heart*." In *Modern American Drama: The Female Canon*, edited by June Schlueter, 229–245. Madison, N.J.: Fairleigh Dickinson University Press, 1990.

Kauffmann, Stanley. "Dark Sides." *New Republic*, 15 December 1986, 22–23.

_____. "Lone Stars." *New Republic*, 10 November 1986, 26–28.

_____. "The Three Sisters." *New Republic*, 2 February 1987, 26–27.

_____. "Two Cheers for Two Plays." *Saturday Review*, January 1982, 54–55.

Kelly, Kevin. "*Crimes* Earnest but Without Insight." *Boston Globe*, 18 January 1990, "Arts," 74.

Kerr, Walter. "Offbeat — but a Bit Too Far." *New York Times*, 15 November 1981, D3, D31.

_____. "Two Parts Gimmickry, One Part Discretion." *New York Times*, 24 January 1982, sec. 2, 3, 10.

Keyssar, Helene. *Feminist Theatre: An Introduction of Plays to Contemporary British and American Women*. Basingstoke and London: Macmillan, 1984.

Kilian, Michael. "Perfect Marriage." *Chicago Tribune*, 3 December 1998, sec. 5, 10B.

King, Rebecca. "*The Lucky Spot* as Immanent Critique." In *Beth Henley: A Casebook*, edited by Julia A. Fesmire, 64–87. New York and London: Routledge, 2002.

Kingston, Jeremy, "*Crimes of the Heart.*" *Times*, 18 August 1989, 14.

Kinser, Jerry. "Mississippi in Ranks of Pulitzers." *Biloxi-Gulfport Daily Herald*, 14 April 1981, B1.

Kirkpatrick, Melanie. "Theater: Asians in America." *Wall Street Journal*, 9 November 1990, A8.

Kirschner, Sam, Diana Adile Kirschner, and Richard L. Rappaport. *Working with Adult Incest Survivors: The Healing Journey.* Frontiers in Couples and Family Therapy Series, no. 6. New York: Brunner/Mazel, 1993.

Kissel, Howard. "*Confluence.*" *Women's Wear Daily*, 11 January 1982. In *New York Theatre Critics' Reviews — 1982*. Week of 1 February 1982, 360–361.

_____. "*Crimes of the Heart.*" *Women's Wear Daily*, 6 November 1981. In *New York Theatre Critics' Reviews — 1981*. Week of 6 November 1981, 140.

_____. "Plenty Is Lacking in *Abundance.*" *Daily News*, 31 October 1990. In *New York Theatre Critics' Reviews — 1990*. Week of 19 November 1990, 167.

_____. "*The Wake of Jamey Foster.*" *Women's Wear Daily*, 15 October 1982. In *New York Theatre Critics' Reviews — 1982*. Week of 1 November 1982, 181–182.

Klein, Alvin. "Hooray for Hollywood? More Like 'Horrors!'" *New York Times*, 12 May 1996, "New Jersey," 12.

_____. "*Miss Firecracker* Is Staged at Fairfield." *New York Times*, 20 March 1988, sec. 22, 18–19.

_____. "The Passage Theater Is Reborn." *New York Times*, 12 February 1995, sec. 13, "New Jersey," 13, 15.

_____. "Poignant, Daft *Miss Firecracker.*" *New York Times*, 24 July 1988, sec. 12, 19.

_____. "The Schoolhouse Stages *Abundance.*" *New York Times*, 28 May 2000, sec. 14, "Westchester," 12.

Koenig, Rhoda. "Amusing, Not Amazing." *Punch*, 9 June 1989, 44.

Koyama, Christine. "*Crimes of the Heart* Acquits Itself Splendidly." *Chicago Tribune*, 24 May 1984, sec. 5, 13.

Kramer, Mimi. "Picturing Abundance." *New Yorker*, 12 November 1990, 105–106.

Kroll, Jack. "The Best of Off-Broadway." *Newsweek*, 25 January 1982, 71, 73.

_____. "New Blood in Louisville." *Newsweek*, 19 March 1979, 92, 96.

_____. "Southern Discomfort." *Newsweek*, 1 May 1989, 75.

_____. "Theater." *Newsweek*, 16 November 1981, 123.

Krupp, C. "*Crimes of the Heart* Writer Beth Henley Talks About Sissy, Diane and Jessica." *Glamour*, January 1987, 134.

Kullman Colby H. "Beth Henley's Marginalized Heroines." *Studies in American Drama, 1945–Present* 8, no. 1 (1993): 21–28.

Kullman, Colby H., and Miriam Neuringer. "Beth Henley." In *American Playwrights Since 1945: A Guide to Scholarship, Criticism, and Performance*, edited by Philip C. Kolin, 169–178. New York and Westport, Conn.: Greenwood Press, 1989.

Lasch, Christopher. *The Culture of Narcissism: American Life in an Age of Diminishing Expectations.* New York: W.W. Norton, 1979.

Laughlin, Karen L. "Abundance or Excess?: Beth Henley's Postmodern Romance of the True West." In *Beth Henley: A Casebook*, edited by Julia A. Fesmire, 88–104. New York and London: Routledge, 2002.

_____. "Criminality, Desire, and Community: A Feminist Approach to Beth Henley's *Crimes of the Heart.*" *Women & Performance: A Journal of Feminist Theory* 3, no. 1 (1986): 35–51.

Lawson, Carol. "Beth Henley's New Offbeat Play Is in Rehearsal." *New York Times*, 14 September 1982, C9.

_____. "Broadway." *New York Times*, 20 November 1981, C2.

_____. "Grosbard to Direct and Produce New Beth Henley Play." *New York Times*, 29 January 1982, C2.

Lee, Hyung-Shik. "Female Bonding Through Recognition and Transformation: Beth Henley's *Crimes of the Heart.*" *Journal of English Language and Literature* 37, no. 3 (1991): 719–736.

Leonard, John. "Something Mild." *New York*, 26 October 1987, 165–166.

Levin. Gerald. *Sigmund Freud.* Boston: G.K. Hall, 1975.

Lyons, Donald. "No Faith in Love and Charity." *Wall Street Journal*, 21 October 1998, A20.

"The Man in the Back Row Has a Question, IV." *Paris Review* 39, no. 142 (1997): 226–244.

Mapp, Larry G. "Lessons from the Past: Loss and Redemption in the Early Plays of Beth Henley." In *Beth Henley: A Casebook*, edited by Julia A. Fesmire, 32–41. New York and London: Routledge, 2002.

Masters, Anthony. "*Crimes of the Heart.*" *Times*, 19 May 1983, 15.

McDonald, Robert L. "'A Blaze of Glory': Image and Self-Promotion in Henley's *The Miss Firecracker Contest.*" *Southern Quarterly: A Journal of the Arts in the South* 37, no. 2 (1999): 151–157.

McDonnell, Lisa J. "Beth Henley." In *Ameri-*

can Dramatists, edited by Matthew C. Roudané, 91–107. Contemporary Authors Bibliographical Series. Detroit: Gale, 1989.

_____. "Diverse Similitude: Beth Henley and Marsha Norman." *Southern Quarterly: A Journal of the Arts in the South* 25, no. 3 (1987): 95–104.

McKinley, Jesse. "On Stage and Off." *New York Times*, 4 February 2000, E2.

Merrill, Lisa. "*The Miss Firecracker Contest*." *Women & Performance: A Journal of Feminist Theory* 2, no. 2 (1985): 74–76.

Meserve, Walter J. "Henley, Beth." In *Contemporary Dramatists*. 4th ed., edited by D.L. Kirkpatrick, 245–246. Chicago and London: St. James Press, 1988.

Morley, Sheridan. "Kids on the Skids." *Punch*, 8 June 1983, 52.

_____. "Steamboat Singalong." *Punch*, 5 May 1982, 742.

Morrow, Laura. "Orality and Identity in *'night, Mother* and *Crimes of the Heart*." *Studies in American Drama, 1945–Present* 3 (1988): 23–39.

Morrow, Lee Alan and Frank Pike, eds. *Creating Theater: The Professionals' Approach to New Plays*. New York: Vintage, 1986.

Morrow, Mark. *Images of the Southern Writer*. Athens: University of Georgia Press, 1985.

Mullener, Elizabeth. "Beth Henley." *Times-Picayune* (New Orleans), 8 November 1981, "Dixie," 7, 8, 10, 12, 14.

Myers, Leslie R. "*Firecracker* Cast Arrives in Yazoo City." *Clarion-Ledger* (Jackson), 22 May 1988, E3.

_____. "Mississippi Playwright Downplays Her Success." *Clarion-Ledger* (Jackson), 21 July 1985, E1–E2.

Nachman, Gerald. "Beth Henley's Pioneer Women." *San Francisco Chronicle*, 23 September 1992, E2.

_____. "Western Women, Gay Men in N.Y." *San Francisco Chronicle*, 20 December 1990, E5, E7.

Nelson, Don. "*Crimes* Is Heartwarming." *Daily News*, 5 November 1981. In *New York Theatre Critics' Reviews — 1981*. Week of November 2, 1981, 139.

Nightingale, Benedict. "Asking for Trouble." *New Statesman*, 14 May 1982, 30–31.

_____. "A Landscape That Is Unmistakably by Henley." *New York Times*, 3 June 1984, sec. 2, 3, 7.

_____. "Low-powered." *New Statesman*, 27 May 1983, 25–26.

_____. "Way Out West Leads Nowhere Fast." *Times*, 3 November 1995, 37.

Novick, Julius. "Affirmative Actions." *Village Voice*, 26 October 1982, 103.

_____. "Not in the Cards." *Variety*, 12 May 1987, 99, 102.

_____. "Too Much, Too Small." *Village Voice*, 12 March 1979, 86–87.

O'Toole, Finlan. "New Georgia Play Is Just Peachy; Hunter's a Hoot in Henley's Latest." *Daily News*, 16 October 1998, "New York Now," 59.

Oliver, Edith. "The Theatre." *New Yorker*, 11 May 1987, 80–81.

_____. "The Theatre: Off Broadway." *New Yorker*, 12 January 1981, 81–82.

_____. "The Theatre: Off Broadway." *New Yorker*, 11 June 1984, 112–113.

Paige, Linda Rohrer. "Southern Firecrackers and 'Real Bad Days': Film Adaptations of Beth Henley's *Crimes of the Heart* and *The Miss Firecracker Contest*." In *Beth Henley: A Casebook*, edited by Julia A. Fesmire, 128–153. New York and London: Routledge, 2002.

Paller, Michael. "Getting the Family Together." *Newsday*, 11 April 2000, B9.

Parker, Jerry. "And the Winner Is…" *Newsday* (Long Island), 18 October 1981, sec. 2, 4–5.

Patterson, James A. "Henley, Mary Beth." In *Notable Women in the American Theatre*, edited by Alice M. Robinson, Vera Mowry Roberts, and Milly S. Barranger, 417–421. New York and Westport, Conn.: Greenwood Press, 1989.

Peter, John. "The Shaming Shylock of Dustin Hoffman." *Sunday Times*, 4 June 1989, C9.

Plunka, Gene A. "Existential Despair and the Modern Neurosis: Beth Henley's *Crimes of the Heart*." In *Beth Henley: A Casebook*, edited by Julia A. Fesmire, 105–127. New York and London: Routledge, 2002.

Pogrebin, Robin. "Sharing a History as Well as a Play." *New York Times*, 11 October 1998, sec. 2, 5, 25.

Popkin, Henry. "On Broadway." *Plays and Players*, no. 406 (July 1987): 32–33.

Porter, Laurin. "Contemporary Playwrights/ Traditional Forms." In *The Cambridge Companion to American Women Playwrights*, edited by Brenda Murphy, 195–212. Cambridge: Cambridge University Press, 1999.

_____. "Women Re-Conceived: Changing Perceptions of Women in Contemporary American Drama." *Conference of College Teachers of English Studies* 54 (September 1989): 53–59.

Rafferty, Terrence. "Nobody's Fool." *Savvy* 8 (January 1987): 66–67.

Raidy, William A. "Mississippi Playwright Tells Home-State Tales on and off Stage." *Commercial Appeal* (Memphis), 15 November 1981, 3.

Renner, Pamela. "The Mellowing of Miss Firecracker." *American Theatre* 15, no. 9 (1998): 18–19, 61.

Renold, Evelyn. "Baring Her *Heart* on B'way." *Daily News*, 3 November 1981, C20.

Rich, Frank. "*Abundance*: Beth Henley's Revisionist Western." *New York Times*, 31 October 1990, C15, C19.

_____. "Stage: *Confluence*, 3 One-Acters, at Circle Rep." *New York Times*, 11 January 1987, C14.

_____. "Stage: *Lucky Spot* by Beth Henley." *New York Times*, 29 April 1987, C22.

_____. "The Theater: Beth Henley's *Crimes of the Heart*." *New York Times*, 5 November 1981, C21.

_____. "The Theater: Beth Henley's *Crimes of the Heart*, Comedy about 3 Sisters." *New York Times*, 22 December 1980, C16.

_____. "Theater: Beth Henley's *Wake of Jamey Foster*." *New York Times*, 15 October 1982, C3.

_____. "Theater: *Firecracker*, a Beth Henley Comedy." *New York Times*, 28 May 1984, 11.

_____. "The Varied Use of History in *Good and Plenty*." *New York Times*, 11 November 1982, C21.

Richards, David. "The Gershwins' *Oh, Kay!* Dances to Harlem." *New York Times*, 11 November 1990, sec. 2, 5, 33.

_____. "Olney's Crazy *Contest*." *Washington Post*, 8 August 1985, sec. B, 1, 10.

_____. "Southern Eccentric." *Washington Post*, 2 June 1984, C5.

_____. "Where's the Drama?" *Washington Post*, 8 July 1984, sec. H, 1, 5.

Richards, Gary. "Moving Beyond Mississippi: Beth Henley and the Anxieties of Postsouthernness." In *Beth Henley: A Casebook*, edited by Julia A. Fesmire, 42–63. New York and London: Routledge, 2002.

Ricoeur, Paul. *Freud and Philosophy: An Essay on Interpretation*. Trans. Denis Savage. New Haven and London: Yale University Press, 1979.

Ringel, Eleanor. "*Miss Firecracker* Doesn't Have Spark Despite Stellar Cast." *Atlanta Constitution*, 12 May 1989, C1, C6.

Rochlin, Margy. "The Eccentric Genius of *Crimes of the Heart*." *Ms*, February 1987, 12, 14.

Rogers, V. Cullum. "Beth Henley: Signature of a Non-stop Playwright." *Back Stage* 36, no. 12 (1995): 23.

Rose, Lloyd. "*Abundance*: Wild & Wacky West." *Washington Post*, 22 March 1994, C7.

Rosenfeld, Megan. "At Olney, the Best of *Crimes*." *Washington Post*, 8 June 1984, sec. B, 1, 6.

_____. "Beth Henley's World of Southern Discomfort." *Washington Post*, 12 December 1986, sec. C, 1, 10.

Ross, Laura. "Henley's Late Date." *American Theatre* 2 (April 1985): 19.

Roudané, Matthew. *American Drama Since 1960: A Critical History*. New York: Twayne, 1997.

Royce, Gradon. "Flat Script and Cast Hinder *Marriage*." *Minneapolis Star Tribune*, 13 July 2000, 4B.

Salter, Susan. "Henley, Elizabeth Becker." In *Contemporary Authors — New Revision Series*. Vol. 32, edited by James G. Lesniak, 199–200. Detroit: Gale Research, Inc., 1991.

Sauvage, Leo. "Dark and Shallow Visions." *New Leader*, 15 November 1982, 19–20.

_____. "Reaching for Laughter." *New Leader*, 30 November 1981, 19–20.

Schickel, Richard. "Jagged Flashes of Inspiration." *Time*, 11 June 1984, 80.

Seligsohn, Leo. "The 'L' in Confusion: Beth Henley Veers into the Theater of the Absurd." *Newsday* (Long Island), 27 August 1996, B7.

Senior, Jennifer. "A Marriage of Convenience." *New York*, 14 September 1998, 70–71.

Sessums, Kevin. "Beth Henley." *Interview*, 17 February 1987, 85.

Sharbutt, Jay. "Beth Henley: Mississippi's Own Neil Simon?" *Times-Picayune* (New Orleans), 3 October 1982, sec. 8, 2.

Shepard, Alan Clarke. "Aborted Rage in Beth Henley's Women." *Modern Drama* 36, no. 1 (1993): 96–108.

Shewey, Don. "A Director with an Eye for the Telling Detail." *New York Times*, 10 October 1982, sec. 2, 28, 37.

Shim, Jung-Soon. "Women's Comedy as Transgressive Strategy in Beth Henley's *The Debutante Ball*." *Journal of English Language and Literature* 43, no. 3 (1997): 651–665.

Shirley, Don. "*Freaks* Slips at End but It's a Fun Ride." *Los Angeles Times*, 19 July 1993, F1, F9.

_____. "Stage-Struck in Screen City." *Los Angeles Times*, 5 January 1999, D1, D6–D7.

Siegel, Ed. "*L-Play* Is a Lifeless Lemon, Largely Lackluster, Leaden." *Boston Globe*, 28 August 1996, C5.

Simon, John. "All's Well That Ends 'Good.'" *New York*, 25 October 1982, 77–79.

_____. "Bad Quirks, Good Quirks." *New York*, 11 May 1987, 82–84

_____. "The Boys in the Sand." *New York*, 26 October 1998, 82–83.

_____. "Living Beings, Cardboard Symbols." *New York*, 16 November 1981, 125–126.

_____. "Repeaters." *New York*, 4 June 1984, 79–80.

_____. "Sisterhood Is Beautiful." *New York*, 12 January 1981, 42, 44.

_____. "Slow Flow." *New York*, 25 January 1982, 56–57.

_____. "Soul Twain." *New York*, 7 May 2001, 63–64.

_____. "Yo, Kay!" *New York*, 12 November 1990, 92–93.

Smith, Douglas. "*The Miss Firecracker Contest*." *Variety*, 4 November 1981, 84.

Smith, Lucinda Irwin, ed. *Women Who Write: From the Past and the Present to the Future*. Englewood Cliffs, N.J.: Julian Messner, 1989.

Smith, Sid. "Playwright's Progress." *Chicago Tribune*, 20 September 1990, sec. 13, 12.

_____. "*Wake* Warmed-over Dixie Melodrama." *Chicago Tribune*, 10 April 1985, sec. 5, 4.

Stasio, Marilyn. "Scenes: An Off-Season." *Penthouse*, June 1982, 44.

_____. "Theater." *After Dark*, March 1981, 28–29.

Stearns, David Patrick. "Star Power Can't Save Henley's *Impossible Marriage*." *USA Today*, 20 October 1998, D4.

_____. "Two Powerful Tales of Greed Gone Wild." *USA Today*, 25 May 1989, D5.

Sterritt, David. "*Miss Firecracker* Fizzles—Despite Its Potential." *Christian Science Monitor*, 16 May 1989, 11.

Sullivan, Dan. "All Odds, No Evens at the Ball." *Los Angeles Times*, 11 April 1985, sec. 6, 1, 4.

_____. "A Glow in the Heart of *Crimes*." *Los Angeles Times*, 19 April 1983, sec. 6, 1,4.

Swisher, Kara. "*Crimes* Steals Hearts of Va. Audiences." *Washington Post*, 25 January 1990, "Virginia Weekly," 2.

Tarbox, Lucia. "Beth Henley." In *Dictionary of Literary Biography Yearbook: 1986*, edited by J.M. Brook, 302–305. Detroit: Gale Research Company, 1987.

Taylor, Markland. "*The Wake of Jamey Foster*." *Variety*, 27 January 1982, 90.

Thompson, Lou. "Feeding the Hungry Heart: Food in Beth Henley's *Crimes of the Heart*." *Southern Quarterly: A Journal of the Arts in the South* 30, nos. 2–3 (1992): 99–102.

Thornber, Robin. "*Crimes of the Heart*." *Guardian*, 3 October 1986, 14.

_____. "*Crimes of the Heart*." *Guardian*, 13 June 1995, sec. 2, 9.

Torrens, James S. "Trying Them Out Off Broadway." *America*, 8 December 1990, 453–454.

Travers, Peter. "*Crimes of the Heart*." *People Weekly*, 15 December 1986, 12.

Viswanath, Ganga and Christine Gomez. "Woman's Quest for Identity in Beth Henley's *Crimes of the Heart*." *Indian Scholar* 8, nos. 1–2 (1986): 1–10.

Walker, Beverly. "Beth Henley." *American Film*, December 1986, 30–31.

Wardle, Irving. "More Drawl Than Ball." *Times*, 31 May 1989, 21.

Watson, Charles S. *The History of Southern Drama*. Lexington, Ky.: University Press of Kentucky, 1997.

Watt, Douglas. "*Jamey's* Wake Is Gravely Shallow." *Daily News*, 15 October 1982. In *New York Theatre Critics' Reviews — 1982*. Week of 1 November 1982, 181.

_____. "*Miss Firecracker Contest* Just Doesn't Have the Spark." *Daily News*, 28 May 1984. In *New York Theatre Critics' Reviews — 1984*. Week of 21 May 1984, 251.

_____. "Three Plays in Search of an Audience." *Daily News*, 11 January 1982. In *New York Theatre Critics' Reviews — 1982*. Week of 1 February 1982, 361.

Wattenberg, Richard. "Challenging the Frontier Myth: Contemporary Women's Plays about Women Pioneers." *Journal of American Drama and Theatre* 4, no. 3 (1992): 42–61.

Weales, Gerald. "American Theater Watch, 1981–1982." *Georgia Review* 36 (Fall 1982): 517–526.

Weber, Bruce. "Plan Your Family Reunion in Rehab." *New York Times*, 11 April 2000, E1, E3.

Weiner, Bernard. "Berkeley *Crimes of the Heart* Keeps Its Balance." *San Francisco Chronicle*, 16 November 1985, 37.

_____. "*Crimes* Captures the Heart of a Family." *San Francisco Chronicle*, 15 May 1984, 41.

_____. "First Place Prize Stuns a Playwright." *San Francisco Chronicle*, 25 April 1979, 52.

_____. "A Rich Comedy-Drama on Three Odd Sisters." *San Francisco Chronicle*, 2 May 1979, 55.

_____. "S.E.W. Theater Switch — Lightweight Sit-Com." *San Francisco Chronicle*, 22 January 1985, 58.

Weiss, Hedy. "Beth Henley Takes the Director's Chair for *Control Freaks*." *Chicago Sun-Times*, 20 September 1992, "Show," 1.

_____. "Henley's *Control Freaks* Doesn't Deserve a Stage." *Chicago Sun-Times*, 22 September 1992, sec. 2, 32.

_____. "Henley's *Revelers* No Fun at All." *Chicago Sun-Times*, 10 September 1996, 34.

Whited, Lana A. "Suicide in Beth Henley's *Crimes of he Heart* and Marsha Norman's *'night, Mother*." *Southern Quarterly: A Journal of the Arts in the South* 36, no. 1 (1997): 65–74.

Wilmington, Michael. "*Miss Firecracker*: Beauty in Bursts of Affection." *Los Angeles Times*, 28 April 1989, sec. 6, 16–17.

Wilson, Edwin. "Beth Henley: Aiming for the Heart." *Wall Street Journal*, 6 November 1981. In *New York Theatre Critics' Reviews — 1981*. Week of 2 November 1981, 138.

_____. "Beth Henley's New Play." *Wall Street Journal*. 20 October 1982, 32.

Wimmer-Moul, Cynthia. "Beth Henley." In *The Playwright's Art: Conversations with Contemporary American Dramatists*, edited by Jackson R. Bryer, 102–122. New Brunswick: Rutgers University Press, 1995.

Winer, Linda. "Another Bad Day for the Sisters Magrath." *Newsday*, 17 April 2001, B2–B3.

_____. "Beth Henley's *Abundance* in a Bizarre Old West." *Newsday*, 31 October 1990. In *New York Theatre Critics' Reviews — 1990*. Week of 19 November 1990, 168–169.

Winn, Steven. "Southern Playwright Gets Bay Exposure." *San Francisco Chronicle*, 7 May 1986, 66.

Wolf, Matt. "*The Debutante Ball*." *Plays and Players* 429 (July 1989): 31.

Woods, Alan. "Consuming the Past: Commercial American Theatre in the Reagan Era." In *The American Stage*, edited by Ron Engle and Tice L. Miller, 252–266. New York and Cambridge: Cambridge University Press, 1993.

World Encyclopedia of Contemporary Theatre. Vol. 2: Americas, edited by Don Rubin. London and New York: Routledge, 1996.

Yaeger, Patricia. *Dirt and Desire: Reconstructing Women's Writing, 1930–1999*. Chicago and London: University of Chicago Press, 2000.

Index

223